Information Age Economy

Information Age Economy

F. Rose
The Economics, Concept, and Design
of Information Intermediaries
1999, ISBN 3-7908-1168-8

S. Weber
Information Technology in Supplier Network
2001, ISBN 3-7908-1395-8

K. Geihs, W. König and F. von Westarp (Eds.)
Networks
2002, ISBN 3-7908-1449-0

F. von Westarp
Modeling Software Markets
2003, ISBN 3-7908-0009-0

D. Kundisch
New Strategies for Financial Services Firms
2003, ISBN 3-7908-0066-X

T. Weitzel
Economics of Standards
in Information Networks
2004, ISBN 3-7908-0076-7

J. Dibbern
The Sourcing of Application
Software Services
2004, ISBN 3-7908-0217-4

Florian Steiner

Formation and Early Growth of Business Webs

Modular Product Systems in Network Markets

With 29 Figures
and 5 Tables

Physica-Verlag

A Springer Company

Dr. Florian Steiner
Deisenhofenerstraße 38
81539 München
E-mail: florian.steiner@vodafone.de

ISBN 3-7908-1552-7   Physica-Verlag Heidelberg New York

Cataloging-in-Publication Data applied for
Library of Congress Control Number: 2004114418
A catalog record for this book is available from the Library of Congress.

Bibliographic information published by Die Deutsche Bibliothek
Die Deutsche Bibliothek lists this publication in the Deutsche Nationalbibliografie; detailed biblio-graphic data is available in the Internet at *http://dnb.ddb.de*.

Physica-Verlag is a part of Springer Science+Business Media

springeronline.com

 © Physica-Verlag Heidelberg 2005
Printed in Germany

Softcover Design: Erich Kirchner
Production: Helmut Petri
Printing: Strauss Offsetdruck

SPIN 11014409   88/3130 – 5 4 3 2 1 0 – Printed on acid-free paper

Preface

These days, emergence and functioning of networks of organisations are among the most exciting research subjects in MIS and organisation theory. Networked value added systems consisting of multiple, principally independent economic actors are a characteristic of the Information Age Economy. They allow for efficiency of each unit specialising on certain components or services and exploiting economies of scale by serving a global market. At the same time collaboration of such networked organizations enables highly flexible development, production, and delivery of bundled products and services according to technological progress and customers' demand.

Florian Steiner's book addresses a specific form of networks which is of even greater importance to ICT-driven industries and markets: business webs. This mode of inter-organisational coordination is especially suited for markets with network effects (product systems and communication products). With an entrepreneur offering a dominant design or standard in its center (so called shaper) and a multitude of organisations providing complementary products to that center (so called adapters), a business web increases its value through positive feed back loops. These are created by new entry of customers adopting the network's services which increases the attraction of the business web for adapters which again increases the attraction of the web to customers etc. At the same time, a business web not only consists of cooperative partners, but also of competitors, especially among adaptors. Thus, a business web unfolds co-opetition.

This book explores in an innovative way the coming into existence of business webs, i.e. the formation and growth of such inter-firm organisations. It combines theoretical analysis, in-depth case studies, and creation of an explanatory framework. The overview of relevant theories is a very informative exercise for all who are interested in learning about instruments for analysing network industries and modular organisations. Furthermore, Florian Steiner presents a couple of very interesting, real cases of business webs. Thus, based on his systematic study, he gains inspiring insights. Finally, he develops a new and stimulating framework which will improve the explanation and the management of business webs.

I hope that this book will be well accepted in the community of interested researchers and practitioners and that it will spur the debate, the understanding, the emergence, and the functioning of successful business webs which shape to a considerable degree the age of the information economy.

Munich, June 2004   Arnold Picot

Acknowledgements

Many insights in this book would not have been possible without the generous help and support of numerous people.

Firstly, I wish to thank my parents for establishing the basis for this work by educating me and supporting me in so many ways throughout the last three decades.

I am grateful to Dr. Bernd Wiemann, Günther Weber, Birgit Hölker, and the staff of Vodafone Pilotentwicklung in Munich for their passion in bringing together the disparate worlds of scientific research and practical real-world application.

I wish to thank Prof. Dr. Dres. h.c. Arnold Picot who played a pivotal role in the inception of the present book. Thank you also for your constructive criticism, useful suggestions and encouragement throughout the research. To Prof. Dr. Thomas Hess, co-chairman of my doctoral committee and Prof. Dr. Theo Siegert my sincere appreciation for their guidance and interest in my studies.

I would like to express my gratitude to my fellow students for their support and assistance in developing the ideas in this book in innumerable conversations and courses in the post-graduate program. I owe special thanks to my peers at the Institute for Information, Organisation, and Management at the Ludwig-Maximilians University in Munich, in particular Ulrich Löwer, Stefan Riedel, and Carolin Wolff who had a great impact through our debate club on research methods and theoretical constructs. Many thanks to Dr. Marina Fiedler, Dr. Berthold Hass and Guido Zimmer for the meticulous overhaul of early versions of the manuscript.

Furthermore, I am very grateful to the Haniel Foundation which supported parts of the work generously.

I extend my deepest appreciation to my fiancée Elisa Valle, other family members, and a countless number of friends for their prayers, assistance, faith, and support.

Munich, June 2004   Florian Steiner

Contents

Introduction

Technological change gives rise to new industries and markets and often renders the capabilities of established firms obsolete.[1] Outstanding cases are the invention of the microcomputer and internet technologies.[2] Schumpeter was the first who noted the equilibrium-disrupting nature of technological change, which he called "creative destruction."[3] Growth and innovation are among the most important factors for the sustainable success of firms. Growth in sales, revenues, profit, employees, etc. provides the resources for further research and development and the commercialisation of new products that hopefully meet or create market demand.

Of special interest for the present study is the introduction and commercialisation of modular product systems by groups of companies. In many industries, interconnected and modular organisational forms have replaced vertically integrated firms.[4] One of the most recognised cases in business history is the vertical disintegration of IBM with the introduction of the open 360 mainframe system and the open and modular personal computer architecture that led to horizontal specialisation in the computer industry.[5] Recent studies have shown an increasing interest in the management of such modular organisations.[6] Literature distinguishes several theoretical constructs such as strategic networks, virtual organisations, value webs and

---

[1] See Henderson and Clark (1990); Tushman and Anderson (1986).

[2] For the social and economic impacts of the invention and commercialisation of the personal computer see, for example, Negroponte (1995); Chandler (1997); Hart and Kim (2002). The altered business challenges with the introduction and the diffusion of internet technologies are discussed by Schwartz (1997); Ghosh (1998); Margherio, Henry, Cooke et al. (1998); Tapscott, Lowy and Ticoll (2000) and Zerdick, Picot, Schrape et al. (2000) among others.

[3] See Schumpeter (1993b).

[4] See, for example, Grove (1996); Göpfert (1998); Zerdick, Picot, Schrape et al. (2000); Garud, Kumaraswamy and Langlois (2003b); Gawer and Cusumano (2002).

[5] See Langlois (1992a); Ferguson and Morris (1994); Grove (1996); Chandler, Hikino and Nordenflycht (2001).

[6] See Langlois and Robertson (1992a); Wigand, Picot and Reichwald (1997); Göpfert (1998); Baldwin and Clark (2000); Galunic and Eisenhardt (2001); Schilling and Steensma (2001); Langlois (2002); Garud, Kumaraswamy and Langlois (2003b).

business webs to describe such modular organisations.[7] Business webs are groups of companies that collaborate on the basis of technological and economic standards to provide a product system.[8] This shift in the organisation of economic activities has taken place largely and most obviously in the financial, microelectronics, and telecommunications industries.[9] These so-called network industries are characterised by the presence of network externalities, rapid technological change, and the supremacy of architectural innovations that often create entirely new markets.[10] The subject of this study is to examine early growth processes of business webs in such industries. Even though establishment and emergence is the most critical phase, characterised by many risks and high uncertainty, scientific theorising and practical advice for business strategists is practically nonexistent. Especially in their early stages, network industries can be chaotic and dangerous places for firms. Bad strategies and mistakes made early on can be fatal. However, since only a few competing firms are likely to survive because of increasing returns dynamics, the potential rewards are enormous. Once a dominant design is adopted by existing users, the technology becomes increasingly attractive to new users. In markets with competing increasing return technologies, small changes in initial conditions, be they by chance or by strategy, may result in a lead sufficient for one technology to become the dominant standard.[11] This leads to an advantage for the technology that achieves to attract a large number of users early on. Telephony and computer networks are important examples for such market dynamics. Hill (1997) gives some examples from the high-tech industry that are very illustrative for the challenges. He explains:

"From the perspective of the sponsoring firm, the key strategic issue is how to establish its technology as an industry standard and capture the substantial profits that flow from ownership of that standard. The annals of business history are littered with examples of firms that have failed in this endeavour. IBM created the dominant standard in today's per-

---

[7] See Jarillo (1988); Jarillo (1995); Campbell (1996); Wigand, Picot and Reichwald (1997); van Aken, Louweris and Post (1998); Hagel III (1996); Selz (1999); Allee (2000); Tapscott, Lowy and Ticoll (2000); Zerdick, Picot, Schrape et al. (2000); Franz (2003). In the following, these modular organisations are labelled "business webs". In chapter 3 the specific attributes of the other terms will be discussed.

[8] See chapter 3 for further elaboration of the term "business web" and a working definition for the study.

[9] For the financial industry see for example Evans and Schmalensee (1999); Evans and Schmalensee (1993), pp. 49-50 and pp. 70-72. Selz (1999); Langlois and Robertson (1992a) and Chandler, Hikino and Nordenflycht (2001) provide historical insight into the evolution of the micro-electronics industry. Disintegration of the telecommunications industry is described in Song (2000); Fransmann (2002); Li and Whalley (2002).

[10] See chapter 1.

[11] See Arthur (1989); Munir (2003); Witt (1997).

sonal computer industry, but lost control over the standard to Intel and Microsoft. NeXT came to market with an arguable superior personal computer system, but was locked out by the dominance of the Wintel standard. Similarly, Apple Computer is being increasingly marginalised by the dominance of the Wintel standard. Sony lost a classic battle with Matsushita to establish a standard for VCRs. And first Sony, then Phillips, tried to create a new standard for recordable digital audio technology, with their DAT and DCC systems, but both appear to have failed."[12]

The present study places emphasis on the analysis of innovating firms that shape these business webs, create new markets, and define the customer value propositions.

Literature Review

Although considerable work on entrepreneurship and the growth of single firms already exists, little work explores the establishment and growth of firm networks.[13]

Classical economists such as Smith[14] and Marx[15], who were occupied with explaining economic growth, first discussed the role of entrepreneurs. In the view of Marx, the entrepreneur is only the provider of capital and is consequently defined as a capitalist. Marx was among the first to distinguish different roles in an economy arguing that there are industrial capitalists, productive capitalists and industrial managers. The focus of neoclassical Austrian economics[16] is the equilibrium-destroying, innovative role of the entrepreneur. For Schumpeter, entrepreneurs are revolutionaries of the economy that pioneer social and political revolutions. Additionally, entrepreneurs show a strong will to succeed; they like to fight and consider dimensions such as profits a measure of success in market competition, which they view as sporting as a financial sprint or a boxing fight. Finally, Schumpeter holds that entrepreneurs are motivated by the thrill of building and designing an economy in spite of or even precisely because of the resistance they encounter. Kirzner (1982), (1985) models entrepreneurship as a market disequilibrium because of asymmetric information and bounded rationality in markets. Incomplete market transparency leads to imperfect coordination between supply and demand. The entrepreneur dis-

---

[12] Hill (1997), p. 24.

[13] See Shan (1990); Autio (1997); Sexton and Landstrom (1999); Miller and Garnsey (2000); Murtha, Lenway and Hart (2001). More recent works include Hite and Hesterly (2001); Garud, Jain and Kumaraswamy (2002).

[14] See Smith (1776).

[15] See Marx (1867).

[16] See Schumpeter (1993b); Schumpeter (1993a).

covers opportunities to exploit friction in existing markets.[17] The difference in Schumpeter's and Kirzner's understanding of entrepreneurship is that the former emphasises the role of opportunity creation whereas the latter emphasises the exploitation of opportunities. Kirzner notes that there are two possibilities to exploit opportunities in space and time – a speculation function that expresses profit opportunities arising from differences in current and future prices and an arbitrage function that expresses differences in current prices at different locations. More recent approaches to assess the roles of entrepreneurs have a more extensive view of the nature of entrepreneurs in stating that entrepreneurs take on a combination of roles – for example in the works of Windsberger (1991), Schneider (2001) and Garud, Jain and Kumaraswamy (2002). These approaches try to combine the different views of entrepreneurship and argue that entrepreneurs combine the roles of the innovator, the arbitrageur and the coordinator. Based on transaction cost reasoning, Windsberger (1991) sees one function of entrepreneurs in finding opportunities of arbitrage by exploiting market imperfections.[18] The innovation function considers voluntary acts of creating new possibilities of profit sources in discovering new knowledge and changing economic boundary conditions. In line with these two profit-generating roles, he notes that profit sources can rely either on superior knowledge of the market or on the active diffusion of innovations. The coordinating role of entrepreneurs comprises the institutions governing the division of labour to realise profit opportunities. An optimal institutional arrangement minimises the coordination costs that comprise transaction costs, production costs and cost arising from risk.

Research undertaken to explain the growth of the firm has concentrated on the single firm, seldom acknowledging the embeddedness in larger contexts such as company groups, regional innovation networks and inter-organisational collaboration. Literature has primarily focused on the reasons for the emergence of inter-organisational cooperation and the arising management issues for established firm networks as well as the strategic outcome of such interlinked organisational forms. Sydow (1991), Snow, Miles and Coleman (1992), among others, discuss the management of strategic networks. Tsang (1998) analyses motives for the creation of alliances. Combs and Ketchen (1999) explain performance and outcome of interfirm cooperation. Gomez-Casseres (1994) explains competition between alliances. Sydow (1992) and Hess (2002) provide brief overviews of theo-

---

[17] See also Picot (1982), pp. 279, who sees the opportunity to reduce transaction cost as an incentive for entrepreneurship.

[18] See also Picot, Laub and Schneider (1990).

retical efforts to explain the emergence of firm networks.[19] Literature commonly argues that firm networks emerge because of external drivers. Uzzi (1996), for example, provides an in-depth analysis of the creation of informal business groups in the apparel industry. However, literature continues to almost entirely overlook the establishment and the growth challenges of these organisational forms. Achrol (1997) holds that there is a lack of causal models for the disintegration of firms and the formation of interfirm networks.[20] In her commentary on her much cited article "Towards a General Modular Systems Theory and Its Application to Inter-Firm Product Modularity", Schilling (2000) proposes that in extension to her own model, "a model of the outcomes of the adoption of increasingly modular forms would be valuable, as would be more development of the different ways that a system can manifest modularity."[21] Jones, Hesterly and Borgatti (1997) define such emergent organisational networks as a combination of independent firms that are mutually engaged in producing and commercialising a product based on implicit and open-ended contracts. Eisenhardt and Schoonhoven (1990) showed in their study on the formation of US semiconductor firms that the personal network of management teams plays a vital role in assessing early network partners. Hite and Hesterly (2001) posit that networks of individual firms consist primarily of socially embedded ties of the management teams as organisational networks emerge. The authors characterise these networks as being identity based. As the organisational network moves into the early growth stage, the member firms' networks evolve toward more ties based on the calculation of economic costs and benefits. The persistent ties between the core set of network partners are based on trust from frequent economic exchanges. There have been some efforts to develop formal models of alliance formation.[22] Some scholars emphasise the importance of successful diffusion of product systems and system innovations.[23] With the exception of the work of Aldrich and Fiol (1994), at least to my knowledge, management literature largely neglected the critical and complex problem of market and industry creation. "The study of market creation," Autio argues, "in spite of its practical difficulty, would appear to be of particular relevance for technology-based new firms, due to the importance of posi-

---

[19] The three dominant research frameworks presented are transaction cost theory, resource-dependency theory, and systems theory.

[20] See Achrol (1997), p. 1150.

[21] Schilling (2003), p. 203.

[22] See Höfer (1997); Garfinkel (2001), Weber (2001). Updegrove (1993) and Hofacker (2000) paid special attention to the formation of standard setting consortia.

[23] See Weiber (1992); Größler, Thun and Milling (2001); Funk and Methe (2001).

tive network externalities which generate increasing returns to the adoption of new technologies in many industries."[24]

Gomez-Casseres (1994) was one of the first researchers to stress that marketing of complex high technology products has become more and more dependent on joint efforts of co-operating firms.[25] Researchers, in particular, have almost completely ignored the establishment and growth of business webs. Hagel III (1996) deals with the establishment of business webs but gives only a few general points for action such as "pick the right technology as platform", "accelerate adoption" and "enter market quickly." Selz (1999) in his dissertation on value webs does not elaborate on web establishment. The same applies, to a lesser extent, to Zerdick, Picot, Schrape et al. (2000). Gawer (2000) focuses her analysis on the management processes by which Intel encourages adapters to innovate.[26] Here again, the researchers did not elaborate the initial management processes. This is rather surprising for a time in which an ever-increasing number of firms are failing to introduce their system offerings to the mass market through the establishment of business webs. (There are, of course, a few notable exceptions such as Intel, Microsoft, eBay, and DoCoMo.) Business history provides numerous examples of firms that failed to establish their product offering or to attract a sufficient number of supporters and customers. Companies such as memIQ AG and the mobile electronic payment system PayBox provide recent examples of business web establishment failure.[27] Waltenspiel (2000) and Franz (2003) are, to my knowledge, the first to explicitly consider establishment and initial growth of business webs.[28] However, both analysed the whole life-cycle of a business web and the different management challenges at each stage. In contrast to Franz, who models business web growth by taking advantage of game theory methodology and then showing empirical validity with illustrating cases, the present study is different in the way it uses the case data. I use two in-depth case studies and several historical mini-cases that will provide deeper insight on how business webs actually came into being. The observed cases serve as empirical data for the generated theoretical framework.

The merits of a theory-generating case study approach (in contrast to a theory-testing approach) are that the derived constructs are readily measur-

---

[24] Autio (2000), p. 14.

[25] See also the seminal work of Brandenburger and Nalebuff (1996) on how firms can benefit from a combination of competition and cooperation.

[26] Gawer (2000), p. 22.

[27] See Heise News (2002); Heise News (2003).

[28] See for example Franz (2003), pp. 108-115 there establishment and growth phases are described.

able since they reflect the observed reality in cases. Propositions and hypotheses are likely to be proven false or verified in subsequent research for the same reason. The results are more likely to be empirically relevant because they will have undergone several verification iterations during the research process.

Research Purpose

Massive globalisation of technology, knowledge and production means taken together with the accompanying further specialisation of tasks and increased division of labour between firms is leading to ever higher levels of complexity in the business world. Under these circumstances business webs are likely to be an organisational imperative for many firms trying to establish architectural innovations or product ecosystems for both entrepreneurial start-up firms and big corporations alike. My goal is to emphasise actively managed business web formation in contrast to the more passive notion of business web emergence. Arguably, economic actors voluntarily plan and design organisational networks for their economic purposes, actively seeking network partners and promoting the formation and early growth of the organisational network. Successfully shaping a business web involves many obstacles and management hurdles. The incentives are, nevertheless, quite high. Leading business web shapers tend to have self-fulfilling economic success, growing to dominant players in their respective industries with market shares of over 80% and equally high gross profit margins. Whereas Zook and Allen (2001), in their empirical study on growth across different industries, found that only 13% of all analysed companies met the growth criterion of achieving 5.5 percent real growth in revenues and earnings and recoup the costs of capital over a period of ten years. Especially in times of economic downturns, business web shapers proved their vitality.[29] Compared to their industry peers, corporations such as Adobe, eBay, Intel, Microsoft, DoCoMo and others can still boast of relatively high market valuations. In fact – and this is even more impressive – some of these companies are still growing in terms of sales and net income.

For management research, this gives rise to the question of how these or-

---

[29] Cohen reports, for example, on eBay: "EBay's stock was not immune from the dot.com collapse – by midsummer, it was down 50% from its pre-cash highs. But EBay itself was doing better than ever. When EBay announced its own second quarter results in July, its highly profitable business model and viral growth once again powered it to an array of upside surprises." Cohen (2002b), p. 242.

ganisations were actually established and which strategies the focal firms (shapers) followed in the early growth phase to attract suppliers of complementary goods and services (adapters). Four central questions for management science and business strategy are:

- How and why does business web establishment take place?
- How and why does the shaper convince initial adapters to support the architectural platform?
- How does the shaper achieve and execute leadership?
- How and why does the shaper capture the largest portion of value?

The present study aims to theorise the early growth processes of business webs with a case study research approach. I explore the challenges that the promoter of an architectural innovation faces in the early growth stages of the formation of a business web.

Structure of the Thesis

The structure of the thesis is as follows. The subsequent sections of this first chapter give a short introduction to theories of the firm that represent the theoretical basis for the study. Here, three different approaches for the existence and the determination of firm boundaries are presented. The second and the third chapter then provide the relevant background for the remaining chapters.

The second chapter describes the special attributes of network industries. Starting with a discussion of product systems, I first describe the construct of modularity in technological as well as organisational design and then outline general principals for modular systems design. Next, I lay out the fundamentals of the economics of networks. Throughout the chapter I show the impact of network effects and the importance of common compatibility standards as well as the impact of both on competition in network markets.

In the third chapter, a detailed description of business webs follows to define the actual subject of analysis. The chapter starts with a discussion of the major theoretical constructs and attributes used to classify network forms of organisation. I then proceed to lay out the distinct attributes of business webs.

The fourth chapter is dedicated to case studies that show formation and early growth of selected business webs. The larger first part presents the cases of i-mode and eBay in detail. The smaller second part of the chapter provides evidence from a variety of mini-cases including Adobe, IBM,

Microsoft, Intel and American Express, among others, as well as their historical roles in establishing new industries such as personal computing and digital publishing and payment cards.

In the fifth chapter, I then present a theoretical framework to model and explain the establishment and early growth of business webs based on the findings of the case studies. I argue that the emergence of business webs requires certain environmental circumstances which are discussed in the first part. Next, I propose to model the formation process as acts of institutional entrepreneurship. The early growth is then described as relying largely on external capabilities which are integrated with differing governance structures depending on the attributes of the exchange relationships. Finally, I theorise the value capturing mechanisms for the shaper of a business web. The sixth and last chapter discusses the results and gives directions for future research. Figure 1 illustrates the structure of the study.

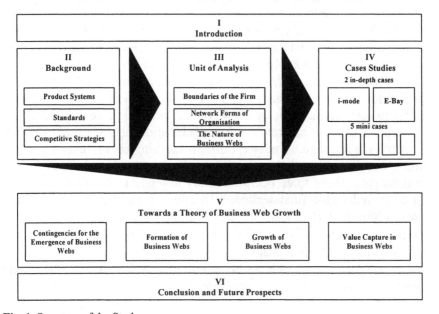

Fig. 1. Structure of the Study

Theory Framework: Theories of the Firm

The questions of how and why hybrid organisational forms such as business webs emerge and how they grow are firmly rooted in theoretical approaches describing the nature of the firm, the division of labour between firms and markets, and the coordination and organisation of economic activities within firms and markets. Theories of the firm aim to answer the following fundamental question:

"Markets appear and disappear; firms expand in scope and then turn back toward specialisation; quasi-firms and quasi-markets proliferate. Why and according to what principles do these things happen?"[30]

Literature broadly distinguishes between vertical boundary decisions and horizontal boundary decisions. Vertical integration refers to the number of value added stages operated within the boundaries of one firm.[31] Horizontal integration refers to expansion on the same value added stage of an industry value chain such as, for example, the merger or acquisition of two direct competitors. Theories of the firm aim to explain the boundaries of the firm – stated differently these theories try to explain why firms perform some activities internally while others are outsourced to external third parties or bought on the market.

In the following sections, I present the major theoretical streams that aim to explicate the existence of the firm and its size and scope. I begin the discussion with exchange-based theories that see the transaction and the associated cost through incomplete contracts in resource exchanges as the main reason for the existence of firms. The next section then describes the complementary resource-based view, which sees the existence of firms in path-dependent idiosyncratic resource combinations that yield a sustaining competitive advantage. A related position focusing on routines and capabilities that give organisations an advantage over markets is presented in the third part. These three complementary approaches are then compared and discussed in the final section.[32] The three presented frameworks are important for the further analysis of two questions:

- Why do integrated firms disintegrate under changing institutional settings and technological change?
- Why are some firms able to benefit from these changes while others cease to exist?

---

[30] Winter (1991), p. 183.

[31] See Porter (1985); Porter (1998); Holmström and Tirole (1989).

[32] "Some theories [of the firm] have their strong point in explaining conditions of existence, others in pricing, distribution, managerial behaviour or growth. To this extent, theories of the firm are inherently complementary rather than substitutes. In any case, only after a period of peaceful co-existence and competition will it be possible to see whether one of the different approaches could be taken as the point of departure for a generalization, or whether a completely new paradigm may be created, incorporating the earlier approaches as special cases." Gustafsson (1990), p. viii.

The next section starts with the exchange-based approach to address these questions.

Exchange-Based Theories of the Firm

Ronald H. Coase was the first to raise the questions of why firms exist and what would constitute their most efficient size and scope in his famous 1937 article.[33] The article provided the fundamental building blocks for transaction cost theory – one of the most prominent theoretical frameworks for analysing boundary decisions of the firm.[34] In this context firms and markets are seen as different governance modes for economic transactions.[35]

The division of labour in firms and between firms causes costs of control and coordination. The transfer of resources and the enforcement of rights over these resources are not costless by any means. These costs are subject to theorising in the transaction cost economics framework. As Williamson writes, "the transaction is the basis unit of analysis" for transaction cost economics.[36] A transaction occurs when property rights on resources, be they goods or services, are transferred between technologically separable stages of production. This implies that transaction cost economics presumes that nonseparable activities are organised under one roof, i.e. a firm. The transfer of property rights brings about transaction costs for finding an exchange partner, negotiations, contracting, controlling etc. "Transaction costs can be interpreted as cost of information and communication that have to be taken into account in order to come to a consensus on an equitable exchange."[37] The aim of transaction cost analysis is to find the appropriate organisational form for a given transaction which minimizes the transaction costs given the characteristics of a transaction, production costs and production performance. Consequently, transaction costs represent a measure of efficiency for the assessment and selection of different institutional arrangements.[38] The major influence factors of transaction costs, originally developed in the organisational failure framework of Williamson (1975), are behavioral assumptions and environmental factors

---

[33] See Coase (1937).

[34] See Williamson (1975); Williamson (1985); Picot (1982); Powell (1987); Powell (1990); Picot (1991); Wigand, Picot and Reichwald (1997).

[35] See Williamson (1975); Picot, Dietl and Franck (2002).

[36] Williamson (1985), p. 41.

[37] Picot (1993), p. 733. See also Picot, Laub and Schneider (1990), p. 190.

[38] See Wigand, Picot and Reichwald (1997), p. 37.

as well as the transaction atmosphere, the availability of capital and know-how and the transaction frequency.[39]

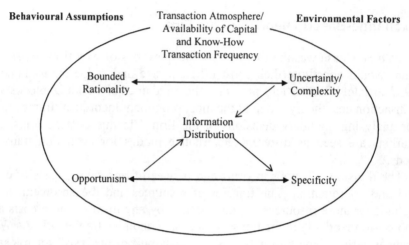

Fig. 2. Organsational Failure Framework[40]

The key behavioural assumptions of transaction cost theory are bounded rationality and opportunism. In contrast to the classical assumption of hyper-rationality, transaction cost economics assumes that economic actors intend to be rational but are in reality only boundedly rational, because of insufficient information processing capabilities.[41] Specificity plays an important role in determining transaction costs. Asset specificity refers to the degree to which an asset can be re-deployed in alternative uses. It is determined by the value difference in deployment for the intended use and the second-best use. Williamson (1985) distinguishes four types of asset specificity: (1) site asset specificity, (2) physical asset specificity, (3) human asset specificity and (4) dedicated asset specificity.[42] Site asset specificity occurs when a production site is built in geographical proximity to suppliers and/or customers. The asset is thus specific to a certain location. Dedicated purchases of specialised tools and machinery give rise to physical asset specificity. Human asset specificity results from transaction-specific investments in human capital such as training and accumulated

---

[39] See Williamson (1975); Williamson (1985); Picot (1991)
[40] Williamson (1991), p. 36. See also Wigand, Picot and Reichwald (1997), p. 38.
[41] See Simon (1955).
[42] In later works, Williamson adds brand name capital specificity and temporal specificity. See Williamson (1996); Williamson (1999).

implicit knowledge through learning-by-doing. Dedicated asset specificity requires non-contemporaneous dedication of assets for a transaction.

Asset specificity as a source of inefficiencies arises because of post-contractual disputes over rents. Such post-contractual problems will only arise if the assets cannot be redeployed elsewhere without cost. Specificity becomes a problem only in conjunction with the behavioural assumption of opportunism, which characterises self-interest seeking behaviour of e-conomic agents at anothers' cost, for example strategic behaviour, guile or deliberate disguise.[43]

At the centre of transaction cost economics as pioneered by Williamson are exchanges and the included contracts. In this framework, firms are often characterised as a nexus of both explicit and implicit contracts linking the individuals of a firm and its stakeholders.[44] Problems with asset specificity occur because contracts are incomplete. Contracts are necessarily incomplete because economic actors are only boundedly rational and thus cannot provide in advance or in sufficient detail for all relevant contingencies that might occur. First and most obvious there are legal contracts such as sales contracts, employment contracts, etc. These belong to the category of formal contracts. However, for many economic actions and organisational behaviour occurring in real life there are no formal contracts because the costs of writing contracts for every exchange or transaction would, in most cases, be too high. Economists, nevertheless, do not consider these transactions to take place without contracts. They consider such arrangements to be based on informal or implicit contracts.

Transaction cost economics can give important insight to thw question of which tasks to govern internally and which to source from outside. In particular, it directs attention to the characteristics of transactions and associated costs. Transaction cost economics is also used to explain shifts in the efficient boundaries of the firm by varying transaction cost based on technological changes. It is also a fruitful framework for illuminating competitive challenges and threats arising out of inter-organisational collaboration. These findings can be utilised for division of labour between modules of individual firms in modular systems based upon their degree of specificity and the prescription of governance modes for the distinct modules. However, the transaction cost framework and the associated theoretical building blocks of contracts and property rights show weaknesses in explaining either the critical role of internal resource combinations that

---

[43] See Aoki, Gustafsson and Williamson (1990), pp. 12-13; Wigand, Picot and Reichwald (1997), p. 38.

[44] See Aoki, Gustafsson and Williamson (1990); Wolff (1994).

lead to above average returns for distinct firms or why firms differ in organising the same transactions in a different manner.

Resource-Based Theories of the Firm

Based on the works of Penrose,[45] alternative theorising on the nature of the firm emerged during the 1980s. Wernerfelt (1984) pioneered the resource-based view of the firm arguing that firms are bundles of idiosyncratic resources. The resource-based view is rooted in strategic management research and initially intended to explain why firms differ in their ability to appropriate above average returns.[46]

The central unit of analysis for the resource-based view is the individual firm and its ability to generate above average rents. The central research question is thus, why do firms differ? According to the resource-based view, organisations are idiosyncratic because of corporate history and path dependencies resulting in resource asymmetries. Resource asymmetries occur because of imperfect factor markets. These market imperfections arise due to information asymmetries between economic actors and the existence of transaction costs that prohibit transferring highly specific assets. Resources in the framework include tangible resources such as capital, production means, information systems and so forth. Human capital, social capital, structural capital, brands, trademarks, knowledge, competencies and capabilities are referred to as intangible resources. Whereas tangible goods exhibit decreasing economies of scale, intangible assets increase their value with usage under some circumstances and hence exhibit economies of scale. Resource asymmetries lead to sustaining competitive advantage if these resources are valuable for the consumer, rare, inimitable and non-substitutable. The framework is illustrated in figure 3.

---

[45] See Penrose (1959).

[46] Resource-based theorists provided a contradictory approach to industrial economics pioneered by Bain (1956). The works of Porter (1985) gave this approach widespread recognition. Porter himself employed it as a tool for competitive analysis in the five forces framework in which firms are treated as being homogenous.

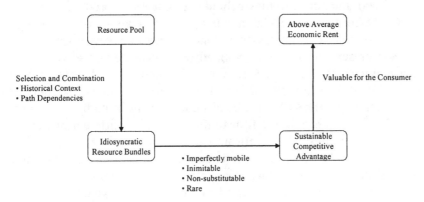

Fig. 3. Resource-based View of Sustainable Competitive Advantage[47]

Reasons for limited inimitability are historical context, path dependency, social complexity, and causal ambiguity. Historical context refers to the decisions and behaviour of managers in the past that led to advantageous resource bundles. This can be attributed to superior management vision in selecting and building specific resources or simply lucky circumstances that rendered resources valuable because of economic change. Barriers to imitation arising out of resources requiring time to build are referred to under the label of path dependency. Examples for path dependent inimitable resources include tacit knowledge accumulated through learning-by-doing and corporate culture. Social complexity describes barriers to imitation attributable to high levels of complexity in imitation. Examples of this are reputation, trust and corporate culture that cannot be bought easily through market means. In the case of social ambiguity, the nature of value contribution of resources remains unclear for competitors. Such resources are invisible to prospect imitators.[48] Again, tacit knowledge is a well suited example, but also "organisational routines"[49] and "emergent strategies."[50]

Building on the resource-based theory of the firm, Prahalad and Hamel (1990) developed the core competencies approach in the early 1990s.[51]

---

[47] Adapted from Rühli (1995), p. 95.

[48] See Wernerfelt (1984); Barney (1991). Conner and Prahalad (1996); Fahy (2000).

[49] See Nelson and Winter (1982).

[50] See Mintzberg and Lampel (1999).

[51] See Hamel, Doz and Prahalad (1989); Hamel and Prahalad (1991); Prahalad and Hamel (1990).

They define core competencies as a firm's skills for collective learning and internal coordination activities behind the process of product and service creation.[52] Core competencies are unique combinations of technologies, knowledge, and skills possessed by one distinct company.[53] Core competencies represent the source of competitive advantage and serve as a base for a company to deliver a variety of new products and services on the market. According to Prahalad and Hamel, core competence should fulfill three criteria: (1) The skill must be difficult to be imitated by other companies. (2) It has to enable the firm to move between different markets and industries. (3) It must add significant value to the market.[54]

The resource-based view suggests that firms exist because the combination and control of valuable, rare, inimitable and non-substitutable resources within the boundaries of a firm enables the stakeholders to derive higher returns. These higher returns are the result of interdependencies between resources. A resource A for example might increase the value of resource B while both resources are independent of a third resource C. If an entrepreneur bundles resources A and B under one roof, the combined value is higher than the single resources or the bundles A and C or B and C.[55] Teece (1986) developed a framework to explain the modalities of value appropriation for innovations in which the value of interdependent resources is illustrated. Teece distinguishes between general assets, co-specialised assets and specialised assets. Co-specialised assets are necessary complementary assets that a firm needs to access or to control in order to appropriate profits. Teece showed that firms were achieving higher performance through the exploitation of complementary assets. The control of complementary assets such as sales channels manifested advantages for incumbents commercialising innovations. Hence, the control of complementary assets helps incumbents to survive technological change and disruption.[56] Confronted with resource dependencies many firms seek to gain access to critical co-specialised assets. There are three possibilities for gaining access to relevant resources. One possibility is to access resources through inter-organisational relationships. A popular way to gain access to critical complementary resources is to form joint ventures or strategic alliances. These relationships can themselves be thought of as resources for a sustainable competitive advantage. "In fact, a firm's network can be thought of as creating inimitable and non-substitutable value (and con-

---

[52] See Prahalad and Hamel (1990).
[53] Core competencies were introduced by Prahalad and Hamel (1990).
[54] See Prahalad, Hamel (1990), pp. 79.
[55] See Conner (1991).
[56] See, for example, the case of Linotype in Tripsas (2000b).

straint!) as inimitable resource by itself, and as a means to access inimitable resources and capabilities."[57] Gulati, Nohria and Zaheer (2000) label these resources as network resources. A second way to reduce resource dependencies is to integrate the resources vertically or horizontally under common ownership. Wigand, Picot and Reichwald (1997) and Barney (1999) assert that the decision to integrate vertically is not exclusively determined by asset specificity but also dependent on the costs to achieve control over those assets. Under some circumstances, neither acquisition nor internal creation is feasible. Under imperfect mobility it may be prohibitively costly to achieve ownership of certain resources. The firm may also encounter limits to imitation if the capabilities are path dependent. The value of resources might be causally ambiguous or socially complex thereby limiting internal creation. „Thus, for capabilities to play a significant role in determining a firm's boundary, it must be costly for a firm to create these capabilities on its own, and it must also be costly for a firm to acquire another firm that already possesses these capabilities."[58] Diversification and focusing patterns of firms can be explained using capabilities-based reasoning about firms. The central hypothesis is that firms expand in markets that utilise similar capabilities. Lockett and Thompson (2001) provide an overview over a number of empirical studies that show a relationship between success and similarity of capabilities. With growing diversification, profitability tends to decrease. Thirdly, a company can simply acquire another firm that possesses the critical resources, if it can afford to do so and if it has the "absorptive capacity,"[59] i.e. existing knowledge and a learning base to successfully integrate the acquired company.[60] The dynamics of building firm specific knowledge and capabilities and the change over time through learning and adaptation to technological change and change in environmental boundary conditions is treated in particular by capabilities-based theories of the firm.

Capabilities-Based Theories

Exchange-based theories of the firm largely address incentive problems which can be efficiently controlled with economic institutions such as firms. Resource-based theories explain differences in firm performance with heterogeneous resource distribution. However, both approaches are mainly comparative-static in their analysis. Capabilities-based theories in

---

[57] Gulati, Nohria and Zaheer (2000), p. 207.
[58] Barney, Wright and Ketchen (2001), p. 140.
[59] See Cohen and Levinthal (1990).
[60] See Picot (1991) for capital and knowledge barriers to vertical integration strategies.

contrast are comparative-dynamic, analysing creation and utilisation of firm capabilities over time. Constructs such as dynamic capabilities enriched the discussion with explicit modelling changes in the knowledge base of the firm. The origins of organisational capabilities can probably also be traced back to Penrose (1959). The idea was put forward by authors such as Nelson and Winter (1982) and Teece (1982). Capabilities-based theories cope explicitly with change in organisations and the ability of organisations to adapt to changing environments by learning in an evolutionary process. An important factor for explaining the „existence, boundaries, nature and development of the firm is the capacity of such an organization to protect and develop the competencies of the groups and individuals contained within it, in a changing environment."[61]

Evolutionary theorising in economics tries to overcome the limits of equilibrium thinking and explains dynamic processes such as innovation, growth and change more realistically. What makes this approach unique is that well defined and well known decisions, stable relationships, mature technologies or settled firm boundaries in stable industries are not of particular interest. "In particular, evolutionary theory can be argued to be needed for analyses of behavior in contexts that involve significant elements of novelty, so that it cannot be presumed that good responses already have been learned, but rather that they are still to be learned."[62] The main unit of analysis is not the transaction, but the firm. The explanation includes variables that are subject to change over time, the emergence of new variables and the disappearance of variables over time, as well as a description of the environmental conditions and the selection systematic that alters observed variables.[63] The concrete units of analysis are human artefacts such as technologies, policies, economic institutions that can be modified and improved from generation to generation. As an example, one can consider a societies selection of competing technologies over time. For instance, evolutionary economists would analyse the competition between the Apple Macintosh operating system and its competitor Windows and the eventual success from Windows over MacOs by selection of the personal computer user population. Criteria proposed for economic selection in the literature include, for example, profits and prices, but also product quality, service offerings, etc. Finally, evolutionary theories are concerned with the processes by which economic actors learn and adapt their behavioural patterns to changing environmental circumstances such as emerging new technologies and institutional change. The basic hypothesis is that

---

[61] Hodgson (1998), p. 189.
[62] Dosi and Nelson (1994), p. 158.
[63] See Dosi and Nelson (1994).

economic actors "follow various forms of *rule-guided* behaviours which are *context-specific* and to some extent, *event-independent* (in the sense that actions might be invariant to fine changes in the information regarding the environment). On the other hand, agents are always capable of experimenting and discovering new rules and, thus, they continue to introduce behavioural novelties into the system."[64]

Central to capabilities-based theories of the firm is the concept of organisational routines. These guiding rules for actors in organisations are relatively invariant and emerge from the learning paths of the individuals, determined by pre-existing knowledge and institutions as well as personal beliefs. Organisational routines, for example, shape the specific relationships between a firm and its owners, customers, and suppliers.[65] Nelson and Winter (1982), differentiate between three types of organisational routines. "Standard operating procedures" refer to the organisational capabilities a firm needs for its current size and scope to produce the core products and serve its core customer segments. Second, there are routines that determine the future growth or decline of a firm in terms of investment behaviour – the management decisions of future size and scope of the firm represented by product extensions and engagement in new markets through organic growth or mergers and acquisitions, so to speak. Third, deliberate processes of the firm are aimed at searching for better operating solutions and are guided by organisational routines.[66] Such deliberate processes correlate to what management scientists refer to as strategies.[67] Nelson argues that "[t]he performance of [a] firm or organization will be determined by the routines it possesses and the routines possessed by other firms and economic units with which the firm interacts, including competitors, suppliers, and customers." The organizational capabilities are based on a hierarchy of organisational routines. In an early paper Nelson (1991) notes that the "[...] notion of a hierarchy of organizational routines is the key building block under our concept of core capabilities."[68] Chandler, Hikino and Nordenflycht (2001) argue that organisational capabilities are based upon three types of knowledge. The authors distinguish between technical, functional and managerial knowledge. Technical capabilities are those skills and applied know-how which are necessary to apply scientific and engineering knowledge to invent new products and processes. Functional

---

[64] Dosi and Nelson (1994), p. 157.

[65] See Winter (1991).

[66] See Dosi and Nelson (1994).

[67] Especially process orientated strategic management researchers have a similar interpretation of strategies. See Burgelman and Rosenbloom (1997); Eisenhardt and Sull (2001); Lovas and Sumatra (2000).

[68] Nelson (1991), pp. 67-68.

knowledge is product-specific and describes development and production capabilities to actually develop and produce products and commercialise them. Finally, managerial capabilities are the management knowledge and experience that are necessary to maintain the financial health and growth of the firm. These "dynamic capabilities" in particular comprise the ability to coordinate activities, make decisions and allocate resources.[69] "Dynamic capabilities consist of specific strategic and organizational routines like product development, alliancing, and strategic decision making that create value for firms within dynamic markets by manipulating resources into new value-creating strategies."[70]

Evolutionary theorising of the firm emphasises learning, the critical role of technological change, and contributes important building blocks for the emergence, growth, and decline of organisations. It explains patterns of growth and shows why some firms are better under regimes of rapid technological change than others are. Further, a firm's changing size and scope as well as the diversification of its knowledge base in adjacent markets can be explained.

Conclusion

The theoretical approach to assess the size and scope of a firm contributes important and complementary findings. The existence of a firm can be explained by transaction cost advantages over the market and the possibility of appropriating above average returns from idiosyncratic resource bundles. The exchange-based response to the question "why do firms exist?" argues that transaction costs in firms are lower than they would be if production were coordinated through the market. At the heart of this argument is the reduction of costs associated with transactions between certain individuals. Hodgson (1998), however, presumes that this argument ignores the possibility of activities, which are in principle non-contractable, including elements of the production process. Furthermore, the reliance on comparative-statics in transaction cost economics downplays the human learning that takes place within firms. Resource-based theory is more centered on explaining the sources of sustainable competitive advantages. Firms exist because bundling of complementary and idiosyncratic resources give them a competitive edge. Evolutionary economics focuses on changes in time and is particularly concerned with growth patterns. The construct of organisational routines shows similarities to intangible resources as put

---

[69] See Teece, Pisano and Shuen (1997) and Eisenhardt and Martin (2000).
[70] Eisenhardt and Martin (2000), p. 1106.

forward in resource-based approaches for explaining the superior performance of firms. The key essence of the three main streams in the theory of the firm is that each approach emphasises particular problems or circumstances that must be integrated in order to retain a holistic picture.

For the subject of this study, the three approaches provide the analytic framework and toolset to explain the dissolution of firm boundaries and the emergence of network forms of organisation. The distribution of resources throughout the business web and the potential to capture above average economic returns can be analysed using the resource-based theories. Growth and change in capabilities can be explained using dynamic capabilities reasoning.

However, the presented frameworks are still very generic and applicable to any firm. For this reason I shall elaborate the special boundary conditions for business webs in the following. Product systems and modularity in connection with specific attributes of network markets require specific organisational arrangements and capabilities. The following chapter will present these unique challenges and refer back to the fundamental principles of theories of the firm as appropriate.

On Network Industries

Why were modular product systems most successful in microelectronics, information technology and telecommunications? All these product systems exhibit network effects. The reason for network effects is the desire for standardisation in network industries leading to increasing returns, positive feedback, and customer lock-ins. The arising switching costs to rival dominant designs for customers create winner-take-all markets. Coyne and Dye (1998) give such diverse markets as aviation, banking, railway, telecommunications, logistics and health maintenance as examples. Firms in these industries transport people, funds, and information through their networks. Firms operating in network industries often share a common infrastructure such as airports, railways, roads, telecommunication networks, ATM networks, etc. and compete for customer value on the basis of these infrastructures. Telecommunication firms have interconnection contracts; banks share payment networks and ATM's for their customers, airlines share frequent flyer programs, airline lounges and, in the case of chartering airport slots, aircraft, crew and boarding facilities. Network-based businesses exhibit strong cost advantages with increasing network coverage due to economies of scale. "If", Arrow writes, „complementary services are produced under increasing returns, then again the utility to a user increases with the number of users."[1] The presence of positive network effects and increasing returns through positive feedbacks leads to the emergence of natural monopolies. For this reason, big players in network industries used to be state owned or regulated monopolies. All these industries are built around product systems whose attributes are the subject of the next section.

The following sections serve as an analytical framework to describe the boundary conditions for the emergence of business webs for the remainder of the study. First, I describe the attributes of product systems. Second, I show the interplay of modularity in technology and in organisation. Then, I present general principles for modular system design that are also applicable to organisations. The second part of the chapter then illustrates the

---

[1] See Arrow (2000), p. 179. See also Evans and Schmalensee (1993), p. 35; Kelly (1998), p. 27.

economic impacts of networks. In the first part so-called network effects are elaborated. The subsequent section then deals with compatibility standards that play a major role in network industries. The impact of network effects and compatibility standards on competition is discussed in the third section. The chapter closes with a summary and brief discussion of the results.

Product Systems and Modularity

Many of the technologies in use today are systemic in nature, meaning that the product consists of multiple parts that are mutually dependent and interconnect with each other.[2] "Product systems consist of various parts or services that can only be used together even though they might be sold separately."[3] Further, product systems require investments in many complementary assets, resources and technologies. The whole system creates utility for the customer only as the interplay of a set of components.[4] The performance of the components and their interoperability determine the performance of the product system.[5] Interoperability is a relational attribute that defines the rules of fit and interaction between components with interfaces. Modularity helps divide those complex systems into many subsystems or modules to keep them manageable. Modules are interdependent in their inner workings but independent among each other, connected only with simple interfaces which hide the complexity of the module to the outside.[6] Figure 4 gives a simplified illustration of a product system.

---

[2] See Winter (1987).

[3] Haucap (2003), p. 30.

[4] "This means that when customers judge the product value it is not the individual part that counts but the product as a whole (in other word the system product)." Zerdick, Picot, Schrape et al. (2000), p. 177.

[5] See Henderson and Clark (1990); Tushman and Rosenkopf (1992).

[6] See Baldwin and Clark (1997); Baldwin and Clark (2000).

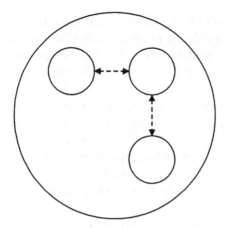

Fig. 4. Simplified Illustration of a Product System[7]

At the beginning of a product system is an architectural innovation that defines the components, the interoperability and the interfaces between components.[8] In Figure 4 the architecture is represented by modules within the system boundaries and their respective connections. This simple architecture consists of three modules connected by interfaces.

Attributes of Product Systems

According to Garud and Kumaraswamy (2003), product systems show three attributes: (1) Modularity, (2) Integrity and (3) Upgradeability. There are a variety of trade-offs within these attributes. The authors show, for example, that higher degrees of modularity negatively affect system integrity because it is impossible to control or eliminate all subordinate interactions between components in nearly decomposable systems. Modularity also affects the ability of the system to evolve and its ability to change. The authors mention the limiting function of pre-specified system architectures which may not allow the system to evolve to a new architecture. A modular innovation,[9] i.e. an innovation within a module, which is independent of the architecture, may be introduced into the market by any firm because it does not require adjustments to other sub-systems as long as it

---

[7] See Henderson and Clark (1990), p. 12; Christensen (2000).
[8] See Henderson and Clark (1990); Galunic and Eisenhardt (2001); Morris and Ferguson (1993).
[9] See Langlois and Robertson (1992b), p. 301-302; Sanchez and Mahoney (1996), p. 68-69.

does not touch predefined interfaces.[10] An architectural innovation,[11] however, requires a significant re-modification of the sub-systems and is dependent on a new standard which can only be achieved by cooperation between all crucial players in order to commonly create a new market in the quickest possible way.[12] Finally, Garud and Kumaraswamy (2003) present tradeoffs between integrity and upgradeability. These trade-offs are manifested in the choice between a maximum efficient present design and an efficient design over time. The hypothesis is that there exist only local maxima that provide an architecture with efficiency at one point in time but most likely inefficiency over time.[13]

Modularity enables reuse of components and increases the speed of innovation. The nature of innovation in a modular system differs significantly from closed vertical systems. Innovations on the system level – architectural innovations – affect the structure and the interplay of modules. These radical innovations occur rarely and typically introduce a new dominant design while starting a new lifecycle. Modular innovations take place at any time in any module simultaneously, leading to fast independent and unplanned trial and error processes without altering the existing system architecture. The decentralised network of participating firms contributing modules to defined standards that are compatible to specified interfaces permits faster adaptation to technological change and market uncertainty than in huge vertically integrated firms. Garud and Kumaraswamy (2003) labelled these enhancements "economies of substitution." The authors posit that economies of substitution "arise when the cost of designing a higher performance system through the partial retention of existing components is lower than the cost of designing the system afresh."[14] Modularity in design also gives rise to the exploitation of external economies.[15] These economies arise from the efforts of third parties producing knowledge spill-overs and complementary assets for a business ecosystem. Modularity in the design of products leads to modularity in the design of a firm's internal structure and organisation.[16]

---

[10] See Teece (1998).
[11] See Henderson and Clark (1990), pp. 9.
[12] See Antonelli (1998).
[13] See Langlois and Robertson (2003), pp. 70-72.
[14] Langlois and Robertson (2003), p. 69, emphasis omitted.
[15] See Langlois (1992a); Langlois and Robertson (1992a).
[16] See Sanchez and Mahoney (1996), pp. 63; Picot, Ripperger and Wolff (1996) pp. 161 and Göpfert (1998), pp. 129.

Modularity in Technology and Organisation

Modularity was a major research topic throughout the nineties of the last century.[17] It refers to the ability to decompose technological and organisational systems in such a way that the internal functioning of a subsystem does not significantly affect the functioning of other sub-modules. "Modularity is a general systems concept: it is a continuum describing the degree to which a system's components can be separated and recombined, and it refers both to the tightness of coupling between components and the degree to which the 'rules' of the system architecture enable (or prohibit) the mixing and matching of components."[18] A product system with high levels of modularity is called nearly decomposable. "A decomposable system is one that is cut into pieces or 'modularized' in such a way that most interactions (which we can think of as flows of information) take place within the modules; interactions among modules are kept to a minimum and are regularized through formal 'interfaces'."[19] The idea of "near decomposability" goes back to Simon (1962) and describes that in the short run the behaviour of a module is nearly independent of other modules, in the long run the module depends on other modules in an aggregate way only. Systems are only nearly decomposable because humans and machines alike have bounded rationality preventing the ex ante design of a system consisting of completely independent components. Other authors, particularly Weick (1976), have put forward the concept of coupling. Integrated products with specific (and often exclusive) interfaces for interconnections and exchange with other modules are tightly-coupled. In contrast, modular products architectures that adhere to a common interface standard to connect to, interact with, and exchange resources between components are loosely-coupled.[20]

---

[17] See, for example, Langlois and Robertson (1992b); Sanchez and Mahoney (1996); Baldwin and Clark (1997); Göpfert (1998); Baldwin and Clark (2000); Schilling (2000); Galunic and Eisenhardt (2001); Schilling and Steensma (2001); Langlois (2002).

[18] Schilling (2000), p. 312.

[19] Langlois (2001b), p. 6.

[20] See Weick (1976); Sanchez and Mahoney (1996); Orton and Weick (1999); Schilling (2000).

Tight Coupling   **Loose Coupling**

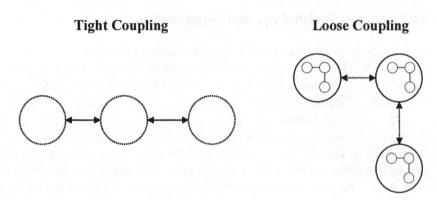

Fig. 5. Tight and Loose Coupling of Modules

The extent of coupling is indicated by the necessity for spatial or tempo-ral links between production steps. Tight coupling requires that production steps have to be executed at the same time in the same place. "In loosely coupled systems, however, each step or component of production is sepa-rated from every other step in space and time. Thus, the production steps can be done in any sequence at any location. Tight coupling requires close supervision in order to contain problems that might otherwise spread quickly to other processes, but loose coupling permits less centralized con-trol because errors in system components do not easily affect the entire system. In short, the more tightly technological elements are coupled, the more control needs to be centralized."[21]

For producing a tightly coupled technological system, high financial in-vestments and huge vertically integrated firms with high levels of control are necessary.[22] Loosely coupled technological systems can be produced in networks of small specialised firms with relatively small requirements for financial investments and permit decentralised control.[23] If coordination is replaced by standardised interfaces, decentralised governance in modular networks has a clear competitive advantage over vertically integrated firms and hierarchical coordination.[24] The challenge for an architectural innova-tor, however, is to coordinate complementary adjacent production steps that are subject to change. "This is particularly important if some of the ex-isting asset-holders, or the factors complementary to the existing assets,

---

[21] Hart and Kim (2002), p. 2.
[22] See Christensen (2001); Afuah (2001).
[23] See Hart and Kim (2000).
[24] See Langlois (2001b); Langlois and Robertson (2003).

have the power to block innovation (...) to protect their rent streams."[25] This challenge arises if an architectural innovation renders one or more established production stages in an industry obsolete, for example, due to technological progress or through the introduction of a new system architecture requiring a major or complete redesign of autonomous modules.

Large systems such as computers, information systems, telecommunication networks, or markets and business organisations exhibit increasing degrees of complexity. To handle this increased complexity firms break integrated products into subsystems or modules which are easier to maintain and change without affecting the system as a whole. In his seminal paper, Simon (1962) defines a complex system roughly as "one made up of a large number of parts that interact in a nonsimple way. In such systems the whole is more than the sum of its parts, not in an ultimate, metaphysical sense but in the important pragmatic sense that, given the properties of the parts and the laws of their interaction, it is not a trivial matter to infer the properties of the whole."[26] Linear, predictable systems are simple; iterative, interactive systems are complex. A typical example for a simple system would be an assembly line or a rigid value chain. Complex systems have large information requirements that overload the capacity of centralised governance structures. Here, good examples are the Internet or a fluid value network. Therefore, complex systems favour decentralised governance coordinated through network connections. Technologies with low/medium levels of coupling and medium/high degrees of complexity require decentralised governance structures. Modern information and communication technologies in particular represent such technologies. Cooperative networks of module suppliers decrease investment risks and increase flexibility for the participating firms.

Principles of Modular System Design

The main target of modularisation is to build "(...) a complex product or process from smaller subsystems that can be designed independently yet function together as a whole."[27] Baldwin and Clark (1997), (2000) have drawn on ideas from computer science to formulate general principles for modular system design. A company can achieve a modular design for its products and services by partitioning information processes into visible design rules and hidden design parameters. Hidden design parameters are

---

[25] Langlois (1992b), p. 117. See also Teece (1986).
[26] Simon (1962), p. 468.
[27] Baldwin and Clark (1997), p. 84.

kept internally within the firm and represent elements which do not affect
a module's architecture, interfaces and standards. They are of great importance to ensure a competitive advantage over other similar firms and companies intending to imitate the underlying modular product or service. In
contrast to hidden design parameters, visible design rules are specified,
disclosed and communicated to the participating companies in the early
stages of modular product and service development. Visible design rules
can be divided into three parts:[28]

- an architecture for specifying coherent modules of the system and its
  functions
- interfaces for defining the connections and communication between the
  modules in detail
- standards for measuring a module's conformity to design rules and performance relative to other modules

Modularity makes it possible to produce components separately and to
use them interchangeably in different configurations without damaging
system integrity.[29]

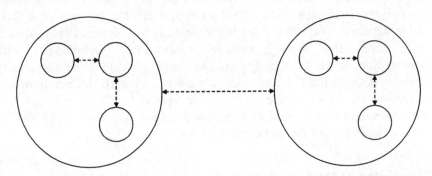

Fig. 6. A Simple Modular Design

Figure 6 shows a design consisting of two aggregate subsystems each of
which is composed of three interdependent modules. The subsystems are
connected via an interface. As long as the modules within a subsystem adhere to a common standard they can be substituted and upgraded without
disturbing the functionality of the whole system.

---

[28] See Baldwin and Clark (1997), pp. 84-86.
[29] See Demsetz (1993).

Economics of Networks

Many connected and interdependent modules constitute a network. In order to function as a whole, a minimum number of modules are necessary. In addition, modules need standardised interfaces to guarantee compatibility between modules.

In the following chapter, I will briefly describe the origins and implications of network economics for modular product systems. In the first section, I describe physical and virtual network effects. In the second section, I then show the importance of compatibility standards to maintain the interoperability of modules. In the third section, I show the impact of network effects and standards on competition for firms operating in network markets.

Network Effects

Katz and Shapiro (1985) and Farrell and Saloner (1985) simultaneously published the basic papers on network effects. According to them, network effects arise whenever the value of consuming a product increases with the size of the installed base of compatible products. The authors postulated that in many industries individual actions affect the utility of other actors. They labelled this effect network externality. The welfare optimal degree of standardisation and welfare destroying effects were at the centre of attention.

Literature on network effects distinguishes between physical connection networks and virtual networks. Physical networks represented by computer networks, telecommunication networks, etc. link users physically, adding value with every new node which in turn represents four new potential communication links to the installed base of users. A telephony network, for example, exhibits direct network effects. Every new user creates utility for the other because he adds potential connection linkages. Indirect network effects or virtual network effects create utility that arises because other users buy the same system and benefit from available complementary products as well as experience and knowledge of other users.[30] These indirect network effects arise because of the availability of compatible products and services around a platform in a market that is positively related to the installed user base. Indirect network effects spur the demand

---

[30] Network externalities were first discussed in Farrell and Saloner (1985); Katz and Shapiro (1985). For further elaboration see Economides (1996); Katz and Shapiro (1986); Shy (1996); Hess (2000) to mention but a few.

for complementary products. Products such as operating systems (e.g. Windows), home video standards (e.g. VHS) or game consoles (e.g. Playstation) that rely heavily on complements represent virtual networks. IBM AT compatible personal computers exhibit indirect network effects insofar as the computing platform's installed base determines the number of compatible software applications and peripherals as well as the available support.

Competition in markets with network effects differs significantly from that in normal markets.[31] "Positive network externalities introduce unique strategic challenges. A new service has relatively low value to its first customer, whereas the costs typically are the highest in the introduction phase."[32] Indirect network effects create a chicken-and-egg problem: A critical mass of users and complementary products is necessary. Without complementary products users cannot be attracted, but nobody wants to create complements for a sub-critical mass product. As illustrated in figure 7, a given product exhibits negative utility for prospective consumers. The negative utility represents the cost of a good with little or no intrinsic value – for example, the initial investment costs of buying a fax machine. Only with an installed base of N* users does the service create utility because the extrinsic value of exchanging documents is dependent on the number of fax machines in the market and the number of people with whom documents can be exchanged. After reaching the critical mass N* of users, the utility function grows even faster than the added number of nodes in the network since every new fax machine adds two new potential connections to the network.[33]

---

[31] See Garud and Kumaraswamy (1993); Besen and Farrell (1994).

[32] Stabell and Øystein (1998), p. 428.

[33] This relation is also known as Metcalfe's Law. See Katz and Shapiro (1992); Katz and Shapiro (1985).

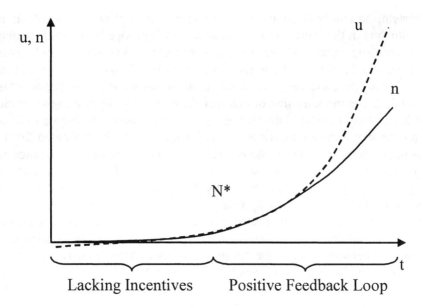

Lacking Incentives   Positive Feedback Loop

Fig. 7. Product Introduction Under Positive Network Effects

Network effects are a source of switching costs. Switching costs arise because it takes time, money, and effort for customers to switch between competing networks. Literature distinguishes between two sources of switching costs.[34]

Exogenous switching costs refer to the nature of a product. These switching costs do not refer to the strategic behaviour of individual firms, but take into account all suppliers of these goods. Examples for exogenous switching costs include telephone numbers or information gathering on new system products. Endogenous switching costs, on the other hand, are deliberately created to attain a competitive edge. Artefacts to create switching cost artificially are, for example, loyalty schemes, costs of contract termination or personalised accounts.

Buyer switching costs result in network lock-ins[35] because users have become comfortable with the architecture – they have got used to it. Lock-ins are in effect ex-post contractual problems arising from incomplete information. A user cannot – at least not without great expense – exhaustively assess alternatives in the market. Once he has decided to buy one

---

[34] For a brief discussion of exogenous and endogenous switching cost in network industries see, for example, Haucap (2003).

[35] See Arthur (1989); Afuah and Tucci (2003), p. 59; Shapiro and Varian (1999), pp. 104 and Witt (1997).

system, he can only switch to a different system if he writes off his investments in the initial system architecture. The property on product architectures and standards gives the property rights holder control and renders the standard asset specific to the buyer, or rather the user.[36] Therefore lock-ins create dependencies that result in above-average prices because they enable the monopolisation of markets. Customer loyalty and high retention rates directly translate into revenue growth, because of the high cost of acquiring new consumers. Reichheld (1996), for example, estimated that a 5 percent increase in the customer retention rate increases the average net present value by 35% for software companies and 95% for advertising agencies. Loyal customers are more likely to spend more and to return more often. This is especially true for online businesses where strong customer retention results in much higher per-customer revenues. The number of users and the market share of a network act as indicators for the existence of network effects, the churn rate of users between networks acts as an indicator for switching costs.[37] The churn rate is the number of customers who disconnect from a network in a given period, divided by the average total number of customers for that same period.

High levels of modularity and gateway technologies that facilitate mixing and matching of components can decrease the cost of switching between different technologies and prevent customers from being locked in to a specific technology. Java technology is just such a gateway technology that enables porting software applications from one operating system to another. Microsoft Services Network (MSN) provides migration software that allows new users of the service to import their addresses, stored e-mails, buddy lists and other personal information from existing America Online (AOL) and Yahoo! accounts, thus diminishing the lock-in effects. Specialised interfaces that coordinate the functions of given component sets constrain mixing and matching and are more likely to lock in customers.

The modular IBM PC compatible architecture illustrates the different attributes of interface standards. Open interfaces such as USB have a very unspecific non-discriminatory nature. Here users can easily switch printing, scanning, and storing devices as long as the new technology adheres to the common attributes of USB. The Windows operating system is more specific in that respect because consumers cannot easily switch the operating system without having to repurchase all of their application software for the new platform, Linux or OS/2, for example.

---

[36] Organisational challenges arising from incomplete contracts are discussed in chapter 1.
[37] See Tewary (2003).

As mentioned earlier, network effects arise in virtual networks because increased sales of critical components of the product system (e.g. operating systems for personal computers) induce a larger availability of complementary components (such as independent software applications). The increased value of complementary components results in positive feedback because of their higher availability.[38] A simple positive feedback loop is illustrated below (Figure 8).

Consider a product system with two components, A and B, with A representing a critical component and B a complementary component. If sales for component A (e.g. the computer) increase, then the sales for B (printers for example) will be spurred. The higher availability of compatible printers for A in turn spurs the sales of A resulting in a winner-takes-most or winner-takes-all market.[39] Such markets are characterised by extreme market shares of only one or two players and inequality of profits.

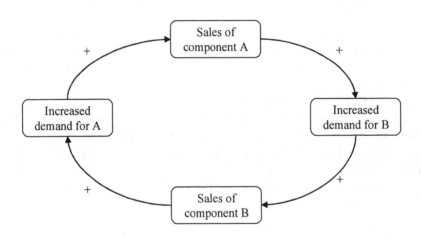

Fig. 8. Positive Feedback Loop

Positive feedback loops result in increasing returns dynamics. It is important to distinguish between network effects and increasing returns, although the two concepts are often treated interchangeably in economics literature. The presence of network effects is the attribute of a product system resulting in increasing returns due to positive feedback loops.

---

[38] See Arthur (1994); Shapiro and Varian (1999); Bettis and Hitt (1995).
[39] For an introduction to "winner-take-all markets" see Frank and Cook (1995).

Compatibility Standards

Although standards have an important role in every industry, in network industries standards are mandatory from the demand side and the supply side alike. [40] Standards enable the combination of elements from different manufacturers and ensure their compatibility. Examples are consumer electronics, broadcasting, transportation, computing systems, telecommunication networks and especially the Internet.[41] Compatibility implies that usage rights on technological knowledge "that has the capability of being used in a system without need for special modification to accommodate it"[42] might possibly be transferred. Universal industry standards are a precondition for compatibility between systems and networks. Compatibility is especially important for products that exhibit positive network effects – the more the technology is shared among users, the more valuable it becomes. Therefore, the demand for standardised products is higher in markets with network externalities. "If technology is hard to use, if it is unreasonably priced, or if ownership rights are difficult to guarantee, then compatibility problems might arise."[43] Recent empirical evidence for this hypothesis is provided by third generation mobile telecommunication technologies where even implementations of various standard releases are incompatible, not to mention the competing standards W-CDMA, TDMA and CDMA2000.[44]

The adoption and diffusion of standards is critical for the exploitation of network effects. "Standards are codified specifications that detail the form and function of individual components and the rules of engagement among them. Together, specifications about the components' function and the rules determining their interaction define the system architecture."[45] Hence, standards represent those specifications that define how different modules

---

[40] "Standards are not new, but they are growing in importance. Why? Because standards are especially important in the sector of the economy that is growing most rapidly, the sector encompassing information, communications, and entertainment, or ICE." Shapiro (2000), p. 2. See also Hill (1997), p. 1.

[41] See Funk (2002).

[42] Hart and Kim (2000), p. 39.

[43] Hart and Kim (2000), p. 42.

[44] A member of the ETSI standardisation body told me that the latest of the 3G standard added much functionality, which is, per definition, not backward compatible. Further, two standardisation bodies standardise the 3G (namely 3GPP and 3GPP2). The air interface is clearly incompatible; efforts in the core network try to balance these incompatibilities. "Unfortunately," he told me, "for (industry-)political reasons, 3GPP is responsible for further developments of GSM and 3GPP2 for CDMA – it has got to be incompatible, doesn't it?"

[45] Garud, Jain and Kumaraswamy (2002), p. 198.

of the system interoperate to provide utility for the consumers of the product system.[46]

Standards play a viable role in the definition and the emergence of components.[47] "That is, the adaptation of modular systems requires standardization, not just quasi independent entities."[48] Standards reduce uncertainty in markets because the "existence of dominant standards plays a critical role in coordinating and integrating all the work of components suppliers."[49] Examples for such dominant standards are VHS (as the dominant standard for video recorders), TCP/IP (as the dominant standard in computer network protocols), GSM (as the dominant standard in mobile telecommunications networks), and Windows (as the dominant personal computer operating system).[50] Under the presence of network effects, multiple networks that cannot interconnect by design can only survive if they offer significantly different services. Critical to standardisation is the history of a standard or technology. As David (1985) showed, even inferior standards may remain dominant in the industry if they were introduced early on and once users have become used to them. For this reason markets that exhibit network effects are described as being "tippy." Tipping is "the tendency of one system to pull away from its rivals in popularity once it has gained an initial edge."[51] The outcome of system competition is largely determined by user expectations about the future dominant standard. Therefore, firms trying to establish a system often use active management of user expectations with so-called vapourware.[52] Such early product announcements can create self-fulfilling prophecies that become reality if users expect that the system will be dominant in the future.

In general, standards refer to products and processes that comply with norms. Standards are recurrent patterns of behaviour that help to coordinate human activity and can therefore be viewed as social institutions.[53] As Antonelli puts it:

"Elaborating upon the large literature, standards can be defined as institutions and more specifically non-pure private goods that: (a) are vectors of technical, commercial and procedural information; (b) emerge in the process of selection and diffusion of technological and organizational changes the result of the interactive cooperative behaviour of learning agents within clubs; (c) change the extent and context of the market and shape the competi-

---

[46] See Garud, Jain and Kumaraswamy (2002).
[47] See Turowski and Pousttchi (2002).
[48] Galunic and Eisenhardt (2001), p 85.
[49] Hart and Kim (2002), p. 5. See also Antonelli (1994) who cites EDIFACT, the dominant document standard in the automobile components industry as an empirical example.
[50] See for example Keil (2002).
[51] Katz and Shapiro (1994), p. 106.
[52] See Bayus, Jain and Rao (2000).
[53] See Langlois (1986); North (1991).

tion process and (d) affect radically the division of labor and the organizational setup of firms."[54]

A wide array of different definitions for and understandings of standards exists in economics literature on compatibility, standards and networks. We find taxonomies of standards including product standards, document standards, compatibility standards, mandatory and voluntary standards, de-facto standards and de-jure standards.[55] Concerning the nature of the standard, we can distinguish between open and proprietary standards. Market-based standardisation describes the efforts of a company or an alliance of companies to gain acceptance for a standard in the market that then will become a de-facto standard. Cooperative standardisation in official standardisation bodies such as IEEE, ITU, DIN, ISO or W3C is community-based and results in de-jure standards.[56] Roughly, one can say that the standards from market-based standardisation are mostly proprietary whereas community-based standardisation results in open standards.

The nature of a standard determines the organisational form. Open standards are mostly governed by standardisation bodies, whereas proprietary standards are mostly governed by privately held companies such as Adobe (e.g. PDF), Microsoft (e.g. Windows) or Sun Microsystems (e.g. Java). Aside from total proprietary hiding of attributes and complete disclosure of all standard specification, there exist an array of hybrid approaches that are often found in business practice. In accordance to the modular design rules prescribed by Baldwin and Clark (2000) many firms followed an approach with hidden design parameters and visible design rules which are specified, disclosed and communicated to third parties. The companies disclose the interfaces for connecting, communicating and interacting, but keep the inner workings closed and proprietary.

"The suppliers for PC assemblers compete with another to supply components that work on a specific platform. These components are designed around standard interface protocols to ensure interoperability among components."[57]

Such open-proprietary standards can yield a competitive edge if the hidden design parameters cannot be circumvented or substituted by reverse engineering. Tripsas (2000b) showed for the typesetting industry, that control of complementary assets can prevent companies from being outpaced by attackers:

"For Mergenthaler, it was not technology itself but the complementary assets of its proprietary typefaces and its existing customer relationships that were a big part of its success.

---

[54] Antonelli (1994), p. 79.
[55] See Farrell and Saloner (1985); Besen and Farrell (1994)
[56] See Keil (2002).
[57] Hart and Kim (2002), p. 3.

Companies that can identify and manage these assets and relationships have a much better chance of carrying their firms across these life-threatening technological chasms."[58]

The coupling of proprietary software and standardised hardware is an often pursued strategy to compete in system markets.[59] The voluntary sponsorship of open standards is used to enable and accelerate sales of profitable complementary products.

"Modular systems offer an attractive compromise. By encapsulating proprietary technology within a component that conforms to an open standards-based architecture, firms can reap the advantages of compatibility with a wide range of complementary goods while still retaining the rent-generating potential of their proprietary component."[60]

In the past, Intel has often pursued a sponsorship strategy in order to increase the performance of the overall Personal Computer architecture and to maintain control over the technological direction. Intel proposed the computer bus standards PCI, USB, and a digital camera architecture to accelerate sales in their microprocessor core business. Intel develops these technologies and gives them away indiscriminately for little or no royalties.[61] Nevertheless, even if these standards are without cost in terms of royalties, adoption is not free of cost, possibly hindering the diffusion process. As Antonelli (1994) noted, the diffusion and the adoption of standards is by no means without cost. The driving agents behind standards face costs in defining and settling standards. The adopting agents have to carry the cost arising from designing their products to the specification of the standard, learning the standard and perhaps attending standardisation meetings which bind management resources. If a new competitive standard is to be established, settled firms are confronted with switching costs, adapting their current products to the product features of the new standard. For the challenges in establishing a business web this implies that even if the shaper gives the specification of standards away for free, the costs for potential adapters may be still too high to support the web.

Christensen, Raynor and Verlinden (2001) argue that prior to technological maturity, integrated companies which design and create end-use products internally appropriate the largest profits because an interdependent, proprietary architecture leads to highly differentiated products and these firms can achieve economies of scale with increasing units.[62] As soon

---

[58] Tripsas (2000b), p. 173, italics added. The crucial role of complementary assets for the appropriation of innovation rents was discussed earlier by Teece (1986).

[59] Church and Gandal (1992) discuss standardisation strategies for hardware and the provision of complementary software.

[60] Schilling (2000), p. 329.

[61] See Gawer (2000); Tripsas (2000b).

[62] See Christensen, Raynor and Verlinden (2001), p. 79: IBM as the most integrated company in the mainframe computer industry made 95% of the industry's profit through a

as the modular architecture and the appropriate industry standards have been defined by a firm or an alliance and are accepted by a majority of industry players, integration no longer represents a competitive advantage and actually turns into a disadvantage concerning speed, flexibility and price.[63] The demand for open standards stems from market forces requiring compatibility. "With an open standard no restrictions are placed on other firms adopting the standard, (...). Even for an open standard there may be an effective leader who defines the standard in the first place or leads technological changes."[64] Open standards lead, in most cases, to decreased margins: "(...) the proliferation of standardized technologies and related 'open system' standards drove down cost structures in the industry. These changes also brought more price-based competition, punctuated by the occasional price war."

Standards act as economic institutions in product systems that coordinate the interplay between modules. In modern economic organisation theory, institutions are defined as "socially sanctionable expectations, related to actions and behaviours of one or more individuals."[65] They provide structure for exchange and enable specialisation.[66] Examples for institutions are firms, markets and states, but also contracts and organisational structures.[67] Standards affect both supply and demand for products and therefore shape the market structure. Standards reduce transaction costs in several ways:[68]

First, they reduce asset specificity because they make products complying with standards more valuable for a greater set of producers and consumers. Standardised components act as general purpose technologies.[69] Therefore, they can be utilised for a broad variety of applications and have a low degree of specificity. A standard interface in a modular product system makes assets non-specific, enabling easier adoption of the modular

---

70% market share in the 1960s to 1980s and General Motors, its counterpart in the auto industry, drew 80% profit from a 55% market share in the 1950s to 1970s.

[63] See Christensen, Raynor and Verlinden (2001), p. 76.

[64] Grindley (1995), p. 56.

[65] Dietl (1993), p. 36; Translation by Wigand, Picot and Reichwald (1997), p. 30.

[66] See North (1991); Wigand, Picot and Reichwald (1997).

[67] North (1991), however, insists on distinguishing between organisations as economic actors and institutions as rules and norms that govern the behaviour of actors within and between organisations. He refers to institutions as the rules, and players as the individuals in organisations. Organisations themselves are groups of individuals with a common purpose that come into existence and evolve as determined by institutions. North (1991), pp. 4-5.

[68] See Langlois and Robertson (2003).

[69] See Langlois (2002).

structure. The reduced specificity comes along with reduced dependencies between the involved parties and increases the frequency of transaction and the decrease uncertainty. "Standards in fact reduce the risks for users to be locked into previous vintages of durable products. Consequently, standards help to reduce adoption lags of new products."[70] Garud and Jain (1996) note that standards are at the same time both enabling and constraining. In the absence of standards, there is full flexibility but no incentive for users to adopt the innovative product or technology because they are likely hesitate in committing investments unless a dominant design has emerged. However, if standards are too rigid they hinder progress leading to a dead-end technology with hardly any variation. Only when the institutional environment merely embeds the technological conditions, do standards enable rather than constrain development. By "merely embed" Garud and Jain mean standards that provide coordination today, but at the same time do not constrain the trajectory path to new functionalities in the future.[71] In this case, the institutional environment and the technology co-evolve, "each of these reciprocally and continually shaping the other."[72]

The second way in which standards reduce transaction costs is through the decrease in information asymmetries the bring about as carriers of implicit knowledge.[73] Virtually, standards codify the characteristics of products and processes making the technical specifications explicit, thereby supporting adoption of the standards.[74] These standards hinder opportunism because rationality is built into them. As a result, the space and the possibility for opportunistic behaviour are limited. Standards enable monitoring network members because it is easier to detect whether agents comply with the norms. A standard thereby acts as a functional equivalent to legal institutions. "A firm that creates a well-defined standard interface can allow the individuals working on particular components to work in whatever departmental configuration they deem most desirable (even if that means that the departments are highly autonomous) and still be assured that the components will interact effectively."[75]

Hence standards help to reduce government costs and permit more reliance on market exchanges. Standards increase the division of labour among firms, shrinking, as a consequence, the optimal firm size. Standards, as Garud, Kumaraswamy and Langlois (2003a) summarise, "help

---

[70] Antonelli (1994), p. 83.

[71] See Garud and Jain (1996).

[72] Garud and Jain (1996), p. 393.

[73] See also Dietl (1995); Scheuble (1998).

[74] See Winter (1991). Garud and Kumaraswamy (2003), p. 57 note that the reliance on open standards "allows firms to 'trade' knowledge encapsulated in reusable components."

[75] Schilling (2000), p. 320.

reduce transaction cost by acting as mechanism for coordination and by helping align expectations." In this way, standards can be considered as substitutes for organisations.[76]

Impacts on Competition

The special requirements of system markets laid out in the previous sections imply special competitive strategies that are the subject of the following. If a firm seeks to commercialise a system innovation that exhibits network effects as an architectural leader, competitive strategies aim at placing the dominant standard in the emerging market. This produces standards wars between sponsors and supporters of competing systems. Famous examples for such standards wars in business history are the struggles for supremacy between MacOS and Windows (and more recently Linux) for desktop operating systems, between DEC, IBM, HP and Sun Microsystems for UNIX derivates for workstations, Intel, Motorola and Texas Instruments for the dominating microprocessor architectures, Beta, Video2000 and VHS for video recorder systems and Sony's Playstation, Sega's GameCube and Microsoft's Xbox for video game consoles.[77] Such standards wars take place between firms as well as between nations. For the first mover, incompatibility acts as a means of competitive advantage because herd behaviour and network effects from the installed base may hinder the adoption of new competing technologies even if they are more valuable or more sophisticated.[78]

However, if the value proposition of a new system significantly exceeds that of the old system, consumers will switch because compatibility benefits will then decrease. Product systems usually exhibit huge fixed costs and marginal variable costs. The dominant goal for economic players in standards wars is to maximise the number of users in order to benefit from increasing returns dynamics with decreasing unit costs. Maximising market share is the strategic imperative in network markets with its properties of high fixed costs for the common platform and low variable cost in distribution. "The most important strategy is, then, to develop the market. Sell more units!"[79] Indeed, this is the hardest challenge for management, because product systems are so scale sensitive. If a product offering does not

---

[76] See Demsetz (1993). Langlois and Robertson (2003), p. 58 describe the merits of open standards on modular organisations and conclude: "Thus, open standards create a unique institutional environment that coordinates activities of the organisational system."

[77] See Church and Gandal (1992); Besen and Farrell (1994).

[78] See Choi (1997); David (1985).

[79] Afuah and Tucci (2003), p. 59.

deliver high value to initial customer segments, the standard setter will never reap the benefits of increasing returns to scale. Scholars therefore suggested using penetration pricing or offering system parts for free in order to achieve a critical mass. System innovators therefore often use penetration pricing, anticipating price structures with a huge installed base to attract as many users as possible to join the emerging network.[80]

Hill (1997) proposes four strategic options to compete for the setting of a dominant design in network industries. (1) Licensing (and OEM) Agreements, (2) Entering into Strategic Alliances, (3) Product Diversification, (4) Aggressive Positioning Strategy. The first option entails sponsoring companies licensing their system innovations to competitors to prevent system wars of competing incompatible designs. The second describes a similar approach, but in this case the sponsor ties the competitors more closely within a strategic alliance to promote and set the standard collectively. Product diversification, the third option, proposes in-house production of relevant complementary products thereby creating incentives for third parties to contribute complements themselves. The product system and the early critical complements are necessary to attract an installed-base that, when achieving a critical mass, is an incentive for independent firms to produce goods and services that adhere to the dominant design. Finally, the aggressive positioning strategy describes aggressive penetration pricing for product introduction in order to rapidly create a huge installed base. One, if not the only, way to solve the chicken-and-egg problem. The strategy implies that the company makes losses in the short run and generates profits in the long-run when learning effects and economies of scale decrease overall costs.

Standards enhance diffusion between both competitors and consumers. Competitors have the otherwise firm-specific product knowledge freely available to them in standard descriptions. New entrants can imitate the dominant designs of a maturing industry more easily if they can adhere to open and freely available standards. However, "(as) carriers of technological and commercial information," Antonelli notes, "standards are productive in that they make it possible to take advantage of the benefits of technological and network externalities. Moreover, the disclosure of technical and commercial information can be properly articulated so as to particularly exclude some firms."[81]

---

[80] See Afuah and Tucci (2003), p. 58-61; Shapiro and Varian (1999); Zerdick, Picot, Schrape et al. (2000).

[81] Antonelli (1994), p. 82.

Conclusion

Modularity in technology brought about modularity in organisation. Loose coupling of nearly decomposable modules and defined connection interfaces enable the disintegration of vertically integrated firms and further specialisation on distinct modules. Especially in industries based on modern information and communication technology, product systems play a vital role in competition. Network effects are a crucial property of system products that require special attention for the commercialization of architectural innovations consisting of independent sub-modules. Network effects favour only one dominant solution by positive feedback loops which leads to standards wars and the creation of winner-takes-all markets. Standards, therefore, play a vital role in competitive strategies in these industries. The technological standards act as economic institutions that govern the behaviour of economic actors. Thus, the setting of standards and the process of standardisation is crucial for survival, achieving a competitive advantage and the acquiring the potential to capture value from the product system. As we will see later on, this is one of the major issues a business web shaper has to deal with and get right from the very beginning. Modular standards institutionalise the function of coordination, diminishing the benefits of centralised control in a firm. In modular technological systems, such as product systems, dominant designs prescribe the hierarchy of modules in the system governing the communication and the interaction between modules. The development of standards to govern interaction and exchange among components of many systems and organisations make them more easily recombinable, allowing a great variety of product bundles through mixing and matching.[82]

---

[82] See Schilling (2000).

Business Webs: Decomposable, Modular Organisations

Business webs are nowadays receiving increasing amounts of attention.[1] However, the theoretical construct has remained quite vague with a variety of labels and definitions. The various authors discuss comparable organisational forms with similar firm examples using different labels (virtual organisation, value nets, value webs, economic webs, etc.) and differing organisational forms with differing examples from the field using the same label (business web).[2] For example the network infrastructure manufacturer Cisco is described, among others, as a virtual organisation, a network orchestrator, and a value net.[3] In the following chapter, I will try to develop a consistent framework for identifying business webs and lay out the common attributes found in the existing literature. The chapter comprises three main sections. The first section discusses different network forms of organisation, governance structures that exist between markets and hierarchies. The second section then elaborates on the distinct attributes of business webs as a network form of organisation. The third and last section closes with concluding remarks.

Network Forms of Organisation

At the centre of this chapter are decomposable modular organisational forms between independent firms. Therefore, the next section is dedicated to these so called network forms of organisations and their attributes. Increased competition, globalisation, and technological pace force business

---

[1] Hagel III (1996); Campbell (1996); Zerdick, Picot, Schrape et al. (2000); Tapscott, Lowy and Ticoll (2000); Franz (2002).

[2] See Allee (2000); Anderson and Wood (2002); Bovet and Martha (2000); Cusumano and Gawer (2002); Galbraith (2002); Franz (2003); Moss (2000); Munir (2003); Parolini (1999); Selz (1999); Tapscott, Lowy and Ticoll (2000); Zerdick, Picot, Schrape et al. (2000).

[3] See Bovet and Martha (2000); Häcki and Lighton (2001); Gawer and Cusumano (2002); Kraemer and Dedrick (2002).

corporations to permanently analyse their size and scope. These driving forces support and require the formation of interorganisational networks to remain competitive. "External forces are the main drivers of this growth in interorganisational cooperation, in particular the increasing global competitive pressures and the increasing rate of technological change."[4] Research contributions to interorganisational cooperation have blossomed in the past decade, challenging the former centrality of the isolated firm as a focus of research. Evidence from literature and observation of business strategies in the field suggest a further blurring of firm boundaries and predominantly network organisational forms due to the following developments:

- Increased outsourcing and disintegration of vertically integrated firms[5]
- Increased competition with differentiated business model and organisational designs[6]
- Technological convergence and standardisation blurring the boundaries of industries (especially for information-intensive businesses)[7]
- Increased globalisation rendering many competitive advantages based on location and national rules and regulatory frameworks obsolete[8]
- Competition between value networks as much as between companies with similar core businesses.[9]

The increased need for network organisational forms is ascribed to the necessity of accessing complementary assets[10], gaining access to new markets (new market segments and new geographical territories), acquiring knowledge[11], increasing strategic flexibility,[12] reducing uncertainties, shar-

---

[4] van Aken, Louweris and Post (1998), p. 301.
[5] See Langlois and Robertson (1992b); Robertson and Langlois (1995); Afuah (2001); Afuah (2003).
[6] See Bahrami (1992); Limerick and Cunnington (1993); Andersson and Svensson (1999); Christensen (2001);Galbraith (2002); Afuah (2003).
[7] See Yoffie (1996); Evans and Wurster (1999); Zerdick, Picot, Schrape et al. (2000).
[8] Duysters and Hagendoorn (1995); Gomez-Casseres (1995); Murtha, Lenway and Hart (2001);Ghiladi (2003).
[9] See Zook and Allen (2001); Zerdick, Picot, Schrape et al. (2000); Gomez-Casseres (1994).
[10] See Teece (1986).
[11] See Hamel, Doz and Prahalad (1989).
[12] See Sanchez and Mahoney (1996).

ing risks, and attaining economies of scale and scope.[13] Decisions about size and scope of the firm also include co-operation agreements and contractual arrangements, showing that the simple assignment to either hierarchies or markets does not accurately reflect organisation in reality. The classification of network organisational forms turns out to be more difficult than the simple attribution of governance structures to either firms or markets. There are high levels of ambiguity in defining and classifying forms of interorganisational cooperation. In the literature, the terms joint venture, strategic alliance, and strategic network are often used as though they were synonomous and interchangeable. However, they differ in the number of participating organisations, governance structures, relationships and exchange of resources. Furthermore, the formal structures for organising partnerships are diverse, as illustrated in figure 9.

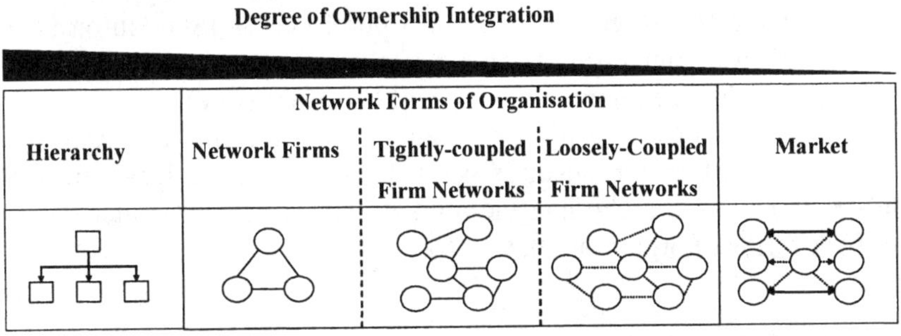

Degree of Ownership Integration

Hierarchy	Network Forms of Organisation			Market
	Network Firms	Tightly-coupled Firm Networks	Loosely-Coupled Firm Networks	

Fig. 9. Continuum of Organisations between Hierarchy and Market

The continuum of institutions for organising economic transactions, as depicted in figure 9, starts with the monolithic, hierarchical firm as described by Chandler and Williamson.[14] This type is characterised by the presence of authority and clearly defined paths of communication. Hierarchical systems represent the structure of an organisation. Transactions within the boundaries of the firm occur under common ownership.

Between the two extremes of the continuum, namely firm and market, there is a range of network forms with organisation of varying degrees of integration and distribution of property rights. To the right of the hierarchy in figure 9 are network firms characterised by less concentrated property rights and lower integration than in a hierarchy. The distinction between a firm network and a network firm lies in the distribution of property rights.

---

[13] See Powell (1987).
[14] Chandler (1962); See Williamson (1975).

When property rights are widely dispersed among elements of the network, we have a firm network. On the other hand we speak of a network firm when property rights are concentrated and elements have common ownership (or at least a controlling majority).

Next to network firms, there are tightly coupled firm networks with more static and stable member organisations than loosely coupled firm networks. Members of these networks often cooperate based on more formal cooperation agreements of longer duration. Loosely coupled firm networks are loosely connected firms with semi-stable relations leading to dependencies. These organisations consist of firms that cooperate with very few or no formal arrangements of short duration.

At the other end of the spectrum, we have arms-length transactions through the market with no common ownership of the production means. This organisation describes anonymous, standardised transactions between economic actors as on a stock market.[15] These transactions can take place between two actors directly (e.g. Firm A purchases an ISO-conform supply such as screws from Firm B) or indirectly through a market maker who balances supply and demand (e.g. a retail hardware store).

Inter-organisational relationships and network forms of organisations play a dominant role in business webs. I will, therefore, leave out further elaborations on hierarchy and the market and discuss in greater detail the network forms of organisation.[16]

Network Firms

As stated above, network firms are networks of firms under common ownership. A good example for a network firm is a joint venture. In a joint venture, two or more legally autonomous participating firms form a new, legally independent organisation for a defined purpose. The new venture most often closely replicates the hierarchical control features of the founding organisations. Each of the joining partners contributes distinct resources that are typically complementary in their nature. In general, the cooperating companies are equals with respect to residual rights of the joint venture. Shared ownership and control involve a great degree of hierarchical control. This control is implemented through the allocation of formal roles. Hierarchical governance structures may also include proce-

---

[15] Refer also to chapter 1.

[16] Further elaborations can be found, for example, in: Williamson (1975); Holmström and Tirole (1989); Holmström and Milgrom (1994); Wolff (1994); Wigand, Picot and Reichwald (1997); Holmström and Roberts (1998); Picot, Ripperger and Wolff (1996); Picot, Dietl and Franck (2002).

dures for resolving disputes, incentive systems and non-market pricing elements. Consequently, joint ventures often have their own autonomous monitoring and control structures. Joint ventures are often found in high-technology research co-operations and sales activities. In the former case, companies try to carry the huge investment burdens mutually or bring interdependent technologies together. The latter case usually pertains to the expansion of one firm possessing a product or technology into a foreign market in liaison with a local firm that possesses sales capabilities, local knowledge and access to relevant sales channels. Joint ventures may be used to exploit new market opportunities, access new markets, share costs and risks or acquire technologies and specific knowledge. In contrast to other cooperation agreements, joint ventures are stable and provide a high degree of formalisation.

Tightly Coupled Firm Networks

As mentioned earlier, tightly coupled firm networks are static and stable networks with more dispersed property rights. Alliances and strategic networks provide examples for tightly coupled firm networks. Alliances involve exchanges, sharing or co-development of capabilities and resources. They are typically horizontal rather than vertical agreements between two or more organisations with the aim of achieving a common goal and may also involve competitors. Most often alliances are based on explicit agreements in form of formal contracts. Firms have increasingly used alliances as a promising way to grow and expand their scope.[17] The relationship between the partners is intended to be long-term and strategically important for all parties. "Strategic alliances are voluntary cooperative inter-firm agreements aimed at achieving competitive advantage for the partners."[18] Contributions to the strategic alliance of the partners aim to complement the contributions of the others. Hierarchical controls institutionalise interactions between the partners. Particularly in high technology industries characterised by fast technological change, high uncertainty and huge investment requirements, strategic alliances appear to have become a strategic imperative. Examples mentioned in the literature include alliances to standardise UNIX and/or alliances to establish RISC microprocessors in competition to Intel.[19]

---

[17] See, for example, Betwee, Meuel, Bergquist et al. (1995); Quélin (1997); Doz and Hamel (1998).

[18] Das and Teng (2000), p. 33.

[19] See Gomez-Casseres (1994); Vanhaverbeke and Noorderhaven (2001).

Strategic networks show vertical and horizontal relationships with other firms, across countries and industries. Such relationships may include, but are not restricted to, suppliers, customers, and competitors.[20] "These strategic networks are composed of inter-organisational ties that are enduring, are of strategic significance for the firms entering them, and include strategic alliances, joint ventures, long-term buyer-supplier partnerships, and a host of similar ties."[21] Network orchestrators or hub firms control the network of companies and determine which players can participate. They define the standards and the relationships for their partners before a widely accepted standard is placed in the market, and can thus better profit from the growth of the network without sharing their core technologies. Network orchestrators are in the position to create a platform on which the network participants or suppliers can interact.[22] The member organisations are often tightly bound to the orchestrator with relational contracts. Examples of such firms are Amazon and Cisco. "Hidden behind the convenient interface we all see when we click onto Amazon.com is a complex supply network of publishers, book dealers, warehouses, and shippers. Building an efficient and effective network and orchestrating it to perform to its highest potential is the greatest challenge."[23]

Loosely-Coupled Firm Networks

A great deal of research has been done on loosely coupled, modular organisational forms.[24] Modularity in design has permitted less hierarchical, more fluid, decentralised control of value-adding activities and promotion of horizontal value chain specialisation. The shift from vertical to horizontal integration and the disintegration of stable linear value chains results in fluid value networks with blurring boundaries. Such loosely coupled firm networks are rather temporal and typically involve less equity exchange and fewer contractual arrangements between participating firms. Examples are treated under labels such as virtual organisation, value web or business ecology.

A Virtual Organisation then is *"an organization network which is structured and managed in such a way that it operates vis-à-vis customers and*

---

[20] See Jarillo (1995) and chapter 6.
[21] Gulati, Nohria and Zaheer (2000), p. 203.
[22] See Häcki and Lighton (2001), p. 29.
[23] Bunell and Luecke (2000), p. 19.
[24] See Langlois and Robertson (1992a); Baldwin and Clark (1997); Baldwin and Clark (2000); Schilling (2000); Galunic and Eisenhardt (2001); Schilling and Steensma (2001); Garud, Kumaraswamy and Langlois (2003b); Langlois (2002).

other external stakeholders as an identifiable and complete organiza-tion. "[25]

This implies that a virtual organisation acts as a normal firm in the market, while it is in fact a firm network. The Airbus consortium, Nike, Puma and Red Bull, among others, provide examples of virtual organisations. Although virtual organisations have their own identity, they have distributed ownership, power and loyalty.[26] In order to assess the term virtual organisation it is helpful to emphasise the meaning of virtual first. Virtual refers to not being real, physically non-existent but appearing as real. A virtual organisation, then, appears to the observer as being a real organisation, though it is not in reality. Byrne (1993) holds that virtual organisations are temporary. Here temporary refers to the fact that the virtual organisation remains effective even when companies decide to leave the firm network and vice versa that companies maintain existence even if the virtual organisation cease to exist.

Moore (1993) suggests viewing a firm as members of a business ecosystem, not only as members of a single industry. "In a business ecosystem, companies co-evolve capabilities around a new innovation: they work cooperatively and competitively to support new products, satisfy customer needs, and eventually incorporate the next round of innovations."[27] Other recent theoretical concepts such as value networks,[28] value nets[29] or industrial market systems[30] also span the traditional boundaries of firms and industries alike and describe the complex network of economic activities that are necessary to deliver a certain value proposition to the consumer. Normann and Ramírez (1993) underlined that many successful companies reinvented the way they capture value in their value-creating system of suppliers, partners and even competitors to co-produce value by analysing their environment on a more holistic level as fixed activities in a value chain.

Value nets as outlined by Parolini (1999) are a tool for competitive analysis that abandons the firm-centric view and takes the end-users point of view for analysing economic activities that add value for a certain value proposition. Bovet and Martha (2000), although using the same terminology, have a different understanding of value nets. They focus on the potential of digital technologies to reinvent value propositions and organise va-

---

[25] van Aken, Louweris and Post (1998), p. 302, emphasis original.
[26] See van Aken, Louweris and Post (1998), p. 303.
[27] Moore (1997), p. 76.
[28] See Christensen and Rosenblum (1995); Christensen (2000).
[29] See Parolini (1996).
[30] See Mathews (2001).

value-adding activities in a more timely and flexible manner. Christensen (2000) describes a value network "as the context within which a firm identifies and responds to customers' needs, solves problems, procures input, reacts to competition, and strives for profit (...)." The central argument is that every firm is embedded in a value network "because their products generally are embedded, or nested hierarchically, as components within other products and eventually within end systems of use."[31] In spite of the confusing terminology, these concepts have some common attributes which are important for the definition of business webs. The authors tried to respond to the same observed phenomenon, that firms responded to technological change, globalisation, ubiquity of digital technology and increasing customer demands for product variety with the formation of firm networks and disintegration of rigid, sequential value chains to achieve a competitive edge. The concepts differ in their reach and their aggregation level. Some claim general applicability whereas others are more focused for certain industries or product categories. To this end, the discussion shows similarities to the construct business webs. The distinct attributes are laid out in the following section.

The Nature of Business Webs

Business webs are container constructs that comprise different organisational arrangements from arms-length market transactions to bureaucratic firms. These organisations consist of relationships that co-generate economic value through complex dynamic exchanges of both tangible and intangible goods, services and benefits. Co-operations are classified upon their degree of integration into first, second and third tier cooperations. As depicted in figure 10, the focal firm (shaper) has tightly coupled relationships with suppliers of core components (core adapter) that are critical for the value proposition. The lines represent contractual relationships (first tier co-operations). Broken lines represent informal relationships (second tier relationships). Businesses in the dark grey inner circle are generally more tightly integrated in the product system and produce critical components. These companies frequently exchange information and drive the evolution of core elements. Companies in the outer circle (third tier co-operations) typically provide rather uncritical components that do not require close relationships to adapt the value-enabling platform and modules interdependently. These modules adhere to the open interface descriptions

---

[31] Christensen (2000), p. 36.

and plug into the system. The contracts between different nodes in the business web and between different business webs vary according to the relations and the underlying transactions. In a similar manner, service provisioning is dependent on the type of network and the services, as is the required network infrastructure for different business webs.

Business webs are customer centric, hetrarchical organisational forms consisting of legally independent but economically interdependent specialised firms that co-opetitively contribute modules to a product system based on a value-enabling platform under the presence of network externalities which are supported by extensive usage of information and communication technologies.[32] Figure 10 shows a simplified representation of a business web.

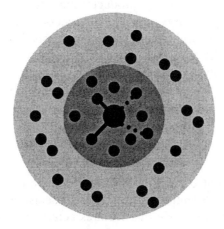

Fig. 10. Simple Illustration of a Business Web

Customer-Centric Product Offering

Business webs follow a customer-centric paradigm. A business web „(...) is a set of companies that use a common architecture to deliver independent elements of an overall value proposition."[33] "The chief concern shifts away from high-volume, low-cost production. Instead, companies knit to-

---

[32] A similar definition is provided by Zerdick, Picot, Schrape et al. (2000), p. 179 who define business webs as "groups of companies that participate in the same value chain system independently of one another and thus exist in a relationship of mutual complementarity."

[33] Hagel III (1996), p. 72.

gether combinations of capabilities (some internal, some external) that support each unique customer value proposition."[34] The overall value of a product is, to an ever larger extent, dependent on the system it is embedded in.[35] A mobile phone without a network connection, for example, is of little value to the customer who wants to make a phone call. In the eyes of the customer, the distinct parts of the system are a completely integrated product system. The consumer demands that this system generates utility for him. It must meet certain functional requirements such as complementarity, interoperability, and general functionality. To sell products, companies in the business web have to jointly optimise the value proposition from the end-user's point of view. Parolini (1999) labels this overall value proposition "absolute net value received by customers." The benefits arising from availability of complementary products and services, the compatibility with other products, quality, quantity of accessories, and so forth, influence the net value. Learning costs, switching costs, information and search costs, etc. reduce the net value. The challenge of system bundling with interdependent modules is that even a minor change in one node can affect the functioning of the overall system, hence influencing the perceived consumer value proposition positively or negatively.

Hetrarchical Governance Structure

Instead of concentrated decision making in a hierarchy, business webs are better described as decentralised, hetrarchical decision making. Heterarchy refers to a governance mode that features centres with different responsibilities and loose coupling between these units. In contrast to hierarchical governance, decision rights are dispersed rather than being concentrated at the top.[36] Companies, which reside in the business web, have different strategic roles based on their network position and the resources they control. Although the business web is characterised by cooperation, it is steered by one or more focal firms. These shaper firms control and provide a value-enabling platform for the adapters. Such a value-enabling platform can be a technical standard, a marketplace, an installed customer base, or a combination of these. Literature distinguishes between technology webs, market webs and customer webs in accordance with predominant characteristics of the value-enabling platform.[37] Business webs can thus be understood as component-orientated business architectures (see Figure 11).

---

[34] Bovet and Martha (2000), p. 29.
[35] Zerdick, Picot, Schrape et al. (2000), p. 177.
[36] See Hedlund (1993); Birkinshaw and Morrison (1995); Pearce (1999).
[37] See Hagel III (1996): Zerdick, Picot, Schrape, et al. (2000).

Product System

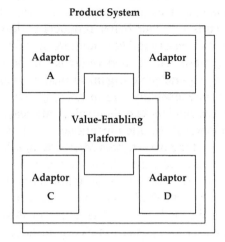

Fig. 11. Business Web Architecture

A value-enabling platform is a socio-technical system that provides the infrastructure for suppliers of complementary modules which are loosely connected via open interfaces. Third party suppliers can innovate independently of the value-enabling platform as long as they adhere to the common interfaces. Two key aspects are highlighted in this definition: the increasing interdependency of products and services and the increasing ability of more actors to innovate in modular systems.[38] Companies that are part of such a platform must pay attention to the following three issues:[39] First, maintaining the integrity of the platform while finding an adequate trade-off between keeping the core product a secret, driving innovations and enabling open interfaces for complementary products. Second, it is important to foster platform evolution. All players have to be aware of which role they adopt in the dynamic innovation process. Third, is the problem of how to achieve or preserve market leadership in at least one of the platform environment segments.

The value-enabling platform acts as an institution to govern the component suppliers within the system market. For shapers it is rational to offer a value-enabling platform for third parties, because in most cases the adapters deliver the innovative applications.[40] The shaper firm focuses on the

---

[38] See Gawer and Cusumano (2002), p. 3.

[39] See Gawer and Cusumano (2002), p. 3.

[40] For example, the World Wide Web, word processors, spreadsheets or digital music compression were all invented by users (respectively adapters) and not by shaper firms. For further elaborations of customers as innovators, see von Hippel (1989); von Hippel

development and the improvement of the value-enabling platform and lets the adapters do the rest. This modularisation allows a high degree of specialisation that results in either better products or lower costs, or both.[41] Business webs exploit quasi-market conditions insofar as adapters develop a myriad of product alternatives and versions for the value-enabling platform. "A modularly upgradeable organizational system allows constituent members to work independently and in unison, even as they evolve over time."[42] The final assemblers can then select the least costly suppliers of standardised components. An often mentioned example is the Wintel business web consisting of the two shapers Microsoft and Intel in providing the core technological standards, the Windows operating system and the Intel microprocessor. On top of the platform architecture, there are myriads of companies voluntarily contributing complementary modules such as power supplies, video boards, modems, printers, and a plethora of software applications. Hart and Kim (2002) refer to this organisation and coordination as Wintelism which they define as "(…) the structural dominance of component providers, such as Intel and Microsoft, over final assemblers, such as IBM and Dell, effected by applying strategies for controlling architectural standards in a horizontally segmented industry."[43] The definition and voluntary providing of the value-enabling platform reduces complexity and environmental uncertainty for the adapters, but leaves them more vulnerable to opportunism of the shaper. Adapters make costly investments in complementary products and services that are specific to the value-enabling platform. The shaper acquires knowledge about the complements that meet strong customer demand and can copy the adapters' most valuable assets and add value by tying the complement more closely to the value-enabling platform – after all, the shaper knows the hidden design parameters of his own platform. Shapers regularly tend to offer mass-marketable or highly profitable complements themselves. A good example for this behaviour are the office applications provided by Microsoft.[44]

---

further elaborations of customers as innovators, see von Hippel (1989); von Hippel (1996); Thomke and Hippel (2002).

[41] See Hagel III and Singer (2000); Bresser, Hitt, Nixon et al. (2000); Picot and Scheuble (2000).

[42] Langlois and Robertson (2003), p. 51.

[43] Hart and Kim (2002), p. 1.

[44] As Campell-Kelly (2001), p. 139 clearly indicates, "Complementors, however, always run the risk that Microsoft will incorporate the functions contained in their software into its own products, either by internal development or by acquiring the technology through a takeover."

Co-opetition between Business Webs Members

The relationships within a business web and the participating adapters is characterised by a situation of continuous competition and cooperation. Literature refers to such relations as co-opetition. The term co-opetition was coined by Brandenburger and Nalebuff (1996) who analysed situations of simultaneous competition using the game theory framework. The central idea is that it is to the benefit of all competing partners, if they co-operate in domains that are not crucial for their competitive advantage. Examples for such co-opetitive arrangements include industry lobbying, basic research, shared storekeeping, and logistics.[45] Business webs consist of legally autonomous businesses that focus narrowly on product-market domains.[46] In the case of the mobile telecommunications industry such product-market domains are network infrastructure, mobile handsets, SIM cards, operating systems, applications, contents etc. The product-market domains are bound to the core competencies of the firms. Core competencies are the basis for competitive advantage in the core products. The core competencies of a mobile network operator are for example scattered throughout network operation, customer acquisition, billing, and customer relationship management. The overall perceived value of the business web, the number of contributing adapters and the installed base are the common basis for value generation for the shaper and the adapters. Hence, it is in the interest of all participants to support the growth and the market success of the platform. Cooperation takes place in supporting activities such as marketing the value proposition of the system, whereas the adapters compete in their distinct competence domains.[47] The philosophy is to grow the business web first and to compete for market shares later.[48] Market forces will eliminate costly and unsatisfactory solutions because of the merits of competition.[49]

---

[45] For a few illustrated examples see Bovet and Martha (2000), pp. 97-99.

[46] "Companies engage suppliers, customers, and even competitors in a unique network of value-creating relationships." Bovet and Martha (2000), p. 5.

[47] See Brandenburger and Nalebuff (1996). Tapscott, Lowy and Ticoll (2000) describe a business web as "a market space in which organizations both collaborate and compete with one another." p. 25.

[48] See Kelly (1998); Tapscott, Lowy and Ticoll (2000), p. 21.

[49] See Evans and Schmalensee (1993), p. 58.; Zerdick, Picot, Schrape et al. (2000), p. 181.

Extensive Usage of Information and Communication Technologies

Business webs have predominately, but not exclusively, emerged in information-intensive industries such as computers, telecommunications, and finance.[50] Even though information plays an important strategic role in almost every industry, for the above-mentioned industries, information itself is the product of the production process. The advances of information and telecommunications technology enable the transmission of information at the speed of light regardless of place and time.[51] Especially the emergence and diffusion of world-wide computer networks such as the Internet facilitated the reconfiguration of market and firm boundaries. Interconnectivity of information systems through universal standards within a firm as well as across firm boundaries lowers transaction costs because the exchange of information is quicker and more efficient.[52] These non firm-specific open standards ease the unbundling of formerly integrated firms and products as they dilute the glue, based on firm specific information, between processes.[53] Taken to the extreme, some examples of business webs would have been virtually impossible without the presence of open architectures and interconnected computer networks. This applies to Yahoo!, eBay and i-mode, but even companies like Apple and Microsoft owe their massive success to the exploitation of digital goods, i.e. the operating software and the complementary applications. Digital goods help firms to exploit what Rayport and Sviokla (1996) call a "virtual value chain."[54] The separation of information from physical goods generates value that is sometimes even higher than the physically traded commodity. Value is generated from knowledge and information, not from physical manufacturing. In contrast to physical goods which exhibit diminishing returns, digital goods exhibit increasing returns to scale because they can be copied and reused at marginal cost.

Increasing Returns Dynamics

Business webs rely on a mediating technology to link consumers. Mediating technology facilitates exchange relationships among customers distrib-

---

[50] Hagel III (1996); Zerdick, Picot, Schrape et al. (2000); Häcki and Lighton (2001).

[51] See Wigand, Picot and Reichwald (1997).

[52] See Picot, Ripperger and Wolff (1996); Wigand, Picot and Reichwald (1997); Tapscott (2001).

[53] See Evans and Schmalensee (1993), Parolini (1999).

[54] See Rayport and Sviokla (1996).

uted in space and time. The shaper itself is not the network. It provides a networking service.[55] Business webs typically exhibit positive demand-side economies of scale. The overall value of the web increases for the user as more companies join the web because of positive feedback loops and increasing returns.[56] The utility of product systems such as computers, telecommunication networks, and financial exchange markets, etc. increases with the number of other users that utilise these products. As the value of a new service depends on the usage of other consumers, a firm cannot initially charge for the service. Cellular telephone subsidies, freeware and shareware computer applications, or even give-aways such as Internet browser software are examples of this management practice. The higher the installed base, the more positive network effects are produced.[57] This leads to positive, self-enforcing feedback loops and supports demand-side economies of scale. If the product system only attracts few users, the installed base will be too small to provide a profitable market for adapters in terms of sales volume. Therefore, business webs often create so-called "winner-take-all" markets under circumstances of demand-side scale economies.[58] Success enforces success, the strong get stronger, and the weak get weaker.[59] "As a result" Shapiro and Varian (1999) conclude, "growth is a strategic imperative, not just to achieve the usual economies of scale but to achieve the demand-side economies of scale generated by network effects."[60]

Conclusion

Network forms of organisation can be classified as network firms and tightly and loosely coupled firms. Network firms expand their boundaries but remain largely integrated and under common ownership. Tightly coupled firm networks have a lower degree of ownership, remain stable over long periods of time, commonly show a coordinating hub firm or orchestrator that coordinates the networks. Loosely coupled firm networks show

[55] Stabell and Øystein (1998), p. 427.

[56] Zerdick, Picot, Schrape et al. (2000), p. 181.

[57] In telecommunications, Cave, Majumdar and Vogelsang (2002) posit, "the availability of an increased number of potential connections can impact on the increasing returns process that underlies the dynamics of information exchange and increase the volume of digital signals flowing through networks." p. 12.

[58] See Frank and Cook (1995); Schilling (2002) and Hill (1997).

[59] See Hill (1997); Evans and Schmalensee (1993), especially chapter 2, and Schilling (2002).

[60] Shapiro and Varian (1999), p. 14.

the lowest degrees of ownership and are largely autonomous and independent.

Business webs are loosely coupled firm networks that may consist of loosely coupled actors. They show common attributes of being consumer-centric, with hetrarchical governance structures that are dispersed and decentral rather than hierarchical and concentrated at one top. The relationships between the member organisations are at the same time collaborative and competitive, and characterised by win-win situations. Business webs have emerged predominantly in digital, technology-intensive industries that predominantly supply information products and knowledge. The firms use extensive modern information and communication technologies for all value-adding activities, including design, production, operation, distribution, etc. Such technologies exhibit positive network effects that give rise to increasing return dynamics and positive feedback loops.

Business Web Growth Cases

Based on the central proposition that business webs exhibit demand-side economies of scale that serve as a foundation for winner-take-all markets, the number of theoretically possible business web shapers is inherently limited. As such, studies with statistically significant sample spaces are effectively not possible. Additionally, problems might arise with the operationalisation of variables such as customer-centricity and co-opetitive relationships which are difficult to measure. Qualitative research methods and, especially, case studies offer adequate research tools to cope with the aforementioned challenges. The research methodology, research process and research sites are explained in the following chapter.

Methodology and Research Sites

The following section deals with the methodology pursued for the present study. After providing a short comparison on research methods, I show why a case study research approach is appropriate for the present study. In the following sections, I describe the research process undertaken, divided into the stages case selection, data collection and case structure.

Research Methods

Various research methods have been developed and proposed for distinct research purposes. Brewerton and Millward (2001) discuss case study designs, correlation designs, and experimental designs. Yin (1984) distinguishes between five major research strategies employed in social sciences: experiments, surveys, archival analysis, histories, and case studies (See figure 12).

Relevant Situations
for Different Research Strategies

Strategy	Form of Research Question	Requires Control over Behavioral Events?	Focuses on Contemporary Events?
Experiment	how, why	yes	yes
	who, what, where how many how much	no	yes
Survey	who, what, where	no	yes/no
Archival analysis (e.g., economic study)	how many how much		
History	how, why	no	no
Case study	how, why	no	yes

Fig. 12. Research Situations for Different Research Strategies[1]

Since this study focuses on how and why questions of contemporary events, it was logical to choose a case study approach. The lack of prior examinations of the phenomena at hand further support the choice of case studies to derive early hypothesises.

A case study involves the description of an ongoing event in relation to a particular outcome over a fixed time. "(… T)he case study allows an investigation to retain the holistic and meaningful characteristics of real-life events – such as individual life cycles, *organizational and managerial processes*, neighbourhood change, international relations, and the *maturation of industries*."[2] Recognition of these perceptions or facts is acquired through experience, observation or judgment of a problem, opportunity, or issue existing in a realistic situation. Case study research is a research approach combining multiple research methods. [3] "A case study is a history of a past or current phenomenon, drawn from multiple sources of evidence. It can include data from direct observation and systematic interviewing as

---

[1] Figure adapted and slightly modified from Yin (1984), p .17.

[2] Yin (1984), p. 14 emphasis added. For an excellent overview of the history of case study research, see Hamel (1993), notably the first chapter.

[3] See Yin (1984); Hamel (1993). In my understanding, it is more an approach than a method, precisely because it takes advantage of multiple methods. Whereas some researchers believe case study research is a method. Hamel (1993) discusses these two views in his monograph "Case Study Methods."

well as from public and private archives."[4] "How" and "why" questions, according to Yin (1984) are likely to favour the use of case studies and histories. However, he actually admits that there exists much overlap permitting (and sometimes arguably even requiring) the combination of two or more research strategies. As figure 12 illustrates, the case study is the research strategy of choice when the research problem addresses "how" and "why" questions and the requirement for control is low. The last variable that speaks for or against the pursuit of a case study approach is the observed timeframe. If the researcher opts for illuminating events in the past where relevant primary sources of evidence cannot be accessed, be it because key observers are already dead or first-hand documents no longer exist, histories are the research strategy of choice. Histories, Yin (1984) writes, "can of course, be done about contemporary events; in this situation, the strategy begins to overlap with that of the case study." There are four major classes of application mentioned in the literature for conducting case study research. The most important is to explain the causal links between real-life events that are too complex to design for surveys or experiments. Second, case studies are applicable to real-life contexts where interventions have occurred. Third, the intervention itself can benefit from an illustrative case study for evaluation purposes. And finally, the case study can be used to explore blurred situations where clear and single sets of outcomes are not expected.[5] Case study research design includes the following components: A research question, propositions (albeit, not mandatory), the unit(s) of analysis, data-linking logic (linking data to the propositions), and criteria for interpreting findings.

I decided to use a case study research approach because the subject is rather new and there is little research to build on which would permit statistical analysis. It would also be hard to find enough firms for such an approach since business webs tend to establish natural monopolies. Additionally, it is almost impossible to identify future business web shapers that are currently establishing and growing their business web. Therefore, a researcher will not be able to go into the field as an ethnographer and observe an emerging business web. This approach would also be overly time consuming since the researcher would not only face the problem of identifying the right corporations in advance, but also the sheer mass of information would be too exhausting to track. The researcher would have to conduct a longitudinal field research from multiple sides and in a multitude of cases. Time and financial budget constraints of the research project prohibited the simultaneous use of replicated multi-case, multi-esearcher, multi-

---

[4] Leonard-Barton (1995), p. 40.
[5] See Yin (1984).

site and participant-observer approaches for the study. For reasons of efficiency, this seemed completely inappropriate. "Moreover, conducting an adequate number of multiple cases at geographically dispersed sites to complement the simultaneous in-depth study is physically demanding, if not possible."[6] To solve the trade-off between data richness and efficiency I for the most part used publicly available data on already existing business webs as a proxy.

Research Process

In contrast to hypothesis testing research, cases are chosen for theoretical, not for statistical reasons.[7] It is impossible to generalise from a single case to a wider population. If a number of cases yield similar results then one can argue that a robust finding has prevailed. The selection of cases is a crucial task because obtaining rich data is important for generalising the findings.

Case Selection
To fulfil the requirements of generalisation, cases should meet the definition of a business web to constrain variation. The question of whether the use of single or multiple cases is more fruitful is widely discussed among scholars.[8] Nevertheless, Eisenhardt (1989) argued that multiple cases provide greater overall generalisation in comparison to single case studies.[9] Even though there is no optimal number of cases, a good rule of thumb is to use between 4 and 10 cases. With less than four cases, it is difficult to generate well-founded theory, with more than 10 cases it becomes increasingly difficult to cope with the resulting complexity.[10] Given the limited number of business web cases available for study, I followed Eisenhardt (1989) and choose cases which showed extreme situations with polar types in which the subjects of interest are transparently observable. I provide two in-depth examples that differ in important dimensions.

An excellent case for the revolutionary growth of a market web is provided by eBay, because it grew extremely rapidly and showed the consti-

---

[6] Leonard-Barton (1995), p. 57.

[7] See Eisenhardt (1989). "In this sense, the case study, like the experiment, does not represent a 'sample', and the investigators goal is to expand and generalize theories (analytic generalization) and not to enumerate frequencies (statistical generalization)." Yin (1984), p. 21.

[8] See Eisenhardt (1989), Eisenhardt (1991; Gibb Dyer Jr. and Wilkins (1991).

[9] Chandler 1962 in his seminal work "Strategy and Structure: Chapters in the History of the American Industrial Enterprise" used the for instance data of four big corporations.

[10] See Eisenhardt (1989).

tuting elements of a business web. I-Mode, an even more current case, exemplifies the rapid growth of the wireless Internet in Japan. Although both cases operate within the virtual realm of the Internet, and have, as such, the same context – or more precisely, the same technological field – their growth histories differ significantly. In contrast to i-mode, eBay is a green field start-up that was not nurtured by a huge company group such as NTT and fuelled its astonishing growth exclusively through generated profits. To fulfil the requirement of corroboration, the derived theoretical constructs are externally validated with several mini-cases from related contexts to emphasise the complementary aspects of business webs thereby aiming for a more complete theoretical picture. "This corroboration helps researchers to perceive patterns more easily and to eliminate chance associations.", writes Eisenhardt (1991) in her response to the Gibb Dyer Jr. and Wilkins (1991) article.

Data Collection

Data collection for case studies may include archives, interviews, questionnaires and observation, irrespective of whether the data is qualitative (words) or quantitative (numbers).[11] The documented evidence may provide grounded hypotheses for further refinement and quantitative and experimental inquiry.[12]

For the collection of data, I systematically searched online databases for relevant keywords such as people, products, corporations, industries etc. Namely, these were EBSCO Business Source Premier[13] for articles from the general business press and TotalTele[14] for the information and communications industry in particular. News clippings provided by wired news[15], ZDNet[16], and online journals supplemented the data. Annual reports and product white papers were available at the websites of the respective companies. Company documents such as white papers, products descriptions, press releases or annual reports and 15 confidential semi-structured interviews with top executives from the information and communication industry comprising major wireless carriers, content providers, software and hardware manufacturers, enhanced data.

The interviews were held prior to the study in cooperation with a masters thesis candidate, which I supervised. The topic of this masters thesis was to identify how a mobile carrier can achieve platform leadership in the

---

[11] See Eisenhardt (1989).
[12] See Glaser and Strauss (1967); Eisenhardt (1989).
[13] www.search.ebsco.com
[14] www.totaltele.com
[15] www.wired.com
[16] www.zdnet.com

emerging mobile business web.[17] The interviews included four major topics for each interviewee and additionally customised questions regarding
the distinct business or industry. The four main topics wre chosesn to un-
veil: (1) the changes in the value system structure and the organisation
with the introduction of mobile data services, (2) the altered relationships
between the main players of the value system (mobile carriers, device manufacturers, content providers, online services and software producers), (3)
the associated risks and opportunities arising from either focussing on data
transmission or diversification as a service provider, and (4) strategies to
achieve platform leadership. The questions in the interviews were deliberately kept very open since they aimed at identifying industry challenges
and opinions of the managers. The candidates for the interviews were chosen because of their long affiliation with the industry and their first-hand
knowledge of firm strategies in the mobile industry. The interviews were
conducted with a dual researcher approach in order to enhance the accuracy of the data. Two researchers were present at each interview, which
took one hour on average. The interviews helped in gaining insight into
management challenges to establish business webs in network industries
and was a valuable input for the study.

However, due to the focus on mobile carriers, data from the interviews
was only used for the i-mode case and is referenced in the footnotes. The
primary sources of data for the presented case studies are publicly available market research reports and articles from the trade press as well as
scientific studies.

Structure of the Cases
The next section roughly sketches the structure of the cases and provides a
description of the terminology used and common to all cases.

Every case starts with a short introduction that gives a brief overview of
the case with a short company history, growth performance and business
web structure. A short acknowledgement of specific contributions to the
case follows. The cases then give a description of the environmental conditions prevailing at the inception of the business web. The environmental
conditions may be regarded as independent variables for each case. Given
similar conditions, other firms in other markets or industries are likely to
encounter the same threats and opportunities, all other things being equal.
In that respect, the environmental conditions describe the technological
field where case results claim a high degree of generalisation.

Next, a description of the business web structure follows according to
the five identified business web attributes developed in the third chapter.

---

[17] See Waltenspiel (2000).

Namely, the product offering, the governance structure, the relationships between participating economic actors, the information and communication infrastructure and the scale sensitivity of the business.

The following part then describes the business model of the shaper firm (or for some of the mini-cases, the dominant business model of the industry). "The business model describes how and where the firm engages in business, who its customers are, and often, who its major competitors are."[18] The business model comprises the definition of the value a firm offers its customers – the value proposition – and what customer segments the firms seek to provide with these offers, as well as the scope of products and services and the addressed customer segments.

Finally, the largest section of the cases focuses on the establishment process and early growth of the business web for the given case. The section analyses four major constructs for each case: achievement of a critical user mass, the scaling of the value-enabling platform across adjacent markets, the leveraged growth through quasi-integration of external capabilities with collaborative arrangements and the geographical expansion. Collaborative arrangements are classified in first, second and third tier linkages. The first refer to more tightly coupled connections between shapers and core adapters as illustrated in the previous chapter. These linkages show long-term durability and great importance of identity. Second tier linkages describe collaborative arrangements that are less intensive and more loosely coupled, still showing importance of the partners' identity. Third tier adapters include independent organisations that voluntarily contribute complementary goods and services without explicit knowledge of the shapers and without formal agreements or involvement from shaper companies. The geographical expansion shows if and how the shapers tried to globalise their value-enabling platform.

The shorter mini-cases attempt to address the same major issues, so far as data is available, but without subdividing the cases in exactly the same manner. Here it was more important to show the establishment and early growth process and whether there were observe similarities or whether findings were contradictory to the two larger in-depth cases.

I-Mode: Formation of the Mobile Internet Industry

"AS THE HIGHEST-VALUED COMPANY on the Tokyo Stock Exchange, the company that Newsweek called Japan's only new multinational to emerge in the last decade,

---

[18] Cartwright and Oliver (2000), p. 25. See also Timmers (1998) and Afuah and Tucci (2003).

and the undisputed leader in the world of the mobile Internet, NTT DoCoMo occupies lofty ground."[19]

Starting in Japan on 22, February 1999 the service "i-mode" was the first of its kind and created the mobile internet industry.[20] The i in i-mode stands for interactive, Internet and "ai" which means love in Japanese.[21] DoCoMo provides the value-enabling platform for third party content providers with a set of customised de-facto technologies, an installed user base, a business model, and billing mechanisms. I-Mode enables consumers to access digital content from the Internet on mobile devices while on the move. As I will show throughout the following chapter, DoCoMo was very careful to underscore the customer orientation in its decisions pertaining to product design, size and scope of the service and the road-map of features. DoCoMo has established a web of partners and allies around its i-mode platform who provide complementary products and services. DoCoMo concentrates its efforts on nurturing the platform, whereas the adapters such as handset manufacturers or content providers compete for market shares in distinct market domains. As an Internet-compatible service, i-mode is naturally based on information and telecommunication technologies. Between July 2000 and October 2001 the service's subscriber base mushroomed from 10 to over 30 million and revenues from i-mode soared 840% during the same time, showing positive feedback loops and increasing returns.[22] As of December 2002 the web phone service had over 36 million users.[23] I-Mode seems to be an ideal case for several reasons. First, i-mode shows all the characteristics of a business web, secondly establishment and early growth took place only recently. Thirdly, i-mode seems to be a very illustrative case since it showed extremely rapid growth and was widely discussed in the industry as well as in management literature.[24]

Environmental Conditions for DoCoMo

Nippon Telephone and Telegraph (NTT) is one of the world's largest telecommunication companies with over 40 million subscribers in its domestic

[19] Frengle (2002), p. 23, emphasis original.
[20] See Funk (2001a); Ratliff (2002); Bisenius and Siegert (2002), p. 21.
[21] See Ratliff (2002), Footnote 8.
[22] See Ratliff (2002), p. 57.
[23] As of February 2003.
[24] See Amaha (1999); Computing Canada (1999); Takezaki (1999); Funk (1999); Funk (2001b); Baldi and Pyu-Pyu Thaung (2002); Gawer and Cusumano (2002); Ratliff (2002), to name but a few.

market.[25] NTT spun off DoCoMo in 1992 as part of the Japanese telecommunication industry deregulation. DoCoMo stands for "Do Communications over the Mobile network" and means "anywhere" in Japanese. After the 1994 liberalisation of the cellular phone market permitting individuals to own cellular phones, DoCoMo faced fierce competition from a number of attackers. Notwithstanding, the company was able to retain the majority of the market. Its share for mobile telephony in Japan is around 56%, and its brand recognition is about 90%. Back in January 1997, Keiichi Enoki initiated the gateway project that laid the foundation for i-mode.[26] Koji Oboshi, at that time President of DoCoMo, thought that the company was then situated on a declining growth trajectory and that future growth potentials had to come from a second trajectory. In addition, DoCoMo encountered technological problems at that time with its network. Service quality used to be poor and DoCoMo lost market share to its competitors, who were aggressively marketing their superior network quality.[27] Hence, Oboshi asked Keiichi Enoki to form a team to start a mobile multimedia Internet service. At that time, he served as a Director Gateway Business Department and later on became DoCoMo's Senior Vice President.[28] Mari Matsunaga became the mobile Internet project's editor-in-chief in 1997. Enoki hired her away from Recruit, a Japanese magazine for job opportunities, as Content Editor for i-mode. In September, Matsunaga brought in Takeshi Natsuno, a former Internet entrepreneur, as Media Director for the Gateway Business Department.[29] Much of the success of i-mode is attributed to these specific persons and their unique combination in a multi-disciplinary, creative, and innovative team.[30]

The I-Mode Business Web

"(...) NTT DoCoMo functions as the nucleus, managing and controlling the network infrastructure and processes that enable the business ecology to thrive and prosper.[31] DoCoMo pursues a "no walled garden approach" that is open to third parties. The business web architecture consists of a technological platform built around de-facto Internet standards, a sound

---

[25] See CommunicationWeek International (2002).
[26] See Natsuno (2003), p. vii, Foreword to the Japanese Edition by Keiichi Enoki, DoCoMo Director, Gateway Business.
[27] See Ratliff (2002), p. 58.
[28] See Rose (2001).
[29] He now serves as i-mode executive director.
[30] See Rose (2001); Batista (2001); Ratliff (2002), p. 58 ; Natsuno (2003), p. 5.
[31] Foong (2002), p. 15.

business model that generates economic incentives for adapters and a winning marketing. Nevertheless, "(...) i-mode is virtually entirely controlled by a single company (...)."[32] Due to its market dominance, DoCoMo achieved total control over the i-mode standard and the i-mode portal platform allowing the setting of handset specifications and restricting access to the official i-mode portal by third party service providers. Control and influence work as a substitute for asset ownership of the modules. "I-mode depends on outside providers for everything from handset to content, yet it's managed so carefully that nothing is left to chance."[33] DoCoMo has close relationships to the handset manufacturers because of the huge R&D expenditures and operator-driven innovations. DoCoMo defines technological features of the handset as well as the product launch and the retail price. DoCoMo requires some basic features such as i-mode button, support for graphics and audio, etc. to be implemented in the handsets which DoCoMo considers critical to enhance customer perception using i-mode services.[34] Japanese handsets are, therefore, far more advanced than those in Europe and the United States. In a similar manner, DoCoMo sets rules for content providers. Through the i-mode guidelines, it defined how content has to be processed to be provided with i-mode. Since DoCoMo uses only a slightly modified adaptation of the common HTML language for the description of content, nearly anybody with some knowledge of HTML code is able to produce their own offerings for i-mode. This led to an amazing 5000 i-mode sites within one year.[35] "By controlling the complete specification of i-mode, including the details of the user interface, NTT DoCoMo has achieved a service that is easy to understand and operate."[36] Consumers are attracted by marketing the service and the value proposition, not the underlying technologies.

Technologically speaking, i-mode itself is not a competing technology to WAP, but a business model, and a service brand, based on a packet communication network and a compact subset of ordinary HTML for enhanced content presentation on mobile phones. In fact, cHTML is closer to HTML, the lingua franca on the WWW than WML, the supposed description language for WAP.[37] Therefore, cHTML sites are easier and faster to

---

[32] Hartman, Ragnevad and Linden (2000), p. 13.

[33] Rose (2001). See also Datamonitor (2002), p. 12.

[34] Interview held with a DoCoMo representative. Hartman, Ragnevad and Linden (2000), pp. 7, 27; Natsuno (2003).

[35] Song (2000). Numbers are as of March 2000.

[36] Hartman, Ragnevad and Linden (2000), p. 30.

[37] "We chose HTML for i-mode because it is the standard for marking content for the Internet. Strictly speaking, the basis used on i-mode is something called cHTML, a subset of

build than WML sites.[38] DoCoMo was well aware of the development of WAP and deliberately decided to use de-facto Internet standards. In sharp contrast to the often-claimed proprietary nature of i-mode technologies by market observers, analysts and the media, DoCoMo utilised mostly open standard-based technologies.[39] In fact, (semi-)proprietary technologies are only utilised on the transport layer between the i-mode terminal and the mobile network substituting TCP with TLP. Additionally, security mechanisms have been added between mobile network and the i-mode server by developing and implementing UITP/NWMP. Nevertheless, the i-mode server and the content provider's server communicate using standard TCP/IP.[40] Figure 13 gives an overview of the service and the system architecture.

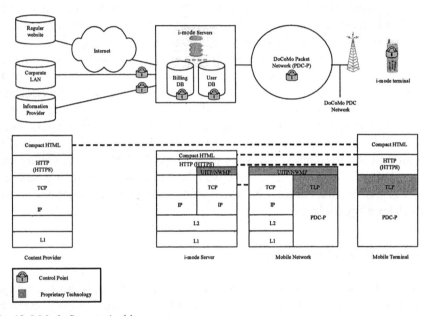

Fig. 13. I-Mode System Architecture

HTML that had been proposed to the World Wide Web Consortium (W3C), the standards organization for internet content." Natsuno (2003), pp. 50-51.

[38] "WML, is not HTML compatible, meaning that ordinary HTML pages cannot be viewed in a WML browser." Hartman, Ragnevad and Linden (2000), p. 14.

[39] See Johnson (2001) or Credit Suisse First Boston (2002) where i-mode is defined as a "proprietary mobile internet technology developed by Japan's DoCoMo for its PDC-P network." p. 127.

[40] See Hartman, Ragnevad and Linden (2000), p. 11 for details.

The genuinely proprietary elements of the platform are the billing system and the structuring and presentation of contents on the mobile handsets. Notwithstanding the restricted listing of application alliance partners on the i-mode menu, the platform is open for any content provider to supply voluntary sites, which are accessible through a variety of search-engines. The decision to embrace open, widely accepted Internet technologies such as HTML, MIDI, and JAVA proved technological foresight regarding widespread adoption by content providers and subscribers.[41] DoCoMo decided to be a first mover and not to wait for a generally accepted WAP solution proposed and guided by Sony and Ericsson. At that time, DoCoMo had an enormous advantage in time-to-market when compared to mobile operators abroad. DoCoMo did not wait for standardisation by standard-setting bodies such as the WAP Forum.[42] In that respect, DoCoMo shaped a de-facto industry standard for the presentation of content on mobile devices in Japan. It proceeded the same way with choosing GIF as the graphics standard and MIDI for ring tones and audio.[43] The adaptation of already existing solutions tailored to the requirements of small devices and wireless networks accelerated the service.[44] A major technological update was to add Java technology to the service with the introduction of i-αppli. This service introduced graphics-rich, dynamic applications for mobile phones.[45] This major step was the result of a tight collaboration with Sun Microsystems that dates back to march 1999.[46] Technology was only half of the story. Next, there was the need for a convincing business model that would ensure win-win relationships offering economic incentives for all participants.

I-Mode Business Model

Figure 14 sketches the i-mode business model with aggregated actors as well as the flows of information, physical goods, and money between them.

---

[41] "The choice was HTML, the existing programming language of the millions of content providers on the Internet. The choice of Internet basics can also be seen as i-mode develops, basing their standards on those of the internet: midi, GIF, soon Java, etc." Hartman, Ragnevad and Linden (2000), p. 26.

[42] Now part of OMA (Open Mobile Alliance).

[43] In contrast, the WAP forum favours its own solutions like Wireless bitmap (WBMP). See Hartman, Ragnevad and Linden (2000), p. 15.

[44] See Datamonitor (2002), p. 13.

[45] "By adding Java technology, i-mode will be able to provide attractive, end-to-end services to consumers." Takeshi Natsuno quoted in Mitsumori (2000).

[46] Natsuno (2003), p. 69.

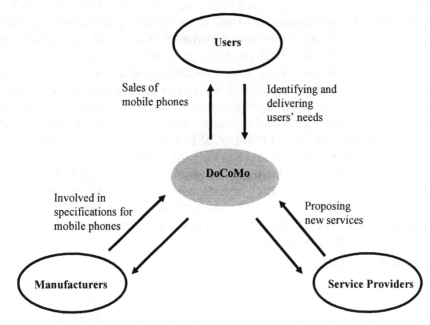

Fig. 14. I-Mode Business Model

Value Proposition

I begin my analysis with the description of the architecture of the product system, which is the value proposition.[47] I-mode is a service offered by DoCoMo that lets customers send and receive information on a cellular phone based on internet technology. Initially, DoCoMo marketed the service to the urban youth segment and thus focused on providing entertainment content. The service package comprises mobile e-mail services, information, and entertainment offerings customised for mobile handsets. Every consumer gets an e-mail address that is bound to the operator and hence creates lock-in effects and prevents churn. There are three possibilities to access content. (1) "My menu" that stores customised links to i-mode content. (2) Bookmarks, in the i-mode menu, which are categorised in the four content categories transactions, entertainment, database, and others. (3) Entering URL's to access independent offerings or any site in the WWW that can be shown on a mobile handset.[48] Much of the success of i-mode is driven by the market and customer orientation – in contrast to

---

[47] See Hass (2002), pp. 94.
[48] See Hartman, Ragnevad and Linden (2000), p. 3.

the technology-driven approach with the European counterpart WAP. DoCoMo never mentioned "Internet" in its marketing and refused to raise expectations of a mobile Internet experience, but instead emphasised the interesting information available through i-mode. Essentially, DoCoMo branded i-mode as an extension to pre-existing mobile services.[49] In spite of the bandwidth of merely 9.6kbit, the service quality always proved adequate, avoiding customer dissatisfaction.[50] I-mode marketing was aimed especially at young customer segments that were willing to pay for the services offered. In April 1999, DoCoMo launched the first i-mode campaign. The commercial showed Ryoko Hirosue, a young actress that checked her bank account using an i-mode handset. "The brand DoCoMo has become associated with quality and reliability, a factor which has enabled it to secure more than 57% of the Japanese subscriber base."[51] Therefore, consumers trust that the information and the contents will be of a certain quality, reliability, and security.

Internal Capabilities
The manufacturers were not allowed to label their brand names on the handsets. DoCoMo sells the i-mode phones branded with the DoCoMo logo.[52] DoCoMo markets i-mode exclusively and controls the i-mode menu. An i-mode button is integrated into the hardware of the handset to guarantee fast and easy access to the i-mode menu.[53] The structure of the available services in the i-mode menu, the ease of payment and ease of use are said to be the drivers behind i-mode's huge success. Signing and paying for a service requires only four clicks right on the phone to add the service to the monthly bill. Unsubscribing a service is even easier; the user only has to delete the service from the menu to stop billing.[54] Screens in i-mode provide a "phone-to" function that permits users to send an e-mail or to establish a voice call easily. Users can, for example, dial a restaurant that they have found using a yellow pages directory service to make a reservation.[55] Push services such as updated weather forecasts are another ex-

---

[49] See Ratliff (2000), p. 16; Funk (2002).
[50] See Datamonitor (2002), p. 9.
[51] See Hartman, Ragnevad and Linden (2000), p. 21.
[52] See Datamonitor (2002), p. 13. The model description indicates the manufacturers by the starting letter, next the series and a closing i for i-mode. For example, N501i stands for a NEC handset complying with the first i-mode generation. For an overview of the mandatory features in the different series, see Natsuno (2003). Available i-mode handsets from different manufacturers and detailed feature description can be found in Hartman, Ragnevad and Linden (2000), p. 8 and pp. 71.
[53] See Hartman, Ragnevad and Linden (2000), p. 9.
[54] See Kuchinskas (2000).
[55] See Natsuno (2003), p. 17. See also Hartman, Ragnevad and Linden (2000), p. 9.

ample of a useful, customer-friendly feature that is convenient since the user is notified of weather changes without being actively involved. Tight coordination of services and handset features and an ongoing dialog with adapters in the business web (e.g. content providers and handset manufacturers) improved services and fostered innovation.[56] "We", Natsuno writes, "were building the environment for emergence and self-organization. To that end, the most important task was to decide on the division of labour between DoCoMo, which provides the platform, and the content providers, which develop the services to run on it."[57]

Revenue Model

Revenue sources for DoCoMo from i-mode are, as depicted in figure 15, threefold: (1) monthly subscription fees, (2) traffic charges, and (3) billing commissions. The black arrows in indicate revenue streams that end up in DoCoMo's pockets. Revenue streams indicated with white arrows go to external third parties. The width of the arrows shows the relative amount of money that is transferred.

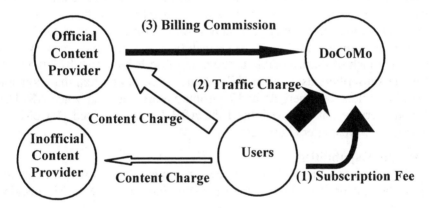

Fig. 15. I-Mode Revenue Model

For the i-mode subscription, a monthly basic subscription fee of ¥300[58] is added on top of the regular subscription. Official i-mode sites may additionally charge between ¥100 and ¥300 per month. For such "pay-for services", DoCoMo collects the fees and bills for service/content providers. DoCoMo retains an administrative fee of 9% for the collection of charges and billing,. However, the majority of revenue comes from increased traf-

---

[56] Datamonitor (2002), 14.

[57] Natsuno (2003), p. 58.

[58] ¥100 roughly equals 1€. In February 1999 1€ was ¥130.

fic triggered by content services. Most of the content offerings (especially non-official sites) are free of charge for consumers, but DoCoMo receives revenues for every data packet sent or received through their network with a volume-based pricing scheme. Data sent or received is billed at a rate of ¥0.3 per 128 bytes on top of the regular subscription fee.

Compared to circuit-switched (that is time-based) billing, the volume-based billing approach was quite transparent to users. They only had to pay for the information they downloaded. The revenues from i-mode contributed significantly to the overall ARPU (Average Revenue per User) of DoCoMo with 19.8% in the first quarter of 2002 according to Gartner Research.[59] In 2000, the ARPU increase generated by i-mode was reported to be 25%.[60] With the introduction of i-αppli, a service based on the Java execution environment, these numbers increased because "Java users generate 2.5 times as much packet traffic as ordinary i-mode subscribers."[61] An average bill ends up with a data charge amount of approximately ¥1,300.[62] In addition to the three main revenue streams, DoCoMo receives revenues from mobile phone advertising for music, movies, and restaurants.[63] The majority of revenues are still voice, accounting for more than 60% of the overall revenues. In summary, revenues from i-mode accounted for 26% of total user revenues in 2001.[64] Nevertheless, voice revenues rose by ¥2.6 billion "much of it attributable to the new subscribers drawn by i-mode."[65] I-mode subscribers use their mobile phones even more often than conventional mobile subscribers do and contribute more data and voice ARPU.[66] I-mode service not only stabilised the ARPU, it also helped DoCoMo to decrease the customer churn rate.[67]

External Capabilities
The question of which activities to perform internally and which to source from the outside is at the center of the sourcing model. DoCoMo decided

---

[59] See Foong (2002). Natsuno (2003) reports that DoCoMo's operating revenue from packet communication was ¥ 200 million in 1998 and soared to ¥ 38,500 million in 1999 with the appearance of i-mode services. He claims that the average revenue per i-mode subscriber exceeds ¥ 2000. Analysis of Credit Suisse First Boston and Booz Allen & Hamilton calculated that for 2000 i-mode users had $12 additional voice volume compared to non i-mode users.

[60] Hartman, Ragnevad and Linden (2000), p. 25.

[61] See Rose (2001).

[62] Datamonitor (2002), p. 10.

[63] Natsuno (2003), p. 84.

[64] Datamonitor (2002), p. 12.

[65] See Rose (2001); Credit Suisse First Boston (2002), p. 93 and Datamonitor (2002), p. 11.

[66] See Hartman, Ragnevad and Linden (2000); Datamonitor (2002); Natsuno (2003).

[67] See Foong (2002); Natsuno (2003).

to concentrate its efforts on providing the i-mode platform, i.e. the mobile portal that was open for third party providers of content. DoCoMo did not buy, but instead only hosted these contents on the value-enabling platform. The business risk was with the provider of the contents. I-mode relied on the innovativeness of the market and the fact that entrepreneurs will offer services through economic incentives. Competition and demand would decide which services would be killer applications and which would not. DoCoMo offered to collect the fees and to handle the billing for the providers. Aside from paying for subscription services, third parties also offered a huge amount of services free of subscription fees. Providers of such services aimed to improve their customer relationships (i.e. customer retention), to decrease costs, or just to create public awareness. See figure 16 for an illustration of aggregated internal and external capabilities.

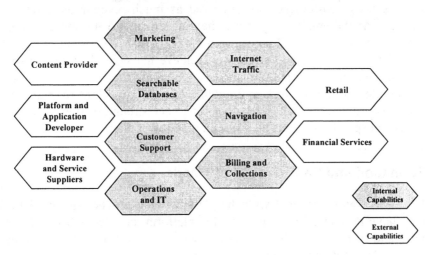

Fig. 16. Internal and External Capabilities of DoCoMo

Competition

In Japan, NTT DoCoMo faces competition from the two local operators KDDI and J-Phone (in the meantime Vodafone KK). KDDI and J-Phone were not able to steal significant market share from DoCoMo with their respective offerings EZweb and J-Sky.[68] Although, EZweb is 1.5 times faster than i-mode, it nevertheless suffers negative feedback loops with steadily

---

[68] As of 2001, EZ web counted for 19.4% of the market followed by J-Phone with 18.7%. NTT DoCoMo's market share for i-mode as market leader was 61.9% according to the Telecommunication Carriers Association (http://www.tca.or.jp/index-e.html).

declining market shares because of lacking content on the platform.[69] On a global level, the main competitors are Vodafone Group Plc., T-Mobile International, Orange S.A. and mmO_2. This distinction is crucial because DoCoMo rules the Japanese market relatively undisputedly, in contrast to the global mobile Internet market struggling with fierce competition from i-mode imitations from the leading global mobile network operators. Its own efforts to establish i-mode as the dominant global design for the mobile Internet with licensing and minority stake holdings in smaller market players in national markets such as KPN and its affiliate E-Plus must be seen as failures regarding adoption rates and usage. Vodafone launched its Live! service offering on October, 24, 2002 in Germany, Italy, the Netherlands, Spain and the U.K. with three dedicated handsets. Thomas Geitner, Head of Global Products and Services said "No service at Vodafone has won as many customers and generated as much revenue as quickly as Live!."[70] At the end of May, Live! had more than 1.5 million customers, generating on average 12 percent more ARPU than voice-centric customers. The Vodafone Group might well achieve the same dominant position as DoCoMo in Japan on a global basis. Operating the first or second largest mobile cellular network in 28 countries with a reach of over 200 million proportionate mobile subscribers is a very strong position to set standards and specify handsets by sheer market power alone.

Formation and Early Growth of I-Mode

DoCoMo was confronted with the classical chicken-and-egg problem. If they have no appealing content on the platform, no user will use the service, and if the service has no active users, content providers will hesitate to provide appealing content.

Achieving Critical Mass

The diffusion strategy of DoCoMo to solve the chicken-and-egg problem was to gain a main group of at least 10 to 20 content providers that would provide appealing content at the start of the service.[71] Actually, DoCoMo introduced i-mode services with 67 initial content providers including banks, newspapers, airlines, and gaming companies. It proved to be a wise decision to employ cHTML as standard for displaying contents on i-mode to convince initial adapters to support the platform. Contents already produced for the WWW could be transformed easily and rapidly for i-mode.

---

[69] See Ratliff (2002), p. 64.
[70] Blau (2003).
[71] A detailed narrative of the events is provided in Natsuno (2003), pp. 136.

Hence, a huge repository of content and a large community of content providers was available right from the beginning. The reliance on de-facto standards such as HTML, MIDI, GIF secured wide spread availability and the prevention of negative feedback loops and a vicious cycle that would have threatened the growth of the installed base. An interviewee from a market analysis company added that e-mail acted as a killer application in the beginning that drove subscribers into i-mode. "We", Natsuno holds, "regarded the one million mark as a crucial milepost, a subscriber base giving us critical mass. Once the level passed, we would be into positive feedback cycle in which people notice what others around them were doing with their i-mode phones and would want to use the service themselves."[72] Figure 17 shows the numbers for i-mode subscribers, i-mode menu sites, and voluntary sites.

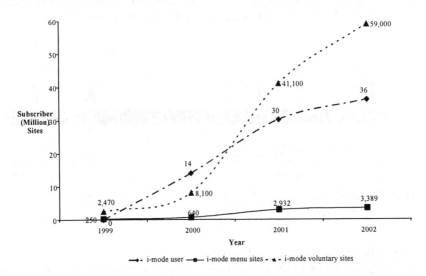

Fig. 17. I-Mode Growth

It took DoCoMo only until August to achieve the goal of 1 million users. In February 2000, one year after launch, the number of users reached 5 million. After 3 years around 30 million or more than three quarters of the overall customer base were i-mode subscribers.[73] In September 2001, subscriber growth still accelerated at a stunning rate of 1.3 million per month. Market research concluded that the openness, the simplicity, and the avail-

---

[72] Natsuno (2003), p. 2.
[73] See Chan (2001).

ability of a wide variety of high quality content were the major success
factors for early growth.[74] Another factor positively contributing to the diffusion of i-mode has been the availability of an adequate number of handsets (six different models in early 2000) sold at reasonable prices.[75] Handsets are heavily subsidised by DoCoMo. A mobile phone that would cost
approximately ¥60,000 retails for less than ¥30,000.[76] Numbers from
Merrill Lynch quoted by Hartman, Ragnevad and Linden (2000) report retail prices varying from ¥12,000 to ¥20,000 in the first quarter of 2000.
Wholesale prices were reported to be between ¥36,000 and ¥43,000. These
numbers calculate to a subsidy of around ¥23,500.[77] This penetration pricing approach has resulted in a fast diffusion of i-mode capable devices because of a short replacement time of approximately nine months in Japan
(compared to 18 months in Europe). In the expansion phase, objectives of
DoCoMo changed to navigation and organisation of information. Figure
18 chronicles the history of key events in the growth phase of i-mode.

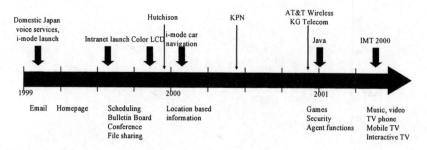

Fig. 18. I-Mode Milestones

Scaling the Value-Enabling Platform
The initial scope of the value-enabling platform of i-mode was broadened
along several directions. First DoCoMo addressed new customer segments
next to the urban youth with offerings targeted at mass-market audiences
and professional business segments. DoCoMo included, for example, electronic retail and commerce services, digital entertainment and information

---

[74] See Hartman, Ragnevad and Linden (2000), p. 5.
[75] Interview with DoCoMo representative. Hartman, Ragnevad and Linden (2000), p. 22.
[76] See Rose (2001).
[77] Supposing wholesale prices define retail prices, we can assume that the subsidy for the
low-end devices is approximately ¥24,000 and that for high-end devices is about
¥23,000. Even if we disregard that wholesale prices determine retail prices, DoCoMo
would have to pay at least ¥16,000 on top if it were to sell the device with the highest
wholesale price at the modest retail price.

services and mobile-enabled productivity tools for business customers. It also tried to broaden the range of supporting devices other than cellular phones. To that end, DoCoMo aimed at in-car navigation systems, game consoles and set-top boxes for home entertainment and television. A third direction aimed at broadening the supported radio interfaces and enabling a trajectory path of i-mode services for 3G and 4G mobile network infrastructure with the introduction of FOMA. Last, but not least, DoCoMo increased the international coverage of i-mode by licensing its value-enabling platform to mobile telecommunication network operators worldwide.

Alliancing: Leveraged Growth

DoCoMo wove a web of partners through various co-operations ranging from joint ventures to alliances in order to tie adapters to its platform (See table 1).[78]

Table 1. I-Mode Co-operations

Date	Event
September, 1999	Announcement to offer corporate intranet solutions with Puma Technologies' product "Intellisync Anywhere" in combination with Microsoft Exchange and Lotus Notes Domino. Softbank handles sales and support.
March, 1999	Alliances with Sun Microsystems (Java platform), Symbian (EPOC platform), and Microsoft (Windows CE) to boost its mobile computing capabilities and hedge its bets on the dominant mobile computing platform.
April, 2000	Investment in Payment First Payment First Corporation to establish electronic settlement capabilities
June, 2000	Joint Venture with Dentsu Inc. to establish D2·Communications, a mobile advertising business.
August, 2000	Exclusive alliance with Sony Computer Enterprises to link up i-mode services with Sony's hugely popular Playstation game consoles and access to games
	Agreement with the Walt Disney Internet Group (the Web business of Walt Disney) for access to Disney's content (cartoon screen savers, songs, news and information).
September, 2000	Acquisition of a 42.3% controlling stake in AOL Japan for 10.3 billion yen to achieve access to AOL Instant Messenger, AOL e-mail and content. AOL Japan is rebranded to AOL DoCoMo.
October, 2000	Joint Venture with Lawson Inc., Matsushita and Mitsubishi Corporation to establish i-convenience, an electronic commerce network, linking i-mode services to Lawson convenience stores.
December, 2000	Agreement to join research efforts with Hewlett-Packard for 4G high-performance multimedia development (MOTO-Media).
December, 2000	Joint venture with Sony, Sakura Bank, Sakura Information Systems, Japan Research Institute, Toyota Motor, Denso, DDI, Sanwa Bank, and Bank of Tokyo-Mitsubishi to develop e-money (an electronic payment system on cellular handsets).
January, 2001	Launch of a wireless music distribution service with three other partners—Sony, Itochu, and Matsushita Communications Industrial Company.
February, 2001	Team-up with Sega to enable access to Sega's Dreamcast video arcade games via i-mode handsets.

---

[78] See Foong and Mitsuyama (2001); Gawer (2000), Foong (2002).

Table 1. (continued)

Date	Event
November, 2001	Joint action plan with Nokia to cooperate specifically in the promotion of open mobile architecture for wideband code division multiple access (WCDMA)-based 3G services.
June, 2002	Collaboration with Oracle to make Oracle's database and global positioning system software compatible with DoCoMo's 3G, or third-generation, wireless technology.
December, 2002	Announcement that Nissan Motor Co., Ltd., and DoCoMo, Inc. have jointly established the Business Telematics Working Committee that will develop business models incorporating mobile multimedia systems and telematics services.
February, 2003	Announcement that DoCoMo and Macromedia, Inc. reached an agreement to jointly deliver Flash™ technology to i-mode platform.
April, 2003	Announcement to start a pilot program with DoCoMo, Inc., to test Visa International, Nippon Shinpan, OMC Card and AEON Credit a service for making credit card payments at bricks and mortar merchants via mobile phones, which are equipped with infrared transmission (IrDA) ports.

First tier co-operations comprise above all the manufacturers of handsets as well as producers of mobile middleware and software clients for the mobile devices. Handset manufacturers are not officially listed as alliance partners, but as co-developers.[79] Official handset manufacturers include NEC Panasonic, Mitsubishi, Fujitsu, and Sony, who, together with DoCoMo, contribute to the handset specifications. In March 1999 shortly after the launch of i-mode, DoCoMo announced an alliance with Sun Microsystems with the aim of adding more graphics-rich, interactive features to the handsets which resulted in i-αppli services based on Sun's Java technology.

Second tier co-operations include approved content offerings for the i-mode portal. These partners are called "Application Alliance Partners". DoCoMo ensures that these sites are technically compliant and that the content is highly attractive to the target segment. Key requirements for being listed on the i-mode menu include novel and up-to-date content, short update cycles and appealing content presentation.[80] Disney, for example, has founded a joint venture with DoCoMo to make Disney's huge content repository available over the wireless Internet in Japan.[81]

Third tier co operations are aimed at broadening the reach of i-mode services. It is DoCoMo's goal not be bound exclusively to mobile phones in the future. For this reason DoCoMo has joined forces with suppliers of other types of computing devices. The company teamed up with Matsushita to bring i-mode to in-car navigation systems and with Sony and Sega

---

[79] Natsuno (2003).
[80] See NTT DoCoMo (2003a).
[81] See Collins and Porras (1994), p. 84.

to have i-mode displayed on ubiquitous game consoles.[82] DoCoMo has even entered into alliances with digital video broadcasters to deliver i-mode right to the living room. In addition to extending the availability of i-mode to non-handset devices, DoCoMo is also expanding the geographical reach.[83]

Geographical Expansion

With DoCoMo's currently addressable market nearing saturation, the company is aiming to expand its service to new geographical regions.[84] It aims to reach approximately one million i-mode users across Germany, Netherlands, and Belgium in 2003 through KPN mobile.[85] At the same time, DoCoMo licensed i-mode to TIM in Italy, Telefónica in Spain, AT&T Wireless in the U.S. and Bouyges Telecom in France. Table 2 shows the regional expansion chronologically.

Table 2. I-Mode Geographical Expansion

Date	Mobile Operator	License Agreement/Stake
December 2, 1999	Hutchinson Whampoa, Hong Kong	20% stake in the telecommunication unit of Hong Kong's Hutchinson Whampoa representing an investment of $1,7 bn.
January 18, 2000	Telekom Italia Mobil, Italy KPN Mobile N.V., Netherlands	Establishment of a Joint Venture with TIM and KPN Mobile to launch mobile portal. DoCoMo holds 25% of the company.
November 30, 2000	KG Telecommunications Co., Ltd (KG Telecom), Taiwan	Acquisition of a 20% equity stake in KG Telecommunications Co., Ltd (KG Telecom) of Taiwan. Licensing agreement for the introduction of i-mode-like services in Taiwan June 18, 2000
November 7, 2001	KPN Mobile N.V., Netherlands	Transfer and license of i-mode technologies to KPN Mobile for the launch of wireless Internet services in the Netherlands and Belgium.
March 16, 2002	E-Plus Mobilfunk GmbH & Co. KG, Germany	Transfer and license of i-mode technologies to E-Plus. The agreement also includes the use of the i-mode Trademark by E-Plus. KPN Mobile holds a 77.5% stake in E-Plus.
April 16, 2002	AT&T Wireless, United States	Launch of a variety of wireless consumer services based on i-mode technology. DoCoMo holds a 16% stake of AT&T wireless representing $10 bn.
April 18, 2002	KPN Mobile N.V., Netherlands	Launch of i-mode in the Netherlands through KPN Mobile. DoCoMo holds 15% stake in KPN mobile.
October 15, 2002	BASE (formerly KPN Orange), Belgium	Launch of i-mode services in Belgium by BASE. KPN Mobile sublicensed the i-mode service to its subsidiary BASE.

[82] Natsuno (2003), p. 86-89.

[83] "No one is going to topple DoCoMo in Japan. But they can't get bigger without risking further regulation. That's why they need to go overseas." Mark Berman, Credit Suisse First Boston, quoted in Rose (2001).

[84] Datamonitor (2002), p. 10.

[85] Personal telephone interview with Executive Board Member of E-Plus GmbH, Germany.

Table 2. (continued)

Date	Mobile Operator	License Agreement/Stake
November 15, 2002	Bouygues Telecom S.A., France	I-mode license and technology transfer agreement in April 2002
Approximately first quarter 2003	Telefónica, Spain	I-mode license and technology transfer agreement with DoCoMo to launch i-mode under the operator's mobile internet brand e-moción

Conclusion

DoCoMo controls all modules of the i-mode business web with control points and has established (quasi-)vertical integration through the externalisation of resources and capabilities that are governed by the gatekeeper position of DoCoMo and the definition of specifications and access to the customers. DoCoMo succeeded in establishing end-to-end control of the service, controlling both the contents and the handsets. The end-to-end control made it possible to maximise the value perceived by the consumer in keeping the service easy to use, reasonably priced, useful and convenient. Interestingly, the control points for DoCoMo are not exclusively technological but rather a combination of an open technological platform, the proprietary customer interface and the billing infrastructure. Thus, DoCoMo managed to create an open-proprietary platform which is highly scalable. Much of the momentum of i-mode is based on its relative openness for third party content providers. The win-win business web created opportunities for entrepreneurs to participate in the value generated. DoCoMo's decision not to buy content from its providers but to provide a platform for third parties was a significant factor in its eventual success because it helped increase the number of users.[86] Thanks to this huge success DoCoMo won awards for being the best mobile operator in the Asia-Pacific region and the coveted award for best mobile operator overall at the 2002 World Communication Awards in London.[87] However, DoCoMo also suffered from the economic downturn and the specific problems which the telecommunication industry encountered worldwide. Especially the strongly needed expansion of the i-mode platform to assure fu-

---

[86] "Plenty of content is the key to the i-mode growth cycle", writes Natsuno (2003), p. 10. "DoCoMo has achieved a huge success because it has marketed its i-mode service to the right segments, ones which will increase usage and drive growth; offer applications, which users want; and form alliances with content partners and vendors (handset manufacturers)." Pescatore (2001), p. 2.

[87] See Molony (2002).

ture growth and to maintain dominance prooved to be difficult in the face of global competition from Vodafone, T-Mobile, mmO$_2$ and Orange.

EBay, Inc.: Formation of the Online Person-to-Person Industry

"I had written hundreds of stories as a journalist, and I had never made such a request before [asking eBay for cooperation]. But it was clear to me then, as it is even clearer to me now, that eBay was easily the most interesting story of the early Internet age, and one of the most important business stories of our time."[88]

The San Jose based eBay is one of the leading Internet companies and the industry market leader for person-to-person auctions. EBay, one of the true success stories of the Internet, mushroomed to the world's largest online person-to-person trading platform. Its market share in the online auction business is about 80%.[89] "There isn't another company on the planet that grew that fast", says Meg Whitman, CEO and President of eBay.[90] In spite of other Internet giants such as Yahoo! or Amazon, eBay was immediately profitable. The company is especially interesting because it managed to retain its leadership against the dominant opinion of market and financial analysts and the overwhelming power in terms of brand and installed user base of Amazon and Yahoo!, both of which tried to establish their own auction platforms. Not surprisingly, many business schools have already published cases covering eBay.[91] In economic research, especially the bidding behaviour has been subject of recent studies.[92] Nevertheless, the growth management of eBay remained widely overlooked. Here, I will elaborate on the strategies eBay pursued to grow its market platform and the community of buyers and sellers.

Environmental Conditions for EBay

Pierre Omidyar founded the business in September 1995 as AuctionWeb. At that point he already had an impressive track history in developing computer technology and founding technology related businesses. Although barely in his mid-thirties, he had already worked as an employee with Data Design, Claris and General Magic. He had co-founded Ink De-

---

[88] Cohen (2002b), p. 9.
[89] See Bradely and Porter (2000).
[90] Hof and Himelstein (1999)
[91] See Bradely and Porter (2000).
[92] See Baron (2001).

velopment. Thus, he already had experience with Internet start-up businesses when he founded eBay. Further, he had the technical skills because he started programming in high school and subsequently graduated with a degree in computer science. Something very special is his attitude to money and prestige symbols. When he founded eBay he was already a millionaire from the sale of Ink Development to Microsoft, but kept his philosophy of being thrifty. He always advised employees to spend the money as if it was their own and even after the IPO that made him a billionaire he kept driving his old VW Beetle cabriolet. In August 1996, he convinced Jeff Skoll, a Stanford MBA and former employee of Knight-Ridder to join the company as his partner. Skoll looked after the business side of the venture whereas Omdyar was occupied with technological issues. Skoll, like Omdyar, had already gathered experience in founding companies. After graduating from university, he founded two high-tech companies – Skoll engineering and Micros on the Move Ltd. Together they build the entrepreneurial team that managed the early successes of eBay.[93] They founded the company in the early days of the Internet diffusion with the emergence of the WWW. The massive diffusion of the Internet in the U.S. is partly explained by the FCC's Computer Inquiry II Decision permitting Internet Service Providers very low connect charges to the incumbent's PSTNs. Due to the huge installed user base, many content providers produced content for the Internet.[94] The company's early growth fell into the new economy bubble hysteria when many technology-based start-ups (such as Yahoo! and Amazon) tried to conquer the new electronic commerce industry sector.

The EBay Business Web

EBay's value-enabling platform is the technological implementation of a marketplace that serves as a venue for the connected community of buyers and sellers. EBay strengthened its strong position by making the site "sticky" with community services, gaining a competitive advantage through consumer branding and positioning the company as a user interface in the value system. Marketplace platforms exhibit strong network effects because the utility of a consumer is indirectly affected by the overall number of participating buyers and sellers. [95] More sellers attract more

---

[93] See Bunell and Luecke (2000), pp. 23; Cohen (2002b), pp. 31.

[94] See Brock (2002).

[95] "Exchanges are inherently subject to network effects, and both buyers and sellers tend to reinforce the regression to the extremes by preferring to do business on the leading exchange." Moore, Johnston and Kippola (1999), p. 339.

buyers that attract more sellers that attract more buyers. The more consumers the more offers and sellers and the more sellers the more buyers
because they can attain higher prices for their goods and can address a larger market giving opportunities of serving specific market segments. The
installed base of buyers and sellers on the eBay platform resulted in a lock-
in for buyers and sellers alike that prevented merchants and consumers
from switching to competitive offerings in the online auction space such as
Yahoo! Auctions, Amazon, etc. because they could not offer the same
breadth and depth of products along with an equivalently huge market. Figure 19 shows EBay's system architecture.

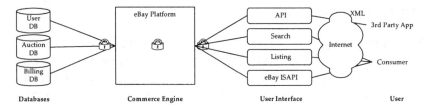

Fig. 19. EBay System Architecture

In the beginning, Omdyar created virtually the entire technological infrastructure himself. He bought a web server that he hosted in his flat. He
programmed the marketplace in PERL[96] scripts. It quickly turned out that
the architecture was not scalable for the ever-rising volume of traffic on
the site, often resulting in major standstills and crashes of the site.[97] The
three major limitations of the initial architecture were flexibility, scalabil-
ity, and manageability. In October 1999, eBay outsourced its backend operation to AboveNet and Exodus. The two firms took over responsibility
for the database servers and the internet routers. The company shifted to
open-standard-based Internet technology replacing the existing proprietary
CGI scripts since the infrastructure technology was not considered a specific asset for eBay. The competitive advantage lies in database content
from the marketplace and ownership of the community interface. The implemented architecture for the marketplace was a Sun Microsystems J2EE
architecture and an IBM Websphere Application Server that was regarded
by observers as the largest J2EE implementation at that time. The server
hardware was sourced from Sun Microsystems and the databases were

---

[96] PERL is a script programming language that can optionally be compiled just before execution into either C code or cross-platform bytecode. Perl is regarded as a good choice
for developing common gateway interface (CGI) programs. See http://www.whatis.com.
[97] Cohen (2002b), chap. 2, particularly pp. 53-59.

provided by Oracle. In sum, eBay relies largely on an open standard-based platform with only limited proprietary extension to keep a competitive edge. One of the proprietary modules that play an important role is the API that enables connections to the marketplace from third parties. EBay disclosed the API in 1999 for adapters to the value-enabling platform. Even before eBay voluntarily enabled technological connections to its platform, adapters emerged in different functions that adopted the emerging standard and provided complementary goods and services to ease and enhance the consumer experience with eBay.[98]

EBay Business Model

EBay first pursued an auction model for collectibles. With growing demand and more listings, eBay added new categories and new market segments as well as new pricing schemes, such as fixed prices. Over time, it evolved to be the largest Internet market maker for almost every imaginable item and for individuals as well as small and large businesses.[99] Viable for the eBay business model is its community of buyers and sellers. The foundation of its success is the establishment of trust among its community members. In its infancy, eBay set rules for establishing trust. "The reputation mechanism was supplemented by rules designed by eBay to govern who could be a member, what members could trade, and how they were to conduct themselves on its Web site."[100] Figure 20 illustrates the eBay business model.

---

[98] See Marshak (2003).

[99] "A *market maker* acts as a neutral intermediary that provides a place to trade and also sets the rules of the market." Afuah and Tucci (2003), p. 22.

[100] Baron (2001), p. 2.

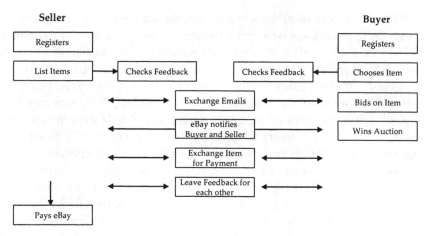

Fig. 20. EBay Business Model[101]

Value Proposition

The company's objective is to build the world's leading online person-to-person trading community.[102] EBay offers an auction platform for individuals as well as small and large businesses on the WWW.[103] The firm's business focus is clearly on being a marketplace. However, the value proposition is not simply providing a venue. EBay provides buyers and sellers a place to socialise, to discuss common topics and to provide mutual feedback. In spite of earlier attempts to describe the value proposition of eBay as a consumer-to-consumer online auction, the site evolved over time into a huge Internet retail giant that is better described as a marketplace for connecting people. EBay introduced, for example, fixed prices for commodity goods and large businesses such as IBM, Sun Microsystems, etc. that already account for around 5% of gross merchandise sales.[104] Thus Tapscott, Lowy and Ticoll (2000) propose that the core value proposition of eBay is liquidity:

"(...T)he ease of converting assets into cash. Agoras achieve liquidity by matching buyers and sellers and facilitating price discovery, whereby buyers and sellers cooperate and compete to arrive at a mutually acceptable deal."[105]

---

[101] Adapted from eBAY INC. (1998), p. 8.

[102] eBAY INC. (1998).

[103] See Baron (2001).

[104] See Shankland (1999); Cohen (2002a).

[105] Tapscott, Lowy and Ticoll (2000), p. 40. Under the term Agora, the authors understand a market where consumers meet, negotiating, and assigning value to goods.

With the advent of eBay, Omdyar created an entirely new market, because the person-to-person online market was virtually nonexistent in 1995.[106] In addition eBay was not only a mere online translation of an off-line business. Since eBay never sees the traded items, it does not serve as an agent for traders. EBay grants no authentication of the traded items, and it is not involved in the transactions of the traders. Whitman says, she thinks, "EBay has created an environment that didn't exist in the land-based world."[107] Consumers adopted the idea because eBay offered some significant benefits over newspaper classified ads, traditional auction houses, and flea markets. The problems with these traditional forms of person-to-person trade are higher transaction costs through the regional nature that make it costly for buyers and sellers to meet and exchange information. Secondly, the supply and demand is restricted when compared to the millions of auctions held every day at eBay. Thirdly, the offer spectrum is nowhere as broad as it is at eBay, where auctions take place in several thousand categories from automobiles to specific niche collectibles. Finally, compared with traditional intermediaries such as auction houses, the fees and commissions for listing items are lower at eBay. In sum, eBay eliminated much friction in the market and provided more ease and convenience to the consumers.

Internal Capabilities
Internally, eBay supports the following activities: Registration of users, auction database operation, bidding handling, service billing and collection of payments, community services. Hence, the core competencies of eBay revolve about brand development, acquisition of users, management and maintenance of the user database and operation of the market platform, facilitating user auctions as well as database maintenance.[108] EBay invests heavily in its community of sellers and buyers because most of the innovations in products and change in layout or rules come directly from community proposals. The control points of eBay that help it to dominate the online auction business are information about users, ownership, and control of the auction databases and control and influence of the user community. EBay gathers information about usage and buying and selling behaviour directly from the user community and voluntary user feedback. The company executes control over the community by setting the rules for the

---

[106] See also Bunell and Luecke (2000), p. 9. Cohen (2002b), p. 114, reports that, during her job interview, Whiteman, the now CEO of eBay, was struck by the fact that "Omdyar had created an entirely new business, one that could not have existed without the Internet."

[107] Himelstein (1999).

[108] See Bunell and Luecke (2000), p. viii.

marketplace and through its ability to exclude community members that do not adhere to these rules. However, community management was not always easy for eBay. In fact, the community always rebelled against major changes regarding the site such as feedback ratings, naming of categories, launch of new features, etc. The lesson eBay had to learn was that it had to involve the community in decisions and to adopt based on feedback from the community.[109]

When a strong community forms the basis for a business like eBay, the company's strongest asset at the same time restricts the company's freedom in taking decisions. When, for example, eBay tried to exploit new revenue streams from advertising the sellers protested strongly. They complained that eBay was trying to steal commerce from them by directing buyers to companies which advertised the same products, thereby selling out on the community for advertising revenue. "Faced with open rebellion from the seller community, eBay backed down. On June 3 [2000], it put up a message on the Announcement Board saying there would be no ads tied to specific search terms."[110] However, eBay never seems to have surrendered earning advertising revenues because it reported in 2002 to have made 61 million dollar net revenues from third party advertising. In 2001 the company reported third-party advertising to have totalled 1%, 3% and 11% of consolidated net revenues for the years ending December 31, 1999, 2000 and 2001 respectively.[111]

EBay tries to secure its strategic assets by hiding information like e-mail addresses of its users that might be exploited by competitors to drive users out of the community. In the past, eBay has successfully taken competitors to court to prevent them stealing their intangible assets. The rules of acceptance, for instance, prohibit postings of third parties to the community. With careful communication of new rules and sensible grounds for the changes, eBay managed to keep the majority of the users calm. To this end, eBay named the protection of users from spam as a reason for hiding e-mail addresses from the public (with the exception of sellers who are indeed able to see who has bid on their items). Some competitors also tried to extract data from eBay using software bots and were (successfully) sued in court for stealing eBay intellectual property.[112]

Revenue Model

The revenue model of eBay comprises several revenue sources. As an auction platform, it charges fees for listing items and takes up to 6% off the

---

[109] See Cohen (2002b).
[110] Cohen (2002b), p. 252.
[111] See eBAY INC. (2002); eBAY INC. (2000).
[112] Cohen (2002b), p. 253.

end price as a transaction fee. In detail, users have to pay an insertion fee first. If they wish to add special listing options such as bold headings, a certain staring time or preferential positioning of their items on the site, as for example in the "Featured Items" section, sellers have to pay extra fees for these additional listing options. After the successful sale of an item, eBay charges a final sale price fee and a fee for selling the item. In 1998 the listing fees accounted for around 45 percent of revenues. The final sale price fee made up the remaining 55 percent.[113] The average sale price (ASP) is an indicator for the revenue potential of eBay. By hosting higher-value auctions, eBay tries to increase its revenues. In 1997, the ASP was roughly $31, in Q4 1998 ASP was $22.57 in Q1 1999 it increased to $23.60. Although eBay stopped reporting the ASP, DB Alex Brown estimated that the number was about $50 in 2002. Market observers argue that eBay does not offer price comparison tools on its site so as not to endanger its high commissions revenues.[114] Figure 21 shows a simple illustration of the revenue sources.[115]

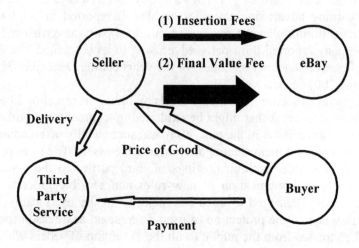

Fig. 21. EBay Revenue Model

Aside from the revenues from its core-business, eBay generates revenues from advertising on its site. Advertising and partnering generate advertising revenue that account for 20% of total revenues. Browsing and

---

[113] See Bradely and Porter (2000), p. 82.
[114] See Arango and Eavis (2001).
[115] As in figure 15, the colour and the width of the arrows indicate who gets how much of the total revenue.

bidding for items at eBay is free of charge. Sellers are charged an insertion fee for listing items, extra charges for different listing options and a final sales price fee. The price for listing on items depends on the opening price and varies between $0.30 and $3.30.[116] EBay offers several listing options that increase the likelihood of selling an item or achieving higher final prices.

Table 3. EBay Insertion Fees

Opening Value or Reserve Price	Insertion Fee
$00.01-$09.99	$0.30
$10.00-$24.99	$0.55
$25.00-$49.99	$1.10
$50.00 - $199.99	$2.20
$200 & higher	$3.30

EBay offers several listing options that increase the likelihood of selling an item or achieving higher final prices. Table 4 provides an overview of the prices for the different options.

Table 4. EBay Listing Options

Listing Option	Description	Insertion Fee
Home Page Featured	Item is listed in a Special Featured section and is also rotated on the eBay home page.	$99.95
Featured Plus!	Featured Plus! Item appears in the category's Featured Item in bidder's search results.	$19.95
Highlight	Highlight Item listing is emphasized with a colored background.	$5.00
Bold	Bold Item title is listed in bold. $1.00	$1.00
Buy-It-Now	Buy-It-Now Allows the seller to close an auction instantly for a specified price.	$0.05

The final sales price fee depends on the final price attained. EBay charges 5% on final prices up to $25, 2.5% for the range of $25 to $1,000 and 1.25% for everything above that. In January 2002, eBay raised its price range from 1.25%-5% to 1.5-5.25%. Along with new product categories, eBay introduced a new pricing mechanism. As long as eBay members were selling unique or rare items, bidding was just perfect, but with more commoditised goods such as CDs, fixed prices were more convenient. EBay introduced fixed prices with the acquisition of half.com, a competitor who pioneered selling used items such as CDs, books, etc. that come with an identification number such as the ISBN for books. With the codes,

---

[116] Fee structure as of March 2003.

half.com could easily provide descriptions of the items for the seller. Sales roughly equal profit since the cost of goods only comprises computing infrastructure and customer service. Thus, eBay achieves gross profit margins of about 80%.[117]

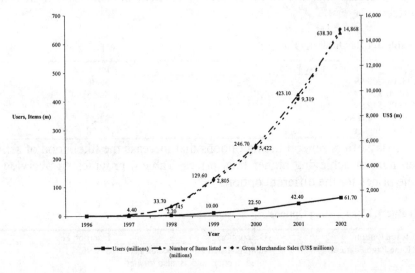

Fig. 22. EBay Growth

The sharp increase of sales on the site starting in 1997 spurred revenue growth.

External Capabilities

EBay concentrates on its core business and lets other businesses handle relevant complementary services such as shipping and handling of goods. "The company does not keep inventory or handle products. It simply collects and manages the sharing of information in a virtual market."[118] The following activities essential for the marketplace are handled by external entities: shipping, payment, payment processing, traffic from Internet portals, inventory, warehousing, sales force.

Users took over many tasks for eBay such as advertising the service, fraud detection and prevention, helpline and support. Users themselves initially handled payment through cheques and money orders or by simply

---

[117] Hof and Himelstein (1999) report gross margins of 70-80%. See also Cohen (2002b), p. 9 who reports that eBay achieved gross profit margins of over 80% six months after foundation then the company began charging fees.

[118] See Cohen (2002b), p. 8.

sending the funds by mail. EBay considered payment as its Achilles heel because payment was the most inefficient link in its transaction chain. This gap was filled by PayPal, an impressive growth story of its own. As pow-ersellers at eBay became aware of the existence of this service, user regis-tration mushroomed by word-of-mouth advertising. The fact that PayPal offered every user a $5 credit supported the viral growth. "[...] PayPal was soon growing at a rate with few precedents in the history of commerce—7 percent to 10 percent a day. The twelve thousand users PayPal ended 1999 with skyrocketed to more than a million over the next four months."[119] By the end of that year, PayPal had already attracted 5 million users giving it a critical mass in the online payment sector. EBay itself tried to establish a payment infrastructure for the site with less convincing success. Billpoint, the acquired PayPal competitor never attracted many users and the service was cut in favour of PayPal in 2002.[120] Although eBay tried to link auc-tions to Billpoint payment, making it easier for customers on the site to use its own service, the installed base, switching costs and the associated net-work externalities prevented PayPal users from switching. The Microsoft strategy of higher degrees of integration by bundling successful modules with the value-enabling platform did not work out. EBay used independent contractors for the help desk. Users also handled marketing and sales in the beginning. In June 1999, eBay opened a customer-service centre of its own in Utah, but staffed with former community members and contractors who became supervisors.[121] Internal and external capabilities of eBay are shown in figure 23.

---

[119] Cohen (2002b), p. 229.
[120] See eBAY INC. (2002).
[121] See Cohen (2002b), p. 178.

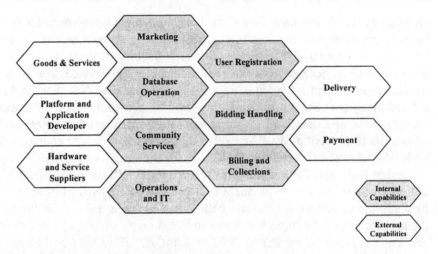

Fig. 23. Internal and External Capabilities of EBay

Competition

Market observers and researchers alike argued that entry barriers for web auctions were particularly low.[122] The key competitors are listed below in the order of their market entry.[123] In October 1997, the first serious competition to threaten eBay appeared with the emergence of OnSale (with person-to-person auctions) and Auction Universe. OnSale actually invented auctions on the Internet and started its operations as early as 1995. In contrast to eBay, OnSale held business-to-person auctions to sell refurbished equipment and tools from a variety of manufacturers. It started offering person-to-person auctions in 1997. OnSale focused on auctions and did not offer community services. To the eBay management, this was their major weakness in combination with poor customer support.[124] Auction Universe, the affiliation of Times Mirror, was launched in January 1998. Incomprehensibly, Auction Universe deliberately decided to prevent users from importing their ratings from eBay. That proved to be a bad decision, because it supported the customer lock-in effects for eBay and prevented users from actually switching to Auction Universe.[125] Further, the company did not offer community features such as eBay giving them a competitive dis-

---

[122] Gomez-Casseres (2001).

[123] For a more comprehensive listing refer to eBAY INC. (2002).

[124] Bradely and Porter (2000), p. 89.

[125] "Auction Universe's site was in many ways similar to eBay's. It offered its own version of the Feedback Forums, although it decided against allowing users to actually import their ratings from eBay

advantage. Cohen elaborates: "In the end, what hurt Auction Universe most was simply a lack of users. When buyers showed up at the site, they found that there was not much for sale – certainly far fewer items than on eBay. Sellers for their part, found that there were few buyers."[126] Later, Amazon made the same mistake when it entered auctions, leaving customers with a site considered too hygienic and clean. In 1998, Excite, Inc. acquired Classifieds2000 offering free classified advertising and person-to-person auctions. Excite integrated the auctions with other features of its portal site such as the shopping search function. However, in the end this competitor also did not fare very well. In late 1998, at the time around the IPO there were serious concerns in the investment community about the sustainability of eBay's success. At that time, Netscape already had a person-to-person auction service and Yahoo! had announced it intended to start such a service in conjunction with OnSale, albeit without user charges.[127] Many observers feared eroding profit margins and decreasing market share for eBay. As it turned out, switching costs for the users (comfort with the brand eBay as well as the huge installed base of buyers and sellers) permitted eBay to keep charging its services at unheard of levels.[128] Amazon started to hold daily auctions in late March of 1999.[129] Additionally it partnered with well established Sotheby's.[130] With the entrance of Yahoo! and Amazon in the market, concerns arose as to whether eBay could resist attackers with a larger installed base and greater brand recognition. Although the jury is still out on the long-term success of eBay, today it indisputably rules the online-auction market.

Establishment and Early Growth of EBay

"We were growing, in terms of traffic, metrics, and everything, twenty to thirty percent a month."[131]

Pierre Omdyar founded eBay as AuctionWeb on September 1, 1995. The domain for the site was already eBay.[132] At its inception the site was free of charge and a place for collectors to exchange collectibles. The legend per-

---

[126] Cohen (2002b), p. 99.

[127] Patsuris (1998). Yahoo! Auctions was completely free. It did not charge any fees to sellers and buyers and did not collect any commissions.

[128] The same phenomenon can be witnessed with Linux vs. Windows or OpenOffice vs. Microsoft Office, where the majority of users refuse to switch to the free offer.

[129] See Hof and Himelstein (1999).

[130] Gomez-Casseres (2001).

[131] Pierre Omdyar, cited in Cohen (2002b), p. 44.

[132] AuctionWeb was hosted on Omdyar's already existent web site eBay.com for his web consulting business Echo Bay Technology Group. See Cohen (2002b), pp. 21.

sists that Omdyar created eBay for his then fiancée who was having trouble finding other collectors of PEZ dispensers and a place to exchange them. Although the PEZ legend was repeated in many reports about eBay, it seems to be just that – a legend.[133]

"The PEZ dispenser story has been told and retold in countless popular accounts of e-Bay's history. But it is, Omdyar concedes, the 'romantic version' of eBay's founding. The truth is, in the summer of 1995 Omdyar was doing what every other smart tech person within a hundred mile radius was doing: obsessing about the Internet and the uses to which it could be put."[134]

In Omdyar's introduction to "The Official eBay Guide" he writes:

"I had been thinking about how to create an efficient marketplace – a level playing field, where everyone had access to the same information and could compete on the same terms as anyone else. Not just a site where big corporations sold stuff to consumers and bombarded them with ads, but rather one where people 'traded' with each other."

Omdyar created the first categories as they came to mind. These were computer Hardware and Software, Consumer Electronics, Antiques and Collectibles, Books and Comics and Miscellaneous. EBay started as a free site, but quickly generated so much traffic, that one year later the site began charging for listing items. Word-of-mouth from early users attracted many new users. By the end of 1995 eBay had already hosted thousand of auctions and some tens of thousands of bids.[135] In fact, in the early days of eBay customers performed all marketing and sales activities for the company. Quickly, traffic on the site increased and Omdyar's ISP forced him to move the site.[136] In order to recoup the increased operating costs for developing and maintaining the site he started to charge 10 cents per listing. In March 1996, the business generated its first profits. In September 1996, Omdyar asked Jeff Skoll, a friend of his, to join the emerging company and to manage the business aspects while Omdyar focused on the technological development of the site.

Achieving Critical Mass

The cultivation of the community and the enlargement of the installed user base were among the most important strategic issues for the growth of eBay. Among the key elements of its strategy, eBay reported in 1999:

"The Company seeks to maintain a critical mass of frequent buyers and sellers with vested interest in the eBay community so that sellers will continue to be attracted to the

---

[133] See Cohen (2002b), p. 83.

[134] Cohen (2002b), p. 18.

[135] See Cohen (2002b), especially the first chapter.

[136] Best, the ISP of Omdyar charged him the business tariff of $250 because the site attracted heavy traffic, though he insisted that the site was free and not a business. Ebay attracted so much traffic that the ISP's systems slowed down. Out of the necessity for paying the bills, he started to charge users. See Cohen (2002b).

service by the large number of potential buyers and buyers will be attracted to eBay by the large number of items listed by these sellers."[137]

First attempts to make the service popular were newsgroup postings from Omdyar.[138] On its first day of operation, virtually nobody visited the auction web site. Omdyar had posted some announcements to newsgroups to extol his site in the growing Internet community. In fact, the team at eBay decided in the first years that publicising the company would only attract attention from competition. As long as the company was not big enough to withstand competition from Internet gorillas such as AOL and Yahoo! they wanted "to fly under the radar" in Omdyar's words.[139] However, later the company realised that it had to market its service to become a household name and to attract mass-market customers. The first users were technologically "safe" users and were not bothered by the site's inconvenient user interface. However, to move the business into the mass-market realm eBay had to re-engineer the site to make it more intuitive and easier for untrained users to navigate while buying and selling. EBay tried to make the service as easy to use and understand as possible and advertised this with savvy consumer marketing. Users should not be hindered from spending money by any obstacles on the site. Therefore, eBay rebuilt the site in 1995, making it easier to navigate. Searching for specific items became easy because of sensible categories that were based on community feedback. This was essential for many prospect users, since many of the new users bought their first PC specifically for trading on eBay.[140] "EBay had always understood the virtue of keeping things simple: the site still offered little more than listings, a search engine, message boards, and the feedback forum."[141]

Additionally, new consumer segments had to be addressed because the market volume for small priced collectors' items was not infinite. The core users of eBay were, in the beginning, mainly collectors trading relatively low-value items such as Pokémons and Beanie Babies. EBay felt that it had to shift to higher-value goods in order to continue thriving and prospering. With higher prices, EBay would have higher revenues through higher final-value fees. To reach this goal eBay introduced new product categories. With the advent of new categories, eBay also introduced category managers to professionalize product management of categories. EBay faced the challenge of transitioning its business from a (loyal) collectors' community to a more anonymous market without impairing the commu-

---

[137] eBAY INC. (1998), p. 6.

[138] See, for instance, Cohen (2002b), pp. 22.

[139] See Cohen (2002b), p. 42-44.

[140] See Bradely and Porter (2000), p. 82.

[141] Cohen (2002b), p. 98.

nity members. EBay also addressed big resellers and corporate customers to bring a broader variety of goods onto the site. Here, it faced the challenge of not upsetting small businesses on eBay that were earning a living solely by selling merchandise in so-called eBay shops. The Marketing and Business Development Group around Steve Westley started to negotiate deals with Netscape, Excite, Angelfire and Lycos to drive traffic to the eBay site. At the same time eBay tried to increase its PR efforts, but most of the audiences they presented the idea to didn't know what to make of it – the basic concept was foreign to them. EBay, Cohen (2002b) reports, "was largely unknown, and the whole idea of online auctions struck many people as vaguely disreputable."[142] Outside of its community, eBay remained widely unknown and ran into problems hiring staff. EBay did not start advertising until 1997 when it changed its name from AuctionWeb to eBay.[143] The company started to advertise its service aggressively in 1999. By the end of that year's first quarter, eBay had attracted a customer base of 3.8 million, giving it a critical mass and positive feedback loops.[144] With branding, heavy marketing, and advertising in online and offline media, eBay had finally become a household name. As early as 1999, Rakesh Sood, a Goldman Sachs analyst, argued that users associated the eBay brand with online auctions. "Branding is huge. It's very difficult for somebody new to come along."[145] Next to deliberate publicity, eBay had strong coverage in the media because of downtime, fraud, pranks and other reports that had to be seen as bad news. Nevertheless, as the old saying goes: "All news is good news." The negative publicity drove new users to the site after first hearing about eBay in the news.

One of the main concerns and obstacles for eBay was the potential threat arising from opportunistic behaviour and fraud on the site. After one year of operation and following suggestions from the community, the company established the FeedbackForum for buyer and seller ratings to facilitate the building of reputations and trust among members. EBay extended the early rules after incidents of fraud crept up. Users began disputing over shipping time, packaging, product descriptions, etc. The feedback of co-users appeared as positive, neutral or negative next to the names of a given registered user. If a user had more then four negative credits, he was removed from the community. The FeedbackForum became the nucleus of a broader initiative, the SafeHarbor, to build and maintain trust, as well as to prevent opportunistic behaviour of community members. SafeHarbor,

---

[142] Cohen (2002b), p. 85.
[143] See Hoovers Inc. (2001a).
[144] See Bradely and Porter (2000), p. 82.
[145] Auerbach (1999).

which was launched in February 1998, includes peer review of users, user verification, integrated escrow services and secure payment means. As the marketplace grew, the company established rules and norms to govern the market place. These rules are formulated in eBay's community values (See figure 24).

Community Values
eBay is a community where we encourage **open and honest communication** between all of our members. We believe in the following five basic values.

We believe people are basically good.
We believe everyone has something to contribute.
We believe that an honest, open environment can bring out the best in people.
We recognize and respect everyone as a unique individual.
We encourage you to treat others the way that you want to be treated.

eBay is committed to these values. And we believe that our community members should also honor these values -- whether buying, selling, or chatting. We hope these community values will help you better understand the eBay community.

Fig. 24. EBay Community Values

The second major obstacle for growth was the increasingly unreliable technological platform which could not hold pace with user growth. From the beginning, the site had often encountered minor crashes and down times, but on June, 10 1999, the site went down for 22 hours following a total system crash, halting all business on eBay.

Gary Bengier who was hired as CFO in December 1997 became the driving force behind eBay going public. Bengier, a Harvard MBA had already amassed two decades of financial management experience with companies such as Microsoft and VXtreme. In advance of the IPO there were several attempts from companies such as Amazon and Yahoo! to buy eBay, but Omdyar thought that going public was more eBayesian and let the market decide what eBay was actually worth. "In the long term," he said, "we are building the company to last."[146] On September 24, 1998, eBay went public on the NASDAQ. With its 88% gross profit margin and amazing growth in users and listed items, it had an extremely successful start on Wall Street. The stock, heavily oversubscribed, rose to 53¼, representing a jump of 197%.[147] Parallel to increasing user numbers, the number of auctions held per day, gross merchandise sales and the number of items sold on the site increased (See table 5).

---

[146] Cohen (2002b), p. 149.
[147] See Cohen (2002b), p. 148.

Table 5. eBay Growth Figures

	1995	1996	1997	1998	1999	2000	2001	2002
Auctions (no.)	15	298	4.394	33.668	n.a	n.a	n.a	n.a
Categories (no.)	10	n.a	1,000	1,500	3,000	8,000	18,000	27,000
Gross Merchandise Sales (US$m)	n.a	n.a	95	745	2,805	5,422	9,319	14,868
Users (m)	n.a	0.041	0.341	2,2	10	22,5	42,4	61.7
Employees (no.)	n.a	6	41	138	198	1,927	2,560	4,000
Net Revenues (US$m)	n.a	32.05	41.37	86.13	224.72	431.42	748.82	1,214
Net Income (US$m)	n.a	3.34	7.06	7.27	9.57	48.29	90.45	249.89
Number of Items listed (m)	n.a	0.289	4.4	33.7	129.6	246.7	423.1	638.3

Scaling the Value-Enabling Platform

Although in August 1999 Meg Whitman emphasised that eBay will continue to concentrate on person-to-person trading, the company enlarged its product range in many directions.[148] The shift in the business mission over time is also documented in the difference between the 1999's SEC 10K filing and the mission statement expressed in the 2000 annual report. In 1999, the company postulated:

"The Company's objective is to build upon its position as the world's leading online personal trading platform."[149]

Whereas, in 2000, eBay describes its business mission as:

"At eBay we do one thing. We work every day to be the world's largest and most compelling Internet commerce platform."[150]

EBay leveraged its existing value-enabling platform as an open proprietary platform for as many customers as possible to further decrease its per unit costs. EBay was able to do so because it already dominated the auction market and did not need to fear that it would loose customers or weaken the brand. EBay could attract even more users with the user base of other popular Internet sites, which wanted to offer auctions without having to develop the technology and a critical mass of buyers and sellers themselves. EBay diversified in three major directions: It tried to address new customer segments other than person-to-person, it added new product categories and it broadened its geographical reach. EBay first transformed the company from a community of buyers and sellers to market platform and then to an Internet commerce brand.

---

[148] "EBay did not want to be a global auction site; it wanted to be what it had long called itself – a global market place." Cohen (2002b), p. 237.

[149] eBAY INC. (1999).

[150] eBAY INC. (2000).

EBay entered new market segments next to person-to-person auction trading, which had previously served as its core business. With the acquisition of half.com, eBay entered into fixed-price B2C market segments, challenging Amazon. At the time of acquisition, half.com had already attracted 250,000 registered users, offering certainty that eBay could not with auctions. Fixed prices are necessary to fulfil the needs of that portion of the population that is under time pressure or is looking for certainty in shopping. For this, eBay introduced the "Buy it Now" feature as a fixed pricing mechanism on its main site. "Buy it Now" enabled sellers to define a fixed price at which they were willing to sell the item without auctioning it. "Buy it Now" also had a positive side effect: it increased auction velocity resulting in a reduced time to cash. In October 2001, EBay absorbed half.com, integrating all listings and merging users as well as feedback ratings.

Among the major extensions of its product offerings, eBay added new categories such as Antiques, Cars and, Real Estate. In a first attempt eBay acquired the well-known auction house Butterfield & Butterfield in April 1999 for $260 million. In the same year, eBay also bought Kruse International, the worlds leading offline car auction company to help its newly introduced eBay category "Automobiles". It turned out that the integration of an offline business encountered many obstacles.

"In part it was a matter of cultural fit between eBay's users and the upscale auction world. Before it bought Butterfield and Butterfield, eBay had briefly considered entering into an alliance with Sotheby's, but the management team decided the Sotheby's name would be a turnoff for the average eBay user. [...] But to many eBay users, Butterfield & Butterfield seemed to be just as evocative of formal wear."

On the other hand, Butterfield & Butterfield's staff could not handle the new challenges of operating in virtual space. "Buyers complained to eBay that they were having trouble getting responses to simple e-mail questions, and high bidders were waiting weeks, even months, for deliveries [...]."[151] Consequently, the acquisitions could only be considered failures. In a later attempt, eBay partnered with Sotheby's to offer high-end auctions.[152] EBay launched the automobile category as a separate site but, due to legal restrictions, offered only used cars. Management thought that automobiles were somehow special and different from "normal" items sold through eBay. For example, buyers of cars were requesting more sophisticated

---

[151] Cohen (2002b), p. 224.

[152] In 1997, Sotheby's partnered with Amazon to host auctions on Amazon's newly established auction platform and eventually established its own web presence. More recently, Sotheby's and eBay have joined forces, integrating Sotheby's listings on eBay. Perhaps the reason lies in the time. Now that more people with diverse backgrounds use the Internet – and the eBay –, things may look different.

search features. In addition, the automotive category needed special services such as inspections, insurance and financing.

Starting with the acquisition of the German auction site Alando,[153] eBay also began offering B2B auctions. In April 2001, for example, Cisco already sold 2.700 items through eBay.[154] In 2001, Gomez-Casseres (2001) reports that Sun Microsystems sold equipment worth $10 million. He also claims that Sun Microsystems was listing between 20 and 150 items per day.[155] In February 2000, eBay disclosed its Application Programming Interface (API) to third parties, which could themselves host auctions by eBay on their sites. By publishing its programming interface in February, eBay made it simpler for outfits to manage auctions on behalf of clients. The payoffs for eBay were deeper inventory, more transactions, higher ASP's, and powerful vendors.

Co-operations: Leveraged Growth

EBay entered into a variety of collaboration agreements and alliances to leverage its growth ambitions and to supply complementary goods and services from third parties.

A strategic partnership with venture capitalist Benchmark Capital enabled eBay to access to the network of professional managers and expert advice for managing growth. For $5 million, the venture capitalist bought 22% of the company in June 1997. Benchmark helped, recruit Meg Whitman as CEO in February 1998. Whitman had a tenure record in big business and brought with her marketing expertise. Jeff Skoll explains: "It was in our heads from the start to try to bring in a world-class CEO to grow this thing as big as it could possibly get."[156] Meg Whitman had years of expertise in brand building for companies such as Hasbro, FDT, Stride Rite and Disney. Whitman employed senior management staff from traditional businesses such as Pepsi and Disney with many years of management experience.[157] Additionally, eBay sought to install experienced managers from related industries into the board of directors in order to benefit from their advice as well as their personal networks. Among others, eBay convinced Intuit founder Scott Cook and Starbucks CEO Howard Schultz to join the board of directors.[158]

Some of the relevant capabilities for the business such as complementary products, and services such as shipping, payment and escrow services

---

[153] Meanwhile rebranded to eBay.de.
[154] Anonymous (2001).
[155] Gomez-Casseres (2001).
[156] Jeff Skoll, co-founder of eBay cited in Cohen (2002b), p. 73.
[157] Gomez-Casseres (2001).
[158] For the current management team please refer to the latest SEC 10k form.

and insurance were integrated into the site but provided by external businesses. These first-tier cooperations included Equifax and iShip which provided shipping services. Escrow services were supplied by Tradenable and iEscrow. Tradenable entered into a contract with eBay, but the fees for the service were to be paid by the users. IEscrow entered into a formal alliance with eBay. Until its acquisition by eBay, PayPal, a third party supplier, provided payment facilitation services. Since fraud on auctions had become an increasingly big problem by 1998 and eBay was afraid of possible regulatory actions, the company made an insurance contract with Lloyds of London. The insurance that eBay offered free of charge covered $200 with $25 deductible. Additionally, SquareTrade, provided dispute resolution. The company made a contract with eBay and offered the service free of charge for eBay users.

EBay concluded several marketing relationships with established customer magnets including AOL, Dega News, First Auction, HotBot, InfoSeek, Lycos, Netscape, Tripod, USA Today, WebTV, Infospace, WhoWhere?, and ZAuction.[159] EBay had developed a strong alliance with AOL over time, starting with a relatively small budget. Its first pay for traffic deal with AOL was signed for $75.000 in early 1998. The original budget increased steadily to $12 million in September 1998, expanding the initial contract for three years.[160] On March 25, 1999, eBay entered into a formal strategic alliance with AOL for four years, paying $75 million for advertising on AOL sites and subsidiary sites to attract user attention. The closer relationship resulted in eBay being granted exclusive rights as the online trading platform for AOL users. EBay co-opted AOL with the agreement and prevented AOL from entering the online auction market itself. AOL benefited from the deal because it made it easier for AOL members to merchandise on the web. The alliance with AOL also helped eBay to fulfil its growth ambitions abroad because AOL was already present in key markets that eBay intended to address. Within a deal closed in March 1999, AOL and its affiliates CompuServe, Netscape, and ICQ agreed to promote eBay to its 16 million subscribers. Steve Westly recalled: "We had gone from $750,000 to $75 million in less than 18 months because both sides saw, and accommodated the others' interest. It was a model partnership."[161] EBay also closed a strategic alliances to strengthen eBay Motors. The site listed more than 1.5 million cars and had linkages to 90% of the U.S. car dealers – a critical complementary asset. IBM entered into an alliance with eBay for the implementation of the J2EE architecture. EBay is said to have

---

[159] See Bradely and Porter (2000).
[160] See Cohen (2002b), p. 103.
[161] Quoted in Bradely and Porter (2000), p. 81.

bound the deal with IBM's assurance that the company will sell IBM products on the eBay marketplace. Preferred solution providers are certified third party developers who contribute support products or services for businesses that use eBay as a sales channel. Major solution providers include Accenture, Andale, Vendio, AuctionWorks, Channel Advisor, CollectorsOnline and FairMarket. Accenture operates the connection to eBay that enables large corporations to dispose of excess inventory. Accenture offers related necessary services and consulting such as transportation management, inventory management and customer service. Andale provides software solutions for auction management with fulfilment features. Similar products are offered by Vendio, Auction Works, ChannelAdvisor, CollectorsOnline and FairMarket, Inc. Microsoft lists similar attributes for its product suite bCentral, a product aimed at the midsize business market.[162]

One of the first of third tier adapters was pongo.com, which handled digital images on behalf of eBay users. The company Cricket Sniper developed eBay bidding software that enabled users to out-compete rival buyers in the very last seconds of an auction. This software became widely utilised and was subject to mixed reactions from buyers and sellers alike. Cricket Sniper eventually broadened its product portfolio and now sells eBay bidding software, sniping software, auction management software and navigation software for eBay message boards. Independent community chats and message boards were among the early adapters of the eBay market platform. One of the more popular and most used is OTWA (short for Online Traders Web Alliance). With growing success of eBay, the larger addressable community of sellers permitted vertical specialisation. Some sellers, for example, saw the demand for shipping supply and resold volume-purchased shipping supplies to small sellers via eBay. One such seller, for example, was so successful she went on to create shippingsupply.com, providing eBay sellers with packing and shipping materials.[163] Although PayPal was recently acquired by eBay it must – at least in its inception – be considered to be a third tier cooperation.

Geographical Expansion
EBay's regional presence became both broader and narrower at the same time. On the one hand, eBay invested in international expansion to enlarge its geographical reach. On the other hand, at around the same time it started so called EBay Cities for merchandise that was not suitable for transport (e.g. boats, real estate and cars). The economic rationale was to

---

[162] See eBAY INC. (2003).
[163] See Cohen (2002b), p. 160.

increase the ASP. In the Los Angeles test market the ASP was 22% higher than in the core business.

The overseas target markets for eBay are (1) Germany, Switzerland, Austria; (2) U.K., France, Scandinavia, (3) Asia (Japan, Korea) (4) China (5) Australia, New Zealand. The goal of eBay is to achieve a leading position in all of these markets. The first step for overseas expansion was the acquisition of Alando, Germany's then number one auction site, in June 1999. At that time, Alando had sold about 250,000 items to a user base of 50,000. On July 4, 1999 eBay launched its U.K. operations at eBay.co.uk. In contrast to Germany, eBay decided against the acquisition of a local brand, building its own site instead. In 2000, eBay had successfully taken control of the new territories, leaving the two biggest European rivals behind with a combined $87 million in sales compared to $38 million for British QXL and German Ricardo taken together. October of the same year saw the launch of eBay Australia. In 2001, the acquisition of the French iBazar, the leading auction Internet platform in France, Italy, Spain, Belgium, Portugal, and the Netherlands, followed. EBay also invested heavily in wireless access to its site because of the discouraging PC penetration in many countries it wanted to address. In the same year, eBay also acquired a majority stake in Internet Auction Ltd., South Korea's largest online trading platform. With the exception of Japan where eBay was struggling with competition from Yahoo! Japan, in 2002 eBay succeeded in becoming the leading auction house in all markets it was present in.

Conclusion

Funk (2001a) argued that i-mode developed from a simple to a complex platform in all relevant dimensions such as network, i-mode menu, applications and handsets. If we look closely at eBay's history, we can observe the same aspects at work. EBay developed from a single geographically operated site with a simple freeware CGI script-based infrastructure and only a handful of product categories to a global business serving many customer segments and hosting almost item every imaginable, from buttons to mainframes, on a now complex J2EE web platform. Although literature on product introduction under the presence of network effects suggests that the only way to overcome the initial chicken-and-egg dilemma is to invest heavily in penetration pricing, eBay showed that the opposite can be true as well. The company managed to price its services early on thereby preventing huge initial losses in the process of attracting an installed base of users. The community of buyers and sellers proved to be the single most important competitive advantage of eBay.

Mini Cases of Other Network Industries

In order to enhance the external validity of theoretical constructs I will now provide data from multiple small cases from the ICT-Industry. I will analyse the establishment and early growth of Adobe, American Express, Microsoft, Visa and Palm Computing because all of these organisations contribute interesting pieces to the overall jigsaw puzzle of business web growth. Special conditions in shaping technology webs are gathered from the history of Microsoft and Adobe. Microsoft in co-operation with Intel established open-proprietary standards to achieve platform leadership over the personal computer business web.[164] Adobe created a business web surrounding its likewise open and proprietary portable document format (PDF) across multiple computer platforms in competition with Microsoft.[165] It is also interesting to analyse the growth processes of firms in the credit card market, such as Visa or American Express, with regard to the underlying business models. Since I will be looking at the entire business web in these mini-cases, I will aggregate the growth histories of the major companies that created entirely new industries under their industries.

Formation of the ePaper Business Web

"As Adobe Systems' twentieth year of helping people communicate better comes to a close, we're pleased to see our customers using Adobe solutions – as well as complementary technologies from our partners – to create, manage, and deliver visually rich information to anyone, anywhere, on any device. For the fourth consecutive year, strong sales of Adobe Acrobat software licenses have contributed to making the enterprise our single greatest market opportunity."[166]

Charles Geschke and John Warnock developed PostScript at Xerox's graphics and imaging lab that that brought forth one of the world's largest software makers.[167] PostScript is a page description language, which tells printers how to reproduce digitized images on paper.[168] The duo left Xerox and founded Adobe in 1982 because Xerox refused to market PostScript.[169]

---

[164] See Borrus and Zysman (1997); Kim and Hart (2001); Gawer and Cusumano (2002); Hart and Kim (2002).

[165] Tripsas (2000a);

[166] John Warnock, Charles Geschke, and Bruce R. Chizen in the letter to the stockholders 2002.

[167] See Campell-Kelly (2001).

[168] More precisely, PostScript comprises a page description language, an interpreter and digital font types. See Tripsas (2002).

[169] See Peak (1996).

Initially, their plan was to produce an electronic document processing system based on PostScript, but the company changed its strategy when Apple Computer asked them to co-design the software for Apple's Laser-Writer printer. Early revenues got a large boost through the collaboration with Apple. In 1984, about half of Adobe's revenues came from Apple royalties. PostScript was disrupting the desktop publishing industry by enabling users to laser print nearly anything they created on a computer in adequate quality.

First, PostScript products were commercialised in a strategic alliance between four component providers that, together, supplied a professional desktop publishing system. Adobe provided the description language, Apple the printing devices, Aldus the layout program for arranging texts and graphics on a Macintosh and Linotype added the necessary type fonts.[170] The company was put on the industry map when IBM, Digital, AST Research, Hewlett-Packard, and Texas Instruments agreed to use PostScript in their printers in 1987. Adobe also entered the PC market by adapting PostScript for Microsoft's operating system. With PostScript, Adobe took over the role of architectural standard setter for printer-page description languages on desktop computer systems.[171] PostScript is an open-proprietary industry standard under the control of Adobe. The language is well documented and the specification was made available free of charge. Adobe encouraged the usage of the language by third party developers by revealing the specification and providing technical support. Geschke recalled, "We made a decision early on that standard itself – the documentation for how you describe the page – would be open, freely available and we would publish it. We would retain the copyright and the trademark, but we would make the interface open to anyone, recognizing that over time, that would invite competition."[172] By 1989 PostScript had become the de-facto standard for printing in the publishing industry and Adobe the unchallenged market leader with close to 100% market share in that segment. In the general laser printer market, the company held no less than 25% at any time. Adobe grew throughout the 1990s by acquiring other software firms in related technology fields including Photoshop and Aldus Page-Maker. In 1993, the company began licensing its PostScript software to printer manufacturers on a royalty basis. For every printing device sold, the company received a percentage fee. The open standard policy and R&D co-operations with hardware manufacturers led to 60 PostScript licensees in 1994. Ownership and leveraging the PostScript standard led to

---

[170] See Tripsas (2002).
[171] See Morris and Ferguson (1993).
[172] Quoted in Tripsas (2002), p. 575.

increasing returns growth with a compound annual growth rate of 70% and an increase in returns from $2.2 million to $762 million from 1984 to 1995.[173] Further product developments, facilitated a move by Adobe towards electronic publishing.

It released Acrobat, a program that enabled a user to create a document and then use Adobe PDF (Portable Document Format) to convert it for electronic distribution, making it a first mover. The PDF document format enabled users to distribute their documents on a variety of platforms in their original appearance.[174] Prior to the introduction of PDF, the appearance of exchanged documents depended on the availability of the publishing software on the required platform because every application had incompatible document formats. Further, the availability of font variants influenced the representation on different computing platforms – even when the original word processor or layout program was installed on the target system. Like PostScript, the definition of PDF was open. Initially, Adobe charged $50 for the reader and up to $695 for software that could create PDF, resulting in sluggish sales. Growing network connections accelerated through growing Internet availability and adoption spurred demand for cross-platform document exchanges. Adobe started giving away the program for viewing PDF contents (Acrobat Reader) for free in order to generate momentum. The formation of an alliance with Netscape enabled the Netscape browser to open PDF documents directly within the browser using a software plug-in. With the release of Acrobat Reader in November 1996, the integration was complete, making PDF the dominant standard for posting and viewing richly formatted documents on the Web.[175] Adobe went into an alliance with AOL to propagate usage among AOL subscribers. The company also established several linkages with major computer manufacturers to have Acrobat Reader pre-installed on the machines. PDF usage grew rapidly and became the de-facto standard for formatting print layouts on the Web. The company made money by selling the full Acrobat program to produce PDF documents. Thanks to many enhancements such as adding annotations, capturing legacy documents in PDF and the ability to sign and password-encrypt PDF files, Acrobat 4.0 spurred sales. Revenues for Adobe's ePaper division skyrocketed from $58 million to $129 million.[176] In 1999, 2 million copies of Adobe Acrobat were downloaded from adobe.com.[177] In 2000, the company felt that it

---

[173] See Tripsas (2002).
[174] See Adobe Inc. (1999).
[175] See Pfiffner (2003), p. 196.
[176] See Pfiffner (2003), p. 198.
[177] See Adobe Inc. (1999).

could leverage its strong reputation and existing relationships in the publishing industry to electronic publishing thereby establishing PDF as the dominating industry standard.[178] By 2000, almost 200 million versions had been downloaded from the Adobe Internet site for free.

Adobe had a significant increase in revenue from Adobe ePaper solution products in 2001 due to increased licensing of the Adobe Acrobat product. By 2002, the company has distributed more than 500 million copies of Acrobat Reader, and the adoption of the PDF format by many industries and governments worldwide has contributed to its widespread use. Sales of Adobe Acrobat software and related products generated $312 million in 2002.[179] Microsoft, which is struggling to introduce its own eBook format as a dominant industry standard, is facing up to Adobe as a major competitor in the ePaper industry.

Formation of the Wintel Business Web

"Microsoft has built the world's largest business ecosystem, made up of six million developers, tens of thousands of companies generating trillions of dollars of revenue, together with Intel and the makers of personal computer hardware."[180]

The key players in defining the so-called Wintel standard for personal computers are IBM, Microsoft and Intel. Microsoft was founded in Albuquerque, New Mexico, in a hotel room and grew by modifying BASIC for emerging personal computer platforms such as the Altair and the Apple Lisa. Bill Gates founded the company after dropping out of Harvard at the age of 19 and teaming up with high school friend Paul Allen to commercialise a version of the programming language BASIC. Gates moved Microsoft to his hometown Seattle in 1979 and began developing software tools for other software developers.

Robert Noyce, Gordon Moore and Andy Groove, three former Fairchild engineers founded Intel with the goal to developing silicon-based chips.[181] Intel started in 1968 as a memory chip business with huge success during the seventies. During the eighties Intel was confronted with major competition from Japan in the memory business it had pioneered ten years earlier. Lower prices and higher quality of Japanese memory production led to decreasing market shares for Intel. Fortunately, Intel had invented micro-

---

[178] See Tripsas (2002).
[179] See Adobe Inc. (2002).
[180] Anderson and Wood (2002), p. 29.
[181] See Hoovers Inc. (2001b).

processors in the seventies as well, and still had a small production facility that was producing them.[182]

IBM first defined the open and modular AT PC Architecture. Intel supplied the microprocessor architecture and Microsoft a compatible operating system for the processor architecture. IBM had set up a newly formed business unit with the goal of commercialising a desktop PC with a one-year time to market. IBM designed a modular product architecture in which it sourced almost everything from external suppliers except the board assemblies and the keyboard. The then leading operating system for the selected Intel processor architecture, 8088, was CP/M from Digital Research, Inc. After Kildal, the developer of CP/M refused to sign the IBM non-disclosure agreement (NDA); IBM approached Bill Gates who quickly agreed to sign. Gates bought a CP/M clone named QDOS (Quick and dirty operating system) from a Seattle programmer for $50,000, renaming it Microsoft Disk Operating System (MS-DOS).[183] "(The) original franchise that IBM granted Microsoft in 1982 for the IBM PC software (...) generated the highest economies of scale and scope in the history of business."[184]

The success of IBM's mass-market PC was astonishing and outpaced all expectations by far. Daily manufacturing volumes increased 600%, sales rose to $5 billion and over 2000 independent software providers wrote over 6000 software applications for the platform.[185] As such, Intel's 8088 processor sold fairly well and Intel increased its R&D efforts with the profits from initial sales. The increased R&D efforts lead to a rapid overlapping evolution of enhanced processor designs. Intel stepped out of the memory chip business and focused on the production of microprocessors after supplying IBM PCs for five years.[186] If IBM had not decided in favour of the technologically inferior processor architecture from Intel, and if the developer of CP/M had agreed to sign IBM's NDA, then the two companies with the strongest influence in the PC industry likely would not be Intel and Microsoft. The turbulent growth story of Microsoft dawned when IBM chose Microsoft to supply the operating system for the AT PC architecture in 1980.

Throughout the 1980s, Microsoft grew mainly with strong sales from MS-DOS, which probably made up 40 to 50 percent of its revenues.[187] In

---

[182] See Grove (1996).

[183] See Lopatka and Page (1995); Chandler, Hikino and Nordenflycht (2001).

[184] Kleiner (2002), p. 6.

[185] See Chandler, Hikino and Nordenflycht (2001).

[186] See Grove (1996)

[187] See Campell-Kelly (2001).

the mid-1980s, Microsoft introduced Windows, a graphics-based extension to MS-DOS that imitated the competing Apple Macintosh operating system. The company went public in 1986 making Gates the industry's first billionaire. IBM lost control and shaping power over its standard to Intel and Microsoft, who drove the evolution of the PC standard and achieved platform leadership leaving IBM as a sole final assembler pressured with fierce competition of manufacturers of IBM AT clones. From about 1990 onward, application bundles were more and more forming the basis for further growth.

Microsoft disclosed the Windows API openly but remained proprietary control of the inner workings of Windows. The programming interfaces permitted third party developers to produce compatible products for the Windows platform. Today the company is the largest producer of software for personal computers in the world with revenues of more than $25 billion and more than $7 billion net income. Microsoft produces a wide range of software applications including the dominant operating system for Personal Computers, Windows, and the major office application suite, Microsoft Office, as well as development tools for the Windows platforms. Microsoft introduced Windows NT in 1993 to compete with the UNIX operating system that was running on the majority of mainframes and large computer networks. Lately, Microsoft's dominant position became challenged by the emergence of Internet applications and the growing popularity of open software.

Formation of the Java Business Web

"Sun saw in Java an opportunity to position itself as a leader driving the internet revolution. In creating a new technological field around Java, Sun would be able to break away the increasingly marginalized Unix field as well as to counter the increasing dominance of the Windows technological field."[188]

Sun Microsystems introduced the first version of Java in 1995 as a common programming language for embedded devices that, in contrast to the personal computer, utilised a variety of operating systems and processor architectures. Java technology was created in a small project by Sun employees, called Green Project.[189]

The project started in December 1990 and in September 1992 the team came up with a working demo of a handheld multimedia device controller. "We focused on products", remembers James Gosling one of the team members. "Business models and end users were as important to us as tech-

---

[188] Garud, Jain and Kumaraswamy (2002), p. 201.
[189] See Gosling (2003).

nology.[190] The device came along with a processor-independent programming language enabling the user to control a wide range of entertainment platforms and appliances. In search of a market, the company first addressed the emerging TV set-top box and video-on-demand industries. "Unfortunately, those industries were in their infancy and still trying to settle viable business models."[191] With the emergence of consumer-friendly front-ends in the WWW and the Mosaic browser, the Internet transformed into exactly the type of network the team was trying to convince cable companies of building. The team went back to work and implemented a Mosaic clone named WebRunner (later renamed HotJava) in 1994 bringing animated and dynamic contents to life on the Web.

In 1995 Sun released the Java source code on the Internet freely to create widespread adoption in the developer community. Within only a few months downloads began to surge into the thousands, showing that Java was an unexpected and overwhelming success. "Soon Sun realized that the Java technology team's popularity was quickly and haphazardly outpacing its own carefully orchestrated popularity, with virtually no marketing budget or plan."[192] The Java technology environment enabled computing devices to run programs written in Java across different operating systems and processor architectures. When the hype about Java took off, Sun executives and Marc Andreessen announced an agreement to integrate Java into the, at that time, omnipresent Netscape Navigator at that year's Sun-World conference.

Beginning in 1996, the company began building Java as an industry standard by licensing the Java technology to all major hardware and software companies.[193] "Sun is giving away Java and HotJava free for non-commercial use, in a fast-track attempt to make them the standard before Microsoft begins shipping a similar product, codenamed Blackbird in early 1996", wrote Wired in 1995.[194] By the end of the year, the JavaSoft division had signed 38 licensees, including Adobe, Borland, IBM, Intuit, Lotus, Macromedia, Mitsubishi, Oracle, Silicon Graphics, Sybase, Symantec, and Toshiba. By the end of 1997, JavaSoft had already attracted 100 licensees and around 10.000 developers showed up at the JavaOne Developer Conference. In 1998 there were 150 licensees and thousands of developers worldwide. The rates for licensing Java's source code for commercial use were a $150.000 upfront fee and an additional $2 per copy. With growing

---

[190] See Gosling (2003).
[191] See Byous (1998).
[192] See Byous (1998).
[193] See Hoovers Inc. (2001c).
[194] Bank (1995).

popularity of the Internet, Java became the preferred solution for distributing and running applications from the network. Java quickly became a common standard on the Internet and the preferred programming language. Sun acted as the standards sponsor and attempted to shape the standard while at the same time retaining ownership of the standard. To achieve a critical mass and to unfold network effects, Sun offered third parties access to its Java technology. The Java Community Process, an organisation consisting of hundreds of vendors, governs the Java standard. Though, quite democratic in design – Sun leaves most development decisions and directions of the standard evolution to the community – the company still retains the intellectual property rights on Java and has a veto right.[195] The technology attracted loyal hordes of programmers, motivated the founding of thousands of Java oriented start-ups.

However, for all its hype and popularity, Java has made generated money in direct software sales for competitors than for Sun Microsystems. Although Sun makes money on Java in charging for Java licensees and compliance testing, Sun, in contrast to Microsoft, struggled to establish Java as a common industry standard and concurrently capture a major wallet share. In fact, it is argued that Sun could not generate much economic profit with Java. Instead, adapters such as IBM and BEA made money with Java in selling application server and programming tools for Java. As one market observer comments, "Sun doesn't have a lock on all things Java. Plenty of other companies – including IBM, Oracle, and BEA – lead Sun in areas such as application servers."[196] Sun went into a three-year alliance with AOL, which had acquired Netscape Communications to develop and sell e-commerce software under the label iPlanet. Eventually, Sun bought back the AOL shares in the venture and now sells its own application server. It hat aslo acquired a commercial development tool provider, Forte. However, Sun, the actual inventor, is a distant third in the market for application servers and it gives away its Java Software Development Kit free of charge.[197]

Formation of the Payment Card Business Web

"The success of the two largest credit card networks – MasterCard and Visa – is critically dependent on the membership of thousands of financial institutions that jointly establish rules, standards, and interchange fees."[198]

---

[195] See Berlind (2002a).
[196] See Berlind (2002b).
[197] See Shankland (2002).
[198] Chakravorti (2003), p. 50.

Diners first commercialised a payment card product and American Express entered the market as a fast follower introducing the first ever charge card. Charge cards have no credit lines and users have to repay charged amount in full within a certain time frame, usually 30 days. The payment card business was first unprofitable for American Express. In 1962 the company made first profits. By 1977 it has overrun Diners fivefold with 6.3 million issued cards. Eventually American Express Cards became the most successful in the industry.

Evans and Schmalensee (1999) argue that payment cards offered a superior value proposition because they reduced the need for cash balances, relaxed liquidity constraints and made it easier for many customers to borrow money. Payment card networks exhibit indirect network effects because the value of a card brand for the customers and merchants increases with every incremental card issued and every incremental merchant that accepts a certain card. For consumers the value of the card increases if more merchants accept it. For merchants the value of the card network increases if more consumers carry the card.

Analytically, a payment card network consists of the following entity classes that pursue distinguishable economic activities: card issuer, merchant acquirer, merchants, processors, card system. Card organisations set the rules for participating institutions that wish to contract with merchants. The business model comprises two pricing dimensions: merchant discounts and cardholder fees. During the seventies competition from the banking industry emerged. The banking card systems MasterCard and Visa are for-profit organisations based on joint venture cooperation consisting of more than 20.000 member banks. These joint ventures set the ground rules, define settlement and authorisation, and establish fees. They act as the rule-making body for the network.[199] Further, they are in charge of developing and encouraging system-wide innovations. The member banks cooperate for standard setting but compete for merchants and card holders with differentiating card products.

Complementary but necessary tasks performed by third parties include: signing merchants, installing terminals, providing authorisation, keeping track of transactions, transferring funds (clearing and settlement), responding to problems of merchants, provision of specialised services (e.g. analysis of purchasing patterns). The first merchants to sign up with Visa were rather smaller because the big merchants had their own card programs and saw the bankcards as competition. The smaller stores, however, saw the benefits of the bankcard system because they did not have to run a billing

---

[199] Payment networks coordinate the behaviour of banks, merchants, and consumers by setting certain prices and rules. Hunt (2003), p. 81.

system of their own. "For a reasonable fee, the bankcard system would guarantee payment and take the billing and collection hassles out the hands of the merchant."[200] Additionally, incremental profits from customers who bought more if they could use the card acted as an economic incentive to pull in more merchants.

At the beginning of the eighties, American Express was confronted with fierce competition from the bankcard systems Visa and MasterCard. However, the company took almost 50% higher merchant discounts and charged an annual fee of $60 for its basic green card product and $85 for the more prestigious gold card. In 1984, American Express even raised the charge for the gold card to 96$, resulting in estimated $370 million net profit alone from its charge card business. With the entrance of credit card organizations, a systems war for market dominance ensued between the competing systems. The systems competed with price, advertising, and innovations for merchant acceptance. The closed-loop system of American Express shows more central control, but almost all work had to be contracted out to third parties. In 1990 American Express responded to languishing market shares with the introduction of the external sales agent (ESA) program to acquire new merchant segments besides travel. Independent sales organisations handle sales activities for small business enterprises. An advantage of American Express is that the company holds all information on cardholders. American Express's internal capabilities include: contract merchants, marketing activities, terminal distribution, Transaction processing.

The advantages of the open-loop business architecture of Visa and MasterCard are better exploitation of economies of scale and pooling of resources. The decentralised governance permits individual members to exploit opportunities without any approval from centralised management as long as they adhere to the ground rules. "The ability of each individual member of an open-loop system to develop features on its cards provides a degree of flexibility and responsiveness to the market conditions that might be difficult to replicate within a closed-loop system. The disadvantage is that the system is more complex in comparison with American Express's closed-loop system. One of the organisational problems with the joint venture structure is a loosening of control and that decision-making can be cumbersome.

---

[200] Evans and Schmalensee (1999), p. 131.

Formation of the Palm Business Web

The PDA (Personal Digital Assistant) market was created and pioneered by Psion as early as 1984. However, John Scully, the then Apple CEO, coined the term PDA with the introduction of the Apple Newton product line which for the first time eschewed a keyboard in favour of pen style handwriting recognition input. Apple started the development of the Newton in early 1990. Apple went into co-operations to produce the product. It bought a stake in the semiconductor manufacturer ARM that provided the microprocessor and wrote the handwriting recognition software together with ParaGraph, a Russian software company. The display was sourced from Sharp, which also manufactured the device. Siemens and Motorola held licenses to develop compatible modules for the Newton. Other partners included telecommunication companies, publishing houses and online service providers. The first devices were available in 1993. In contrast to exaggerated product announcements, the initial Newton 100 was behind schedule and showed major product flaws. Especially the accuracy of the handwriting recognition software never met consumer expectations. Other ventures, small and big alike, including Go Corporation, Momenta Corp., IBM, Microsoft, NEC, and Toshiba failed likewise to profitably establish PDAs in the marketplace in spite of an assumed combined investments of $1 billion.

"And then came along Jeff Hawkins and his 28 colleagues at Palm Computing, who spent only $3 million to develop a working model of the device that would launch an entire industry."[201] Jeff Hawkins founded Palm Computing in 1992 to commercialise handheld computers. Initially, the company aimed only to provide handwriting recognition software and to rely on external resources for the architecture, hardware, operating software and marketing. Being an unfamiliar device with no settled industry hindered the third party investments in such an architecture. Palm, therefore, had to switch its strategy and decided to become an architect itself and developed and designed the operating system, PalmOS, as well as the communication protocols itself. The financial requirements to perform all tasks on its own turned out to be much too large for Palm to carry alone. Thus, the management team decided to search for strong financial partners. None of the initial Palm partners, however, agreed to commit resources because the sales of the first product generation were disappointing. Palm approached US Robotics which eventually acquired the company and pro-

---

[201] Stanford Technology Ventures Program (STVP) (2001), p. 4.

vided the necessary resources to commercialise the Palm Pilot, making the personal digital assistant industry an astonishing success.[202]

The product met, for the first time, user requirements in terms of size, features, ease of use, value proposition and price for PDAs. In contrast to Apple, Palm concentrated on reliability and usability of the device. The companies own handwriting recognition software, Graffiti, showed outstanding reliability compared to the Newton software. The Palm approach did not intend to recognise the user's specific handwriting but increased accuracy with a simplified and standardised way of writing letters that takes about 20 minutes to learn. After conducting extensive market research which revealed that users wanted PC connectivity, used only a handful of applications, and cared much about size and weight, the company produced the PalmPilot, a simple extension to the PC that allowed scheduling while the users were mobile. The company pioneered the palm-sized form factor that fit in a shirt pocket with its Pilot 1000 and Pilot 500 devices, weighing around 155g. Connectivity to the PC was realised with a small docking station that synchronised the stored data with personal information manager programs such as Lotus Notes, ACT! and others by simply pushing one button.

Palm sourced almost everything for the Pilot from outside. The product architecture was built around a Motorola Dragonball processor and a Toshiba memory chip. The Pilot was designed by Palo Alto Design Group and manufactured by Flextronics. Palm Computing sold more than 1 million units in the first year, making it one of the most successful consumer electronic launches in history. "50 applications were posted on the web within the first 2 weeks of the introduction of the PalmPilot."[203] Over 3000 developers showed interest in developing applications for the device and IBM was eager to license the Palm standard to produce clones of the Palm-Pilot under the label IBM WorkPads. With the Pilot, Palm established the dominant design for the handheld computer industry. In 1997 US Robotics merged with 3Com. With the introduction of the Palm V series in 1999, sizes became even smaller, weighing 115 g at a size of 115mm x 77mm x 10mm. The devices had a 160x160 pixel backlit display and were shipped with a suite of personal productivity tools, including date book, address book, to-do list, expense management, calculator, notes and games.

Jeff Hawkins left Palm in 1998 with Donna Dubinsky and Ed Colligan to found Handspring, a company that produces Palm clones with expansion slots for pluggable modules such as radio access or digital cameras.

---

[202] See Baldwin and Clark (1997). Later US Robotics merged with 3Com.
[203] Stanford Technology Ventures Program (STVP) (2001), p. 11.

By the end of 1999, 3Com had spun off its subsidiary into an independent company – PalmComputing. In that year, Palm started to license the Palm devices' operating system, PalmOS to hardware manufacturers such as Sony, Nokia, IBM, Handspring, Qualcomm, and TRG. The phenomenal success of the Palm devices in the late 1990 gave PalmOS a major advantage in the battle of competing palm computing platforms with around 70 percent market share and an established base of over 5 million users and over 20,000 developers for the platform.

By 1999 Palm held an estimated market share of 78 percent and the platform was supported by 70,000 registered third party developers contributing 5,000 plus software programs.[204] The broad acceptance among developers and the variety of available applications and the support of leading enterprise software vendors such as CA, IBM, Oracle, SAP, and Sun Microsystems made Palm the leading platform in the handheld computing industry. The major competitors for Palm are now Psion with the EPOC platform and Microsoft with its PocketPC platform.[205] Psion went into a joint venture with cellular phone manufacturers such as Matsushita, Motorola, Nokia and SonyEricsson, to from Symbian, a standard multimedia platform for next-generation mobile phones with PDA functionality. Microsoft made a major step with the introduction of PocketPC 2002 that eliminated many of the problems with earlier versions and devices such as the HP iPaq that hit the market with major commercial success.

Conclusion

The two in-depth cases of i-Mode and eBay showed that formation and early growth in both cases had quite a lot of similarities. First of all, both benefited from boundary conditions at the inception regarding availability of new technologies and an institutional environment that permitted addressing existing market needs with these technologies. However, it was the vision and the motivation of individuals such Enoki and Omdyar that realised the opportunities and created the business web by defining architectures and standards as well as the active involvement of numerous third parties.

Secondly, both business web shapers took advantage of a modular product architecture which enabled them to rely heavily on external sources for many products and services. The broad availability of these modules was a critical factor for success in achieving a critical mass early on.

---

[204] Stanford Technology Ventures Program (STVP) (2001), p. 5
[205] See PCTECH Guide (2003).

Thirdly, both succeeded in building a win-win business model and in capturing a major share of the value in their business webs.

DoCoMo controls all modules of the i-mode business web with the definition of specifications and access to the customers. The company managed to create an open proprietary modular product system which is flexible and enables innovation within the defined modules, for example handsets and content sites. The win-win business web created opportunities for entrepreneurs to participate in the value generated.

EBay's value-enabling platform is the technological implementation of the marketplace which serves as a venue and the connected community of buyers and sellers. EBay strengthened its strong position over the modular architecture by engineering customer lock-ins into the site, thereby gaining a competitive advantage over its rivals. The community of buyers and sellers proved to be the number one source of competitive advantage for eBay.

The presented mini-cases show strong similarities to the two in-depth cases, but also some differences. Generally, it can be said that open proprietary interfaces play an important role in attracting adapters and capturing value in the business web. The cases also show that establishment of business webs favours neither company groups nor new entrepreneurial firms, but that either can succeed or fail in establishing a business web.

There is also evidence in the data that the ICT-sector is a huge cluster in which different firms engage in multiple business webs, such as Adobe that shapes the PDF standard and adapts to different hardware and operating system platforms with its PDF products. Most obviously, Adobe provides the Acrobat Reader for Unix derivates including Linux, as well as MacOs, Windows, Windows CE, Palm, and even Symbian covering a great range of hardware platforms.

On an abstract level, one can think of the ICT industry as a web-in-web architecture with multiple linkages between firms, constituting an intricate network of embedded firms with ranging degrees of weak and tight coupling relations. Presumably, general-purpose technologies such as TCP/IP, Java, and PDF require similar technological capabilities and similar strategies that enable firms to participate in multiple business webs. Further, shapers seem to have developed the capability to establish business webs around more than just one value-enabling platform. One of the most striking examples is Microsoft, that shapes not only the Wintel business web, but also engages as a shaper in server and network OS markets, online services, game consoles, SmartPhones and Webservices.

First mover advantages, in contrast to predictions in literature, cannot be observed in most cases. Fast followers or even late entrants reaped the returns of industry creation, often stealing away leadership from pioneering firms. Examples can be seen in Psion and Apple in the PDA market, Xerox, Apple and IBM in personal computing and Visa and MasterCard in the payment card industry.

Towards a Theory of Business Web Growth

After having examined the cases, the empirical findings are compared to existing literature and a theoretical framework for general validity is derived. This chapter opens by describing contingencies for the emergence of business webs.

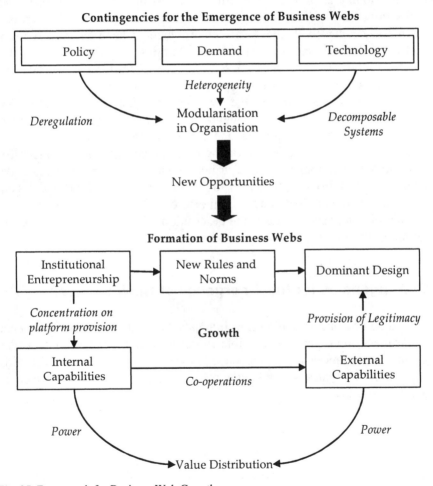

Fig. 25. Framework for Business Web Growth

The institutional environment is divided into policy issues, especially regarding deregulation and liberalisation of markets, increasing heterogeneity in customer demands, and rapid technological change as an enabler. Next follows a conception for the formation of business webs with the three building blocks, institutional entrepreneurship, legitimacy achievement and establishment of a dominant design. The ensuing section models growth patterns of business webs with the sections resource dependencies, internal- and external capabilities. Finally, the relations between network position attributes of the value-enabling platform and value capture are treated. Figure 25 illustrates the framework.

In short, the model starts with contingencies for business web emergence that facilitates and drives modularisation in technology and organisation. Modularisation requires firms to adjust their size and scope. Specialisation and focus on distinct modules leads to increased interdependencies with the firm's environment. Changing market needs and technological properties create opportunities for new market creation leading to the formation of business webs. The establishment of a business web is an act of institutional entrepreneurship, where entrepreneurial firms define rules and standards for the new market or industry. To be successful, firms have to establish the legitimacy of the new market to motivate adapters to contribute resources and customers to adopt the product system. Growth takes place by leveraging external capabilities and unleashing positive feedback loops. Value distribution and capture in the business depends on the ability and the power to influence critical resources with control points of the product system architecture.

The following section starts the description of the model with an elaboration of the contingencies for business web emergence.

Contingencies for the Emergence of Business Webs

Unfolding and understanding the circumstances that lead to the emergence of business webs, make it possible to derive which actions under which given circumstances will foster business web growth. First, I will briefly address policy issues, second some market factors and third some technological issues.

Policy Issues

The market structure of the information and communications industry has changed largely through liberalisation.[1] Antitrust policies of the U.S. government laid the cornerstone of what we call today Wintelism.[2] "The U.S. government's antitrust actions were central in fostering the growth of both the semiconductor and packaged software industries and encouraging value-chain specialisation in the computer industry."[3] The emergence of the IBM compatible PC architecture enabled new entrants to occupy layers in the formerly integrated value chain. In the telecommunication industry, rapid innovation and growth accelerated in the EU and in Japan by the early agreement on common standards such as GSM and PDC and the liberalisation and deregulation of the former state-ruled industry. As shown in the i-mode case, the roots of the service lay in the deregulation of the Japanese telecoms market. Without the emergence of competition from new attackers, DoCoMo would hardly have commercialised i-mode. In general, liberalisation and deregulation of markets is a prerequisite for business web establishment. The impacts on the market structure of circumstances such as globalisation and increased competition accelerated the shift to further specialisation. The last decades of the previous century were characterised by ever-growing globalisation. New challenges for management and the organisation and division of labour arose out of this transition.[4] Increased global competition is driving disaggregation of huge diversified groups of companies.[5] As Picot (1999) puts it: "Such transformations lead to boundless, virtual companies, composed of networked modules in form of companies, business units, teams, and individual workplaces, with each module being able to perform its assigned task in the best possible manner."[6]

---

[1] See Picot, Dietl and Franck (2002),p. 97; Cave, Majumdar and Vogelsang (2002), p. 3; Picot (2003), p. 6.

[2] „The essence of Wintelism is a reliance on open but owned technical standards and extensive outsourcing of component production to enable industrial structures to become less vertically and more horizontally integrated. Hart and Kim (2002), p. 1.

[3] Hart and Kim (2002), p. 8.

[4] See Hitt, Keats and DeMarie (1998).

[5] See Powell (1987); Snow, Miles and Coleman (1992).

[6] Picot (1999), p. 21.

Heterogeneity in Customer Demands

On the demand side, customer empowerment increased because of a shift in demand from mass production to a desire for greater diversity.[7] Customers became more demanding and, due to higher market transparency, more powerful. Furthermore, the success of companies has become bound to time and innovation competition. Innovation has become the primary driver of competition and competitive advantage.[8] All these changes, in conjunction with advances in technology, led to heterogeneity in supply and demand boosting modularity in organisation.[9]

Heterogeneity in customer demands influences the likelihood of a product migrating to a more modular design. If customers require different solutions then a firm can offer product varieties based on different bundles of modules or can even let customers aggregate their own product bundles. Large degrees of modularity make it possible to offer a wide range of possible product configurations.[10] Efforts such as mass customisation attempt to better suit the individual utility of consumers.[11] Mass customisation is a promising strategy to accommodate customers better when their demands are very heterogeneous. It also enables and facilitates flexibility for customers.

A modular design also enables companies to react more flexibly to changes in customer needs and tastes while permitting faster innovation by permanently improving single modules.

Rapid Technological Change

Rapid technological change in the industry is proposed as a major driver for modularisation.[12] Schilling and Steensma (2001) argue, "the loosely coupled organizational form allows organizational components to be flexibly recombined into a variety of configurations, much as a modular product system enables multiple end-product configurations from a given set of

---

[7] See Powell (1987), p. 78.

[8] See Christensen (2001).

[9] "The more heterogeneous the inputs are that may be used to compose a system, the more possible configurations there are attainable through the recombinability enabled by modularity. Furthermore, the more heterogeneous the demands made of the system, the more valued such recombinability becomes." Schilling (2000), p. 317.

[10] See Schilling (2000).

[11] See, for instance, Pine (1993) and Piller (2000).

[12] See Baldwin and Clark (1997); Snow, Miles and Coleman (1992); Schilling and Steensma (2001).

components."[13] Advances in technology enable competition from invaders of previously unrelated sectors. Digitalisation facilitates the disaggregation of value chains.[14] It allows rapid and innovative recombination because digital contents are independent of the technological distribution channel.[15] Media contents, digital video for example, can be distributed via cinema, television (DVB-T, DVD player), Laptop/PC (media viewer application), and even mobile devices such as PDAs or cellular phones. The emergence of open interfaces and standards drive the decentralisation of economic activities and horizontal specialisation.[16] Open standards are likely to lower entry barriers that are key determinants for industry structures in the works of Bain and Porter.[17] Open standards and interfaces between the interconnected parts constitute a decomposable system. A strongly interrelated technological development is the digitalisation of information.[18] The (quasi) absence of marginal costs in the distribution of information goods as software (or standard specifications) leads to increasing returns.[19] "In terms of embedded technology," Langlois (2001a) posits, "software is the paradigm case of knowledge reuse through durable dies. Once written, a piece of code can be stamped out an indefinite number of times at little more than the marginal cost of burning a CD."[20] Scholars emphasised that vertical integration is an advantage when a company finds itself in a situation to compete for the customer whose needs have not been satisfied by the functionality of available products, services and the underlying technology. They recommended disintegration for well established and specified processes and activities which do not serve as a competitive advantage for the company anymore.[21] On the one hand the vertically integrated position of firms in an older technology and industry may experience a negative impact on the future performance in the newer technology and industry. On the other hand, especially in the early introduction phase of a new

---

[13] Schilling and Steensma (2001), p. 1149.

[14] See Cartwright (2002).

[15] Further elaborations of the impacts of media convergence are discussed by Yoffie (1996) and Hass (2002).

[16] See Steiner (2002); Li and Whalley (2002); Fransmann (2002).

[17] See Bain (1956) and Porter (1985).

[18] Claude Shannon already showed in the 1940ties that any information can be digitalised in binaries. His 1948 Bell System Technical Journal publication "A Mathematical Theory of Communication" can be viewed as the birth hour of digitalisation. See Waldrop (2001). The competitive effects of digital convergence are laid out by Yoffie (1996).

[19] See Shapiro and Varian (1999), p. 3.

[20] Langlois (2001a), p. 85. With the coming effective of omniscient broadband Internet connections, even these costs can be diminished to the costs of operating a server and costs for data transmission.

[21] See Langlois (1992b); Christensen (2001), p. 108-109.

technology, a firm may have advantages being vertically integrated.[22] Some argue that firms are better off being vertically disintegrated in dynamic industries with fast technological changes and a high uncertainty since upstream capabilities of a firm are rendered obsolete through the introduction of new technologies.[23] Others regard vertical integration of firms superior to non-integration and suggest that companies create more products and services on their own, the higher the uncertainty of the relationship to other companies is and the more probable the obsolescence of upstream capabilities is.[24] Eventually, it is shown that firms that took a vertically integrated approach to the new technology showed superior performance when compared to those that decided to go for a 'buy on the market' strategy. Firms that were vertically integrated into the old technology showed lower performance than those that were not.[25] All these ambivalent findings show that under regimes of technological change the definition of business boundaries is a critical starting point for businesses. The definition of business boundaries in particular gets hard when boundaries are blurred. Shifts in technologies such as information and communication technology shift the efficient boundaries of the firm.[26] Afuah (2000) showed that this ambiguity in findings represents two sides of the same coin and argues that the efficient boundaries of the firm are dynamic and largely influenced by the technology that the firm exploits.

Formation of Business Webs

The presence of the contingencies described in the previous section opens the door for shaper companies to form business webs. These entrepreneurial activities are the subject of the following section. I describe the formation of business webs in three steps. First, I argue that shapers act as institutional entrepreneurs by defining and setting the business rules and the technological standards for the emerging business web. Second, I describe how shapers achieve legitimacy for the new institutions. Finally, I show

---

[22] See Afuah (2001), p. 34-35.

[23] See Brown, Durchslag and Hagel III (2002); Christensen and Rosenblum (1995); Hagel III and Singer (2000); Teece (1992).

[24] See Chandler (1962); Williamson (1985).

[25] See Afuah (2001), p. 4 and the discussion of efficient firm boundaries in the third chapter.

[26] See, for instance, Picot and Reichwald (1994); Picot, Ripperger and Wolff (1996); Wigand, Picot and Reichwald (1997); Evans and Schmalensee (1993).

how the institutions become accepted and settled with the establishment of a dominant design.

Institutional Entrepreneurship

Schneider (2001) and Garud, Jain and Kumaraswamy (2002) emphasise the role of institutions in entrepreneurship. In their concept, creation, diffusion and maintenance of institutions are the essence of entrepreneurship. The creation of institutions greatly reduces risks for other actors by establishing rules and norms that reduce uncertainty and threats arising from opportunism. Institutions and particularly property rights are a prerequisite for the establishment and the growth of new markets.[27] David Ticoll expressed that "eBay is changing the rules of the business and competition in the e-business marketplace. The consumer-to-consumer online auction model is a new niche that eBay was able to foster."[28] They constrain actions of economic actors and concurrently produce opportunities.[29] Examples would be the division of labour between companies, the underlying business models, industry standards, and dominant designs.[30] "Firm formation is essentially an entrepreneurial act because to coordinate and transmit tacit knowledge the coordination of the firm is required."[31] Routines in evolutionary theories can also be treated as a factualisation of dominant designs and a standard is "essentially a process of building regularity or routines."[32] This interpretation becomes obvious in the definition of technological regimes. Dosi and Nelson (1994) write that by technological regime, they mean "the complex of firms, professional disciplines and societies, university training and research programs, and legal and regulatory structures that support and constrain development within a regime and along particular trajectories."[33] The initial efforts to create institutions deliberately are acts of institutional entrepreneurship.[34] "New institutions arise when organized actors with sufficient resources (institutional entrepreneurs) see them as an opportunity to realize interest that they value highly."

---

[27] Picot, Dietl and Franck (2002), p. 157.
[28] Bradely and Porter (2000), p. 83.
[29] Fligstein (1999), p. 16.
[30] See Zimmerman and Callaway (2001).
[31] Alvarez and Busenitz (2001), p. 761.
[32] Munir (2003), p. 102.
[33] Dosi and Nelson (1994), p. 161.
[34] See DiMaggio (1988), Suchman (1995); Fligstein (1999); Garud, Jain and Kumaraswamy (2002).

Achieving Legitimacy through Co-operations

Institutional entrepreneurs struggle with a lack of legitimacy in a highly uncertain field in which they seek to exploit new market opportunities. Structuring the emerging field (the market) around designs, standards, industry norms and business rules, etc. is viable for successfully establishing the new market or industry. The rules must offer incentives for third parties to join and to support the institutional entrepreneur; otherwise the market remains restricted, as it was the case for Apple computers when compared to the world-wide personal computer market. To gain support from third parties the institutional entrepreneur has to position his dominant design strategically and establish links with key stakeholders in order to achieve legitimacy. Munir (2003) concludes that the "battle for dominance during the era of ferment does not revolve around technological evolution, but includes the generation of acceptance and the buildup of a network of supporters, which in turn, make a particular technology or design more appealing to users."[35] Accumulation of member organisations, contributors of complementary goods and legitimacy sponsors has proven to be critical for survival and establishment.[36] Hence, the institutional entrepreneur actively reduces the risks of other economic actors. New market creation has to struggle for acceptance and legitimacy to convince complementors and customers to devote resources and efforts. As eBay tried to gain more publicity in November 1997 the idea of online auctions was so new to the audience that they did not know how to deal with it. Johnny Wong, the PR agent in charge expressed: "It was such a totally different animal, they didn't know what to make of it."[37] The initial rules, technologies, and practices are referred to as "proto-institutions" as long as they are not widely accepted, established, and diffused.[38] Institutional entrepreneurs "define, legitimise, combat, or co-opt rivals to succeed in their institutional projects."[39] In the case of i-mode, DoCoMo was defining the technological de-facto standards, the business model, and the customer value proposition. DoCoMo acted as an institutional entrepreneur by establishing and creating the market for mobile Internet services.[40] For the successful establishment of institutions, acceptance and support from others is manda-

---

[35] Munir (2003), p. 106.

[36] Barnett, Mischke and Ocasio (2000) developed an ecological model where firms compete for member organisations.

[37] Cohen (2002b), p.

[38] See Lawrence, Hardy and Phillips (2002).

[39] Augier and Simon (2003), p. 196.

[40] "(...) i-mode was the first commercial service of this kind in the world." Ratliff (2002), p. 55.

tory.[41] "The claims of institutional entrepreneurs are supported by existing or newly mobilized actors who stand to gain from the success of the institutionalisation project." These actors benefit from a reduction of production costs (e.g. new technologies) or transaction costs (e.g. new organisational forms) or both.[42] Subsidiary actors provide legitimacy for the new industry. The investment of Benchmark Capital into the online market place provided eBay with legitimacy that was crucial for attracting human resources and corporate partners. These are often companies from related industries. Recruiting supporting actors is the most crucial task for the institutional entrepreneur. Garud, Jain and Kumaraswamy (2002) show that convincing adapters proves to be difficult. In the case of Sun's Java technology, other actors refused to adopt the new standard as long as it was not brought into public domain, because they feared competitive disadvantages. Zimmerman and Callaway (2001) see the challenge predominately in the insufficient legitimacy of the new industry and propose to constitute legitimacy through different resource contributors. "As the number of members of a network grows, so the processes of interfirm coordination become more standardized, and come to approximate what we recognize as a market."[43] Figure 26 illustrates this process. In the first step, an institutional void is replaced by proto-institutions. External provision of legitimacy through subsidiary actors helps to establish and diffuse proto-institutions. Over time, they will become generally accepted institutions.

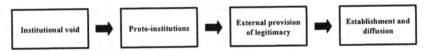

Fig. 26. Process of Institutionalisation

The actors who create the categories, the norms and the standards are suggested to have the most power, hence a first mover advantage.[44] Especially in markets characterised by positive network effects, the early establishment of a critical mass gives the firm a critical edge over competition. "Buyers came to eBay because it was where all the buyers were. Once

---

[41] In some few cases, absolute power renders acceptance and support unnecessary. This obviously applies to monopolies or cartels.

[42] Picot, Laub and Schneider (1990), p. 190.

[43] Mathews (2001), p. 93.

[44] Zook and Allen (2001), p. 45 argue, for instance, that creating a new market segment is a way to build market power and influence through "dominating its experience of a product or service."

eBay achieved critical mass, which it did early on, it would have made no sense for users to go to any other site."[45]

Establishment of a Dominant Design

In early stages of an industry, firms tend to be small and entry is relatively easy due to a plethora of technologies in use. As time passes, competition selects a technology regime and a dominant design emerges that increases entry barriers with growing demands to scale and investment intensity. The emergence of a dominant design is the outcome of a process of variation, selection and retention of innovations. Standards and standardisation play a fundamental role in this evolutionary process that leads to the dominant designs, that themselves have the characteristics of standards.[46] A dominant design serves as a common blueprint for the product architecture that most parties adhere to. "First-Movers, of course cannot create industry by themselves. They have to develop close relationships with supporting enterprises – with suppliers both of capital equipment and materials to be processed, with research specialists, distributors, advertisers, and providers of financial, technical, and other services. Thus the needs of the core firms lead to the creation of a supporting nexus – interconnected and complementary (rather than competitive)."[47] Institutional entrepreneurs may achieve a competitive edge over incumbents in related markets because "they move quickly to define the competitive space, challenging competitors to compete by new and unfamiliar rules."[48] EBay showed that in network industries first mover advantages exist due to an early establishment of a critical mass that is self-reinforcing. Yahoo! and Amazon, as late entrants, struggled to catch up, even thought they had a broader and bigger audience and a more recognised brand when they entered the market. An established learning base, as laid down by Chandler (1992), also helps incumbents with relevant knowledge and organisational routines maintain a competitive edge over attackers. The horizontal expansion of i-mode to game consoles and car navigation devices or the provision of Microsoft Windows derivates such as PocketPC and SmartPhone are examples for this strategic behaviour. This behaviour is quite intuitive because the assets, resources and capabilities of the shaper are not specific to vertical in-

---

[45] Cohen (2002b), p. 100. Even Larry Schwartz, CEO of eBay's competitor Auction Universe admitted, "eBay has done a great job, being the first mover and getting the market established."

[46] See Munir (2003).

[47] Chandler, Hikino and Nordenflycht (2001), p. 5.

[48] Yoffie and Kwak (2002), p. 22.

dustry solutions, but applicable to a horizontal range of industries. DoCoMo benefits when it deploys its resources in a multiple range of applications because it can decrease its per unit costs, achieve a broader deployment of the standard and use available specific resources efficiently.[49] IBM, American Express, Apple and others showed that the creators of markets do not necessarily keep their leadership if new entrants provide a significant better value proposition or if the institutional entrepreneur fails to maintain control over the value-enabling platform. Linkages play a vital role for the early growth of the firms. Leveraged growth through external resources is the subject of the following section.

Growth of Business Webs: Leverage of External Resources

The organisational network environment of the institutional entrepreneur provides resources, which are necessary for the existence and the growth of the firm. Subsidiary actors such as Sun, Matsushita, NEC, Access and Bandai, for example, provided hardware, software, content, and horizontal industry expertise for DoCoMo. Resource dependency theorists suggest that every organisation is dependent on resources that lie outside the organisation.[50] Firms use interorganisational relationships as a way to reduce resource dependencies.[51] These dependencies of the organisations environment are base on resource asymmetries.

Resource Dependencies

"Resource asymmetries occur because of the differential flow of resources among network members, as well as their differential ability to control such flows."[52] Aside from dependence on resources, growing businesses can barely achieve large number cost benefits through economies of scale.[53] The loose coupling of system components through open and standardised interfaces "permits decentralised control"[54] and the establishment of new industries and markets with new rules. Under such circumstances,

---

[49] Williamson (1975); Teece (1982); Picot (1982)
[50] See Pfeffer and Salancik (1978).
[51] See Finkelstein (1997), p. 789.
[52] Gnyawali and Madhavan (2001), p. 431.
[53] See Picot (1991), p. 347.
[54] Hart and Kim (2002), p. 3.

specialised companies are better adapted to particular segments. Vertically integrated firms are hardly able to establish a whole value creating system that is proprietary and idiosyncratic because of immense capital requirements, necessary knowledge, competences, and capabilities that reach far beyond the possibilities of a single firm.[55] Exceptions are very large corporations such as General Electric, Siemens, Samsung, Sony, etc. which can, in principle, produce almost all necessary parts of a product system in-house. Nevertheless, these huge corporations suffer from inefficiencies regarding either transaction cost disadvantages or lack of innovativeness. Therefore, it is economically inefficient to source all complementary modules internally. Products such as Sony Vaio notebooks that run with Microsoft Windows or Siemens cellular phones that are operated by Symbian OS and run applications from various third parties give empirical evidence for this. The German media group Kirch, for example, failed to successfully introduce digital pay-TV with a very integrated approach. The European cellular telephony standard was standardised in a joint effort with the GSM Association even though the French Alcatel had the financial resources and technological capabilities to go alone. Transaction cost economics suggest that firms should concentrate their efforts on tasks that are highly specific and of strategic importance.[56] Picot, Laub and Schneider (1990) showed that the concentration on these tasks and extensive use of hybrid and market arrangements for unspecific tasks to suppliers influenced the success of new businesses positively. Technologies have an impact on transaction cost relations. Information and communication technologies allow more transactions to be coordinated by the market because these technologies lower transaction costs.[57] The modular and highly standardised components of system architectures such as microcomputers or telecommunication networks tolerate even more reliance on the market as a coordinating mechanism because threats arising from opportunism diminish.[58] DoCoMo focused on providing a platform on which third party providers could offer their products and services. The telecommunication network infrastructure, the payment structure and the content format are unspecific to the different contents available through the i-mode platform. The unspecific nature of standardised technologies such as internet protocols and markup languages support horizontal specialisation, because lower transaction costs support governance of economic activities through the market. Picot (1982) already emphasised that the change in institu-

---

[55] See Picot (1982); Picot, Laub and Schneider (1990); Picot (1991).
[56] Williamson (1975); Picot (1991).
[57] See Picot, Ripperger and Wolff (1996); Wigand, Picot and Reichwald (1997).
[58] See Afuah (2003), p. 42.

tional settings such as legislative rules or emerging technologies offer incentives for entrepreneurship.[59] EBay, for example, disrupted many businesses that were based on market friction from asymmetric information. However, the problem of deciding which tasks to operate internally and which to source from the outside proves to be difficult for managers. Therefore the following two sections prescribe "make" or "buy" decisions for business web shapers. First, I theorise which activities should be governed internally, the internal capabilities, and then I do the same for tasks which should be sourced from the outside, the so-called external capabilities.

Internal Capabilities: Concentration on Core Competences

Internal capabilities standard transaction cost theory recommends governing those economic tasks internally which show high degrees of specificity.[60] In the case of business webs, the underlying technology such as software, protocols and the likes are often highly firm specific (at least in the beginning) and inalienable because they are tied to the knowledge of the employees. They are also highly path-dependent, since the routines of individual and collective learning at firm level requires time. To a large degree eBay could fight off its attackers like Amazon and Yahoo! because it had achieved a learning base that was not easily replicable.[61] After the announcement that Amazon would enter the auction business, Whitman told eBay investors that eBay had years of experience in conducting auctions online and community management.[62] EBay concentrated solely on auctions whereas Yahoo! tried to include a wide variety of specific applications, among them auctions on its portal site. Amazon left its traditional core business of being a store when it entered auctions. Whitman recalls that "a refrain emerged at eBay: Yahoo! Auctions had a community without commerce, while Amazon Auctions had commerce without community."[63] Probably, both businesses would be better off if they had partnered with eBay for auctions.[64]

---

[59] Picot (1982), p. 279.
[60] See, for instance, Williamson (1975); Picot (1982); Picot (1993); Picot, Ripperger and Wolff (1996); Williamson (1985).
[61] See chapter 1.
[62] See Cohen (2002b), p. 168.
[63] Cohen (2002b), p. 168.
[64] AOL, that went into a long lasting alliance with eBay and refused to launch auctions itself, did not, by contrast, loose money on auctions but received millions of dollars from eBay for driving traffic to the site.

External Capabilities: Linkages with External Resource Contributors

Scholars in entrepreneurship as well as organisation researchers give evidence that the entrepreneurial firm lacks resources and capabilities, which it must integrate from suppliers, partners, and customers through direct and indirect linkages.[65] First, external resources are approached through personal networks. In the case of DoCoMo the initial management team was partly compiled through personal relationships. In a similar manner, Omdyar approached Benchmark Capital, because he had already established connections to senior management of that venture capitalist from earlier start-up activities.[66] Growth depends on the access to external resources and capabilities from relations with other organisations.[67] Autio, Yli-Renko and Sapienza (1997), and Autio (2000) show the general dependence on resources that lie outside the firm for new, technology-based firms. "For small firms," they state, "necessity refers to the need of the firm to access external resources (…)." Cusumano and Gawer (2002) hold that most "platform leaders do not have the capabilities or resources to create complete systems by making all the complements themselves." In the early stage, firms do not have the funds, the knowledge, or the resources to provide a product system. A major problem in the initial phase of the new business is the decision between what to produce inside the boundaries of the firm at what components to source from the market or through co-operative organisational arrangements.[68] Network entrepreneurs do not have the know-how to serve all horizontal business segments and it is unlikely that they have the financial capital to develop all applications, solutions and services in-house.[69] "Intel's initial commercialization of the microprocessor was a team effort. The development of the 386 and the 486 required funds, knowledge, and the skills that were not available to the start-up."[70] The same is true for the initial growth of Netscape, von Krogh and Cusumano note in their research on growth strategies. "But although Andreessen and the other programmers had most of the essential concepts and technical skills, they lacked the money, managerial insights, and organizational skills needed."[71] Another critical aspect of external sourcing is

[65] See, for example, Yli-Renko, Sapienza and Hay (2001). For a literature review, see Hite and Hesterly (2001).
[66] See Cohen (2002b), p. 74.
[67] See, for instance, Utterback (1974) for research findings on the use of external resources.
[68] Picot, Laub and Schneider (1990), pp. 192 and 197.
[69] Picot (1991), p. 348.
[70] Chandler (1997), p. 99.
[71] Krogh and Cusumano (2001), p. 55.

reduced transaction costs when limited capabilities are concentrated to "specific tasks that build the core of the innovative idea that cannot be delegated to market supply."[72] Hence, the institutional entrepreneur has to grow by the leverage of external resources that reside outside the firms boundaries. I-mode managed the challenges by carefully selecting 67 content providers and four handset manufacturers for the roll-out of the i-mode service.

Besides general valid findings of the growth of the technology-based network firm, business webs show special requirements due to the nature of the product system provided. Important growth drivers are the installed base (i.e. users, consumers, or merchants), positive network externalities, and increasing returns.[73] By assembling a compelling initial service bundle with key players DoCoMo carefully secured a substantial basis that attracted customers. The increasing number of users enabled DoCoMo to realise scale and learning effects. With the increasing spread of fix-costs over a growing customer-base, exploitation of increasing returns dynamic became possible. Annual total revenues for DoCoMo rose from ¥3,718,694 (2000) to ¥5,167,138 (2002), representing a 71% increase.[74] During that timeframe, ARPU from i-mode rose more than tenfold from ¥120 to ¥1,450.[75] Direct and indirect network effects resulted in self-reinforcing growth of adapters and users that accelerated increasing returns. Official i-mode menu sites soared to 3,400 by January 2003. Voluntary sites did even better, achieving an amazing 41,000 sites by the end of 2001 and now number more than 60,000.[76] The i-mode subscriber base mushroomed from 48,000 at the end of 1999 to 36 million as of first quarter 2003.

For many of the observed firms, growth was realised with the expansion into new geographical or product markets. In the case of eBay, the company struggled with some extensions to its core business whereas other extensions went fairly well. For example, the acquisition of Butterfield and Butterfield showed that eBay, with its start-up Internet culture and ambitions, was not able to operate an offline auction house successfully. Additionally, the brand values of eBay were not a close match with Butterfield and Butterfield and the installed customer base was not attracted by the high-priced offerings. Arguably, the culture and the attributes of the in-

---

[72] Picot, Laub and Schneider (1990), p. 192.

[73] See Katz and Shapiro (1992) and also Kelly (1998); Shapiro and Varian (1999); Zerdick, Picot, Schrape et al. (2000).

[74] Wall Street Journal (2003).

[75] See NTT DoCoMo (2003b).

[76] See chapter 4.

stalled base also have to be taken into account if new products are added. Amazon and Yahoo! were not able to market their own auction service launches although Yahoo! had the community of users and Amazon had the skills and the capabilities for doing commerce over the Internet. On the other hand, eBay successfully included other extensions to its core program such as automobiles that went fairly well. In the same way, Yahoo! managed to launch successful complementary services such as instant messaging with its customer base. The answer lies in the nature of the products that are added. If the shaper company transfers its knowledge in the core business of providing and operating the value-enabling platform to other markets without the need of major adoptions, the integration will likely be a success. If the resources and capabilities needed to operate a business successfully differ significantly from value-enabling platform provision and operation, the extension will likely fail. Another source of failure is expectations associated with the brand values. In case a brand such as Amazon not recognised for certain activities within the customer base, enlarging the scope of the firm will prove to be difficult as well. In addition to books, Amazon managed to add new inventory to its site such as CD's, electronic devices and even household goods, but its auction venture lacked acceptance because users did not see Amazon as the place to host auctions on the Internet. These findings are supported by Zook and Allen (2001) who found evidence that sustained value creators focus on one core business where they execute clear market leadership.[77] The authors posit:

"Misdefining the business (whether through poor judgement or plain sloppiness) commits you to invest in areas unlikely to lead to profitable growth or to ignore areas you should reinforce."

This is exactly what eBay's management encountered when it invested in offline businesses that were off the core of managing an online community thereby disregarding necessary investments in technology to keep the electronic marketplace reliable and scalable. Firm diversification is often based on a firm's competencies that can lead to a sustainable competitive advantage. Zook and Allen (2001) come to a similar finding in their study stating, "From focus comes growth; by narrowing scope one creates expansion."[78] Although literature emphasises diversification as a means of growth, Zook and Allen (2001) found in their research on growth patterns across industries that most growth potential steam from the focus on the core business. Zook and Allen (2001) distinguish sharply between adjacency businesses around the core of a company serving as a cushion to

---

[77] Powell (1987), p. 74 makes a similar observation and terms the growth from outsourcing and subcontracting "a strategy of growing by becoming smaller."

[78] Zook and Allen (2001), p. 21.

strengthen and enforce the core business and disjoint diversifications. The authors give evidence that in most cases diversification destroys value and hinders sustainable profitable growth. The movement from core businesses into related businesses, however, usually entails further growth. Nevertheless, it remains unclear why some companies master expanding into formerly unrelated businesses and transform the core business, learning base and organization capabilities successfully. My reasoning would include other variables such as brand images, industry learning curves, degree of specialisation of capabilities and tasks, and organisational structures of diversification as well as the state of technology in a particular observation. Strong consumer brands that have a strong affiliation to the core business will likely increase the chance of failure when diversifying into unrelated businesses and trying to integrate them because the mindshare among consumers does not link the brand with the new offering. The solution is to establish a new brand or to conduct a multiple brand strategy. When a new industry is in its infant state, early movers do not have a big lead in cumulated knowledge and sometimes a new entrant can even draw advantages from established general-purpose complementary assets such as distribution channels giving the early mover a competitive edge. If the capabilities necessary to conduct the business are more general in nature, as for example the capabilities to establish consumer brands or to manage facilities, a diversification also will likely be successful because the company will have already developed the necessary organisational skills. The organisational structure refers to the way in which diversification is organised. Presumably, it will make a difference if the diversification takes the form of a merger or acquisition, the form of a newly founded business as a spin off or new business unit. An integration of an existing business brings a different culture and modus operandi with it almost naturally, making it difficult to unleash the full growth potential for the acquiring firm.[79] A newly formed business unit or spin-off will encounter fewer problems in that respect. Collins and Porras (1994) identify three types of adjacencies. The first refers to a mere product extension, such as adding a new sales channel or a new customer segment for existing products. Options, the second type, describe venture capital nurturing, private equity investments or share holdings of companies that might be relevant to core business in the future. These hedge investments should/are meant to prevent the innovators dilemma, namely being outsmarted in the core business by a disruptive technology. Finally, the third type refers to a sequence of expansions comple-

---

[79] An exception is what Collins and Porras (1994), p. 80 describe as full pluggable acquisitions. Here both firms have natural interrelations that fit together perfectly.

menting the core business in order to expand the boundaries and the capabilities of the same.

Value Creation and Value Capture in Business Webs

Understanding why firms differ in their capability to create and capture value is a central challenge to the theory and practice of strategic management. In a differentiated market, no matter how intense competition is, at any given time some firms appropriate above average profits. Such profits are the returns on innovation in product features, operations or marketing that cannot be imitated easily by competition. Performance of firms for the purpose of the present study is defined as accounting profit. Profit is value captured by the firm. The most commonly used profit measure is the firms formally reported earnings. Examples include net income or earnings per share.[80]

Value Creation

Value is created if the combination of productive assets through technology transformations inputs to products that are valued higher from consumers than the sum of the market cost of input factors. Value creation refers to the difference between goods bought, costs of production, marketing, sales, etc. and the realised margin. Productive assets include land, machinery, plants, human resources, etc. Technology is the process of using human capital and organisational capabilities to add value to these resources through transformation in a production process. In business webs, value is created to a large extent from dependency among users of the network. The value of services increases with each user added because of positive demand side economies of scale such as in the case of microprocessors, software, fax machines and cellular phones. However, the products deliver value for themselves that only increases with a stronger user base. A processor or an application in most cases has an intrinsic value. A fax or a cellular phone obviously has hardly any use without other users. It follows that the extent of intrinsic value has to be taken into con-

---

[80] The return on investment represents the firm's earnings after taking into account the cost of capital invested in the business. The cash-flow contribution is defined as the firm's earnings before taking fixed-asset and capital costs into account (e.g. EBITDA). It represents the amount of cash left from a sale after subtracting the variable costs associated with that sale used as a basis for decision-making in mature, high fixed-cost and cyclical industries.

sideration when other users are an integral part of the value of the product. The institutional entrepreneur requires access and control of external complementary assets to appropriate profits.[81] Without the availability of i-mode-compliant handsets and optimised contents for small screens, DoCoMo would not have been able to sell its services. An installed base is therefore a critical driver of the value in the business web. In addition, the composition of the installed base matters. If only a special segment is represented in the customer base, only a fraction of the potential value can be realised. Consider a Japanese mobile subscriber: unless he does not maintain many linkages to remote citizens all over the world, he will arguably not benefit much from added customers to a network in the EU or the US if none of his Japanese peers have decided to join the network.

Value Capture

Value is captured in beginning by consumers willing to pay more than the costs of goods. Typically, this hidden price expectation is the marginal willingness to pay or the perceived value expressed in monetary units. The difference between the price of the good and the willingness to pay is the consumer surplus.[82] The difference between the cost of goods and the price is the producer surplus. Depending on the nature of exchange relationships between supplier and buyer, the seller's surplus gets distributed backwards in asymmetric portions in the value creating system. If a buyer is strongly dependent on the input resources of a supplier, the supplier will appropriate a larger share than the supplier of homogenous goods from factor markets.[83] Firms can exploit deeper profit pools in deciding which customers to pursue and which channels to use or to guide product, pricing, and operating decisions. Profit pools are the total profits earned in an industry at all points along the industry's value chain. The shape of a profit pool reflects the competitive dynamics of a business. [84] Although a practical concept, profit pools provide only a relative measure for performance in relation to competitors because it does not show absolute levels of growth or profitability. A certain limitation of the concept is that the researcher or analyst has to define the boundaries of a firm and the boundaries of the industry that is being analysed. Especially for business webs with dynamic blurring

---

[81] See Teece (1986); Teece, Pisano and Shuen (1997); Autio and Garnsey (1997); Langlois (1992a); Lee, Lee and Pennings (2001); Funk (1999); Birkinshaw (2000); Autio, Garnsey and Yli-Renko (1997).
[82] See, for instance, Varian (1996).
[83] See Porter (1985).
[84] See Gadiesh and Gilbert (1998).

boundaries this is a major implementation obstacle in management practice. Perhaps one could try to construct profit pools for business web, defining the core activities for the web and the relative share of sales from that activity. Nevertheless, an understanding of profit pool dynamics can help guide important decisions about every facet of a company's operation and strategy, leading in many cases to the development of new, more profitable business models.

Control Points

Key to appropriating large amounts of the overall generated value is market power and an influential position with suppliers and customers. The primary measure for market power is the relative market share.[85] Against common wisdom, scale itself is not the source of sustaining competitive advantage. The logic of scale economics is the other way around. A sustaining competitive advantage results in economies of scale. If a business can differentiate its offerings, more users will likely decide to buy products from this business than from competitors provided the differentiators create value for the customer or make it more difficult to compare offerings. Competitive advantage through differentiation is, for example, achieved through better service, better quality, better products, or the control and ownership of crucial complementary assets that add value to the product. Higher outputs result in scale economies that bring better cost structures with increased specialisation, learning curve advantages and a decreasing fixed-to-variable cost ratio.[86]

The generated value of the business web is distributed among different resource contributors (shaper, adapters, customers, investors) largely through the pricing mechanism or bargaining power over the resource contributors.

---

[85] See Porter (1985).
[86] Zook and Allen (2001) argue in a similar manner.

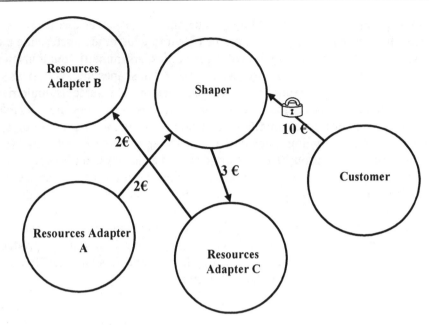

Fig. 27. Value Distribution in a Business Web

Resource-based power refers to the control of resources with enforceable property-rights that potentially translates to power over dependent actors or appropriable resource rents. In the case of physical resources, this is not much of a problem. Challenges arise when a firm seeks to appropriate profits from intangible resources such as technological knowledge.[87] Appropriability refers to the creditability and the enforceability of property rights. Krugman (1987) proposes three types of appropriable knowledge: (1) largely appropriable knowledge, production process knowledge, firm specific learning curves, knowledge integrated in the firm; (2) semi-appropriable knowledge, product designs, reverse engineering; (3) spreadable knowledge, non-appropriable knowledge, often embodied in people, spill-over in social networks. Unilateral dependence on resources translates into asymmetric power relations enabling party A to threaten party B to pursue actions intended by A. Mutually interdependent resource control translates to symmetric power relationships with equal potential to influence the behaviour of either party. Practically, equal power relationships are unlikely. In reality more or less asymmetric relationships exist that give either party incrementally more influencing power over the other party. The power to decide and shape norms, rules and procedures (institu-

---

[87] Appropriability of technological knowledge is discussed in Hart and Kim (2000).

tions) gives rise to structural power. The amount of power one party executes over another is dependent on the extent to which it can determine the structure of the relationship between the parties. Asymmetric relationships from structural power arise because the party that shapes the institutions is able to restrict the potential opportunities of actors. Resource asymmetries lead to a sustaining competitive advantage if these resources are valuable for the consumer, rare, inimitable and non-substitutable. Such resources, create a strong bargaining position and hence above average returns. "The more crucial the resource of the firm is to the network, the better is the firm's bargaining power in respect to cashing the resource."[88] The degree and direction of dependencies lead to distinct power positions in the organisational environment.

Shapers have influence over system architectures and adapters that produce complementary products because they control interfaces, product specifications and technical standards.[89] Borrus and Zysman (1997) write about the power relations in the microcomputer industry.

"Market power has shifted from the assemblers such as Gateway, IBM, or Toshiba, to key producers of components (such as Intel); operating systems (such as Microsoft); applications (such as SAP, Adobe); Interfaces (such as Netscape); languages (such as Sun with Java); and to pure product definition companies like Cisco Systems and 3COM."[90]

Influence or control of critical resources such as architectural designs or standards creates strong dependencies on other industry peers. These critical resources are controlled through "control points."[91] Industry control points[92] or choke points[93] are bottlenecks within business webs that are necessary for other participants to do their business. These bottlenecks are a scarce resource and therefore oppose dependencies that translate into a higher perceived bargaining position. Control points hinder attackers from entering the profit pool and erode margins. Examples for control points include enforceable property rights for critical components in product systems such as the microprocessor and the operating system in personal computers, the control of customer relationships as illustrated by mobile network operators, the definition and guided evolution of proprietary industry standards as recently exemplified by IBM, VeriSign and Microsoft with web service protocol stacks.[94] In addition to the ownership of a tech-

---

[88] Keil and Autio (1997), p. 307.
[89] See Cusumano and Gawer (2002), Christensen (2001).
[90] Borrus and Zysman (1997), p. 150.
[91] See Hagel III (1996).
[92] Munir (2003), pp. 104.
[93] Gadiesh and Gilbert (1998).
[94] "Choke points can arise for many different reasons: the granting of a patent for a core component of a product, the establishment of an industry wide operating standard that all

nology platform, control points arise from the control or the ownership of customer relations, transaction platforms, or powerful brands. Control points limit the freedom and scope of strategic flexibility of other members in the business web. By defining the rules and standards, the shaper exercises power over the adapters and imposes sanctions where necessary. The ability to expose sanctions is dependent on the underlying value-enabling platform. In a technology web, sanctioning potential is restricted by the disclosure level of the technology. If the technology is at least partly proprietary, it is sufficient to restrict access to relevant information. Microsoft used this approach to sanction adapters of the Wintel business web.[95] In the case of an installed base of customers, access to the customers has to be prevented by legal or technological means. Yahoo! could, for example, remove shops from its shopping directory. The same applies to the marketplace. EBay, for instance, developed strict rules that prevent buyers from seller fraud.[96] Achieving control over the architecture is a powerful means for attaining competitive advantage because a competitor would not only have to invent a similar architecture but would also have to convince adapters to change their designs.[97]

A further source of superior performance based on inimitable differentiation is a strong consumer brand that guides consumer buying behaviour and permits higher margins due to premium prices. "Moreover, consumers are willing to pay more for the brand with the highest market share (since it has more associated applications), and therefore profits associated with this brand can be a large multiple of profits of other platforms."[98] Kodak rules about 70% percent of the photographic film market because of its brand strength.[99] EBay's control points are foremost the community of buyers and sellers, in essence the control over the buying relationships, and the marketplace with its infrastructure and applications to conduct commerce. However, the brand also represents a powerful control point be-

---

companies must obey, or the consolidation of control over the customer interface, to take just three examples." Gadiesh and Gilbert (1998), p. 143.

[95] "By strategically excluding some vendors from access to the full details of the interface, Microsoft retains more control over what products can be made compatible. This enables Microsoft to protect its market power in product categories that might otherwise have been overrun with competitors, and it gives the company great control over the evolution of the architecture of personal computer software." Schilling (2000), p. 330.

[96] See Bunell and Luecke (2000).

[97] See, for instance, Katz and Shapiro (1994); Shapiro and Varian (1999); Zerdick, Picot, Schrape, et al. (2000). Examples for system competition provide Langlois and Robertson (1992a).

[98] Economides (2003), p. 242.

[99] See Munir (2003), p. 105.

cause eBay became a familiar household name synonymous with online auctions. "eBay's advantage was that buyers and sellers thought of it as the place to go for auctions. (...) Amazon had hardened in the public's mind as a fixed price book, music, and video destination—not as a place to go for auctions."[100] The organisational capabilities and routines to exploit resources can also be a powerful source of control points.[101] Consider, for example, tacit knowledge or experience that is necessary to provide certain products or services. DoCoMo's control points are the control of the i-mode menu in combination with the overall product architecture definition and the ownership of the customer data and the billing relationship. Economic activities controlled by the shaper are the sweet spots of the business web, the places where the highest profits are realised.[102] "But even a small percentage of a huge number translates into a major business potential, and eBay is well situated to grab the lion's share of it. And though bargain hunting may be a hobby, it has created a vast community of eBay users."[103] The higher the bargaining power of the shaper over its customer and adapters, the higher the proportion of the value captured by the shaper.[104] This is the reason why firms such as Intel and Microsoft take a lion's share of the revenues in their business web.[105] Microprocessors and software, as depicted in figure 28, realise the highest operating margins in the PC Industry.

---

[100] Cohen (2002b), p. 169.
[101] See Park (1996), Mathews (2001).
[102] See Gadiesh and Gilbert (1998).
[103] Bunell and Luecke (2000), p. 16.
[104] See Park (1998).
[105] See Hagel III (1996). "In the decade between 1987 and 1997, Intel generated an astounding average annual return to investors of 44%. Even more impressive, recently Intel's annual earnings equalled those of the top ten personal computer firms combined." Eisenhardt and Brown (1998), p. 59-60. More recent research by Häcki and Lighton (2001); Christensen, Raynor and Verlinden (2001), Christensen (2001), Gawer (2000) and Cusumano and Gawer (2002) give support for these findings.

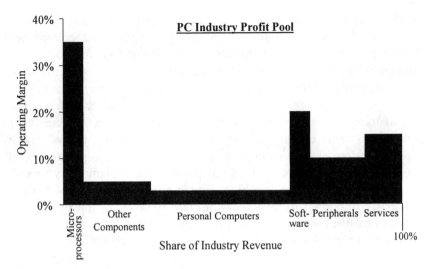

Fig. 28. PC Industry Profit Pool[106]

In order to function properly as a tool for competitive advantage, control points have to be the key input for the value creation of other businesses or scale sensitive, creating "winner-take-all" markets. Shapers leverage their control horizontally across distinct businesses by permanently creating lock-ins and exploiting network effects. EBay creates a customer lock-in through the feedback rating which prevents customers from churning because they cannot take their history of integrity and honest behaviour with them to another site. The company is well aware of the competitive advantage controlling this critical control point offers. EBay tried to keep its feedback rating exclusive and inalienable much in the same fashion as Microsoft looks after its API's, file formats and protocols. Yahoo!, eDeal and others who have tried to import eBay user feedback rating were sued by eBay claiming that the companies offended eBay's intellectual property rights.

Conclusion

The emergence of business webs is constrained by the institutional environment. Political, market and technological institutions that permit horizontal specialisation and vertical control of economic activities are a prerequisite for the establishment of business webs. In particular, these are

---

[106] See Gadiesh and Gilbert (1998), p. 145.

liberalisation and deregulation of markets, larger global markets, and modular technologies. The shaper firm (i.e. an institutional entrepreneur) drives the establishment of a business web. The shaper firm defines the system architecture, the technological standards, and the business rules and seeks legitimacy from subsidiary actors. For success, the introduction of a product architecture requires the necessary complements and a critical mass of users at the beginning. Partnerships and alliances secure the access, and to some extent the control, of complementary assets. For the shaper of a core system element it is viable to tie adapters through alliances. These adapters are in charge of providing complementary products and assets that must be compatible. Demand-side economies of scale are particularly important in markets with huge fixed costs and positive network externalities such as in the information and telecommunication industries. Once the shaper has managed to "cross the chasm" between early adopters and an early majority of the mass market, turbulent growth unfolds.[107] In order to successfully cross the chasm between early adopters and an early majority the shaper has to broaden the utility of its value enabling platform. At eBay, technologically savvy collectors were the early adopters. They did not care too much about technological obstacles and helped themselves. For eBay, achieving mass market acceptance meant ensuring the stability of its technological platform and making it as easy as possible for sellers and buyers to engage in commerce. Mass-market demand also required new listings and categories other than collectibles and the introduction of new pricing mechanisms. EBay used its cash flow and its stock assets to quickly integrate these necessary elements through acquisitions of companies (respectively adapters) that were already offering the sought after functionality. At some point, a lock-in into a dominant design takes place. The case of i-mode illustrates that a customer (respectively adapter) lock-in is by no means exclusively tied to proprietary technologies but also to reputation, brand and the bundling of products and services. Due to positive network effects, a vicious cycle starts and the network starts to become self-reinforcing. At this point, the shaper encourages even more network externalities to keep the vicious cycle of positive feedback going. Conner and Rumelt (1991) posit that it is the best strategy to encourage clones in order to establish a critical mass of users and to create positive network externalities by spreading the standard through the whole market.[108] This may be achieved by licensing or freely distributing the standard and the interface specifications to competitors and adapters. DoCoMo tries to broaden its geographic reach and the worldwide sub-

---

[107] See Moore (1995; Moore, Johnston and Kippola (1999).
[108] See Conner and Rumelt (1991).

scriber base by investing in minority stakes of US and European mobile network operators or by licensing its service as in the case of Telefónica, Telecom Italia Mobile and Bouyges Telecom. At this stage, the early growth process has ended and the shaper now has to manage and govern the adapters of the business web. These issues are beyond the scope of the early growth phase and, hence, not subject to further analysis.[109] The establishment and the early growth is summarised in figure 29.

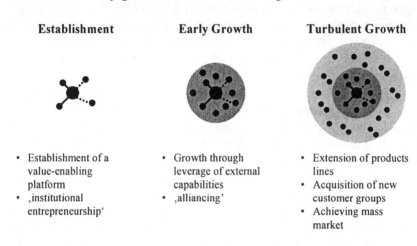

Establishment	Early Growth	Turbulent Growth
• Establishment of a value-enabling platform • ‚institutional entrepreneurship‘	• Growth through leverage of external capabilities • ‚alliancing’	• Extension of products lines • Acquisition of new customer groups • Achieving mass market

Fig. 29. Growth Stages of Business Webs

The thick dot in the middle of the business web in establishment illustrates the shaper of the web. As elaborated earlier, the core business is about developing and nurturing a proprietary open technological platform, a community of customers, a market place or some combination of the three. Crucial adapters are attached to the core with strong ties (---) or weak ties (- - -) that provide legitimacy for the emerging business web. Shaper firms use more formal contracting with complementors where knowledge and skill are vital for the functionality of the product system and quality is important. Standardised activities with little asset specificity or products with uncertain market demand are likely to be coordinated through market relationships.[110] The shaper and the first core adapter pro-

---

[109] For further elaborations of management topics of business webs see particularly Franz (2003). More general issues of network management can be found in Sydow (1991); Limerick and Cunnington (1993); Mathews (1994); Park (1996); Gulati and Singh (1998); Ireland, Hitt and Vaidyanath (2002).

[110] Transaction cost economic reasoning on efficient boundary decisions supports these finding. See Powell (1987); Picot (1993); Wigand, Picot and Reichwald (1997).

vide the invariant core group of businesses in the business web. In the subsequent phase, early growth takes place with initial adapters joining the web and establishing the inner circle of the emerging business web (dark grey circle). The inner circle is characterised by companies that join the web for further collaboration and the emergence of the first adapter companies that voluntary commit to the business web by inventing and commercialising products and services for different customer segments. This happens without the knowledge of the shaper companies and is based on entrepreneurial opportunities and economic incentives offered by the value-enabling platform. In the third stage, the web reaches its critical mass resulting in a flood of new adapters that try to commercialise complementary product offerings for a wide array of customer groups. On the basis of general-purpose, value-enabling platforms, adapters develop solutions for niche market applications and mass marketable solutions alike. Powell (1987) argues in his research on hybrid organisational arrangements that a division of labour between a large generalist organisation and small, specialised firms is a fruitful strategy to overcome the disadvantages of "bureaucratic inertia and the lack of clout and legitimacy that plagues small companies."[111] Accordingly, the division of labour between the shaper, concentrating on the value-enabling platform, and the adapters, concentrating on responsive development of innovative complements, strengthens both parties and decreases weaknesses. At this stage, shapers will strengthen their market position by acquiring or reengineering the most profitable mass-market products and starting to integrate them into the value-enabling platform. The influence and control of control points such as architectural design, proprietary technology, de-facto standards, and customer profiles defines the ability to appropriate profits. Profitability and competitive advantages are tightly bound to the control of the architecture of the product system and the interconnecting interfaces. The shaper benefits from positive network externalities that led to a competitive advantage over other market players since an established dominant design makes it more difficult to introduce architectural innovations in the market.[112]

---

[111] Powell (1987), p. 80.
[112] At least if they are not compatible with the actual dominant design.

Conclusion

The properties of network industries such as supremacy of modular product systems and network effects create unique challenges for product introduction, organisation and competitive strategies. The analysis showed that modular product systems play an increasingly important role in economy-altering competition. Many of the most important industries today build on networks and have to take the economics of standards and network effects into account. The properties of network industries favour and support decentralised governance of economic activities. Business webs are an organisational answer to cope with the requirements of decentralised governance. The present study aimed to illuminate the growth patterns of business webs and to respond to the question of how and why the ability to capture profit differs among business web participants. Business webs were defined and five constitutive dimensions (consumer-centricity, heterarchy, co-opetition, information basis, and scale sensitiveness) were identified from existing literature. The growth histories of several business webs showed how selected companies established their product offerings under the presence of network effects and established new industries around their value-enabling platform. I-mode and eBay were chosen as major research sites to assess the research phenomenon because the firms showed the relevant characteristics of a business web and an establishment process that took place only recently. The external validity of the findings was enhanced with several mini-cases from other network industries. The two in-depth case studies illustrated the growth processes and gave some important insights to the theory. The growth model structured and aggregated the findings. The major elements of this model are contingencies that drive the emergence of business webs, the institutional entrepreneurship of shapers to set the rules and standards for the emerging business web and the leverage of external resources for growth. The relation between internal and external resources and their properties are determinants for the value capturing potential in the business web.

I started the analysis by asking, "How does business web formation actually take place?" The cases showed that the establishment process is a co-evolutionary process at a time where interdependent actors such as shapers, adapters, and consumers co-operate to achieve an overall value proposition. Institutional entrepreneurship of the shaper helps in coordinating the tasks and in the division of labour. These rules are legitimised by supporting actors and help diffuse the product system in the market. Consumers adopt the system innovation when they assume that the system has been legitimised and find the product system useful and easy to understand. The second question, "How does the shaper convince initial adapters to support the architectural platform?" is targeted at the way the shaper achieves legitimacy. Shaper firms initially attempt to get the backing of reputable and established businesses such as banks and venture capitalists or large established corporations to achieve legitimacy for the emergent industry and the product system at hand. A key driver for initial support of the architecture is to offer the core adapters economic incentives. These include an enhanced value proposition, customer relationships, decreased cost, new customer segments, or additional revenue streams. The third question, "How does the shaper achieve and execute leadership?" is intended to illuminate the strategic leadership of the shaper. Leadership is bound to the influence and control of the architectural design, the standards, and the business rules. Shapers exercise leadership by defining the components and the interfaces between the components as well as the business model. A rather interrelated question is the fourth and last one, "How does the shaper capture value?" concerning the potential for appropriating rents. Rent appropriation is closely related to the control and the influence of control points that are valuable, rare, inimitable, and non-substitutable.

Implication for Practice

For the introduction of an innovative product system, the timing of market entry is crucial. Product management throughout the whole business web is another key issue for the strategic leader. As a shaper, a company should manage the overall product system from end-to-end by controlling all parts through quasi-vertical integration of core adapters.[1] This is achieved by tight coupling with organisations already established in related, matured industries, thereby lending legitimacy to the new industry. The shaper firm needs to communicate the architecture as well as the standards and rules to decrease uncertainty for prospect adapters. In order to achieve an overall compelling value proposition of the product system, the distinct modules have to be aligned carefully in order to maximise the perceived value.

---

[1] An issue also heavily stressed by the interviewees in the study.

Market entry should not take place before interoperability of the components can be guaranteed and a sufficient offer of complementary goods is available. A critical mass of initial, attractive complementary goods and services acts positively on adoption by users. Using open platforms and general-purpose technologies eases the process of convincing adapters to provide modules to the product system. The economic benefits for the adapters must be clear and sufficiently high. At the same time, everything possible has to be undertaken to secure the optimal customer perception in all relevant service dimensions such as quality, price, up-to-dateness, and reliability. Rapid growth is achieved by concentrating on development of the value-enabling platform and consequent leverage of external capabilities. The value-enabling platform has to be protected from imitators with control points that are hard to imitate. These control points need to be scarce bottlenecks for adapters and users in order to gain a lion's share of profits generated in the business web. Most promising are interface standards to technical systems, user interfaces, customer data and strong brands.

Limitations and Future Prospects

A certain limitation to the general applicability of the findings is the fact that a case sample cannot claim statistical significance of the findings for a population.

Challenges in following a case study approach arise from generalisation, documentation and validation. One criterion for the validity of cases is the significance of findings. Significance broadly refers to theoretical and practical interest of the case. Another indicator for validity is completeness, meaning the communication of the whole case. Internal validity can be achieved by data triangulation with further data sources. Multiple sources of evidence, if they lead to similar results, increase the convergent validity of theoretical constructs. A retrospective case study has the advantage that the researcher does not become too involved, thereby losing objectivity. Data sources for triangulation in the study included databases, newspapers and magazines, news clippings, and qualitative interviews. The advances of Internet technology support this approach since large numbers of technology and business related information resources are available on-line in full text. Finally, validity can be achieved by considering alternative perspectives through comparison of results with existing literature and the cases of other researchers. Linking research results to existing literature is crucial for theory generating research, because the findings only rest on a limited number of cases. A weakness of this approach might be that it most likely generates only "modest theories."[2] Theories derived from case study research typically lack the broad applicability of theories including resource dependence, resource-based view, transaction cost, or population ecology. They are narrower in their applicability because they are tightly matched to the observed cases.[3]

The coherence of the findings of the cases in this study allow the presumption that the derived model is quite robust. Further, rigor of data might dilute the reliability of findings. One serious challenge to the pursued case studies approach for the researcher is the careful choice of references for the cases. It did in fact happen that, on occasion, even reputable and reliable sources reported ambiguous facts. Additionally, one cannot simply assume a fact is true, simply because several sources report the same. The PEZ legend of eBay might serve as an example here. This is a big challenge for data triangulation and internal validation. To that end it seems promising to compare the findings derived from published data with first hand impressions from the involved managers in interviews. Insufficient general applicability is a problem inherent to the case study approach and does not weigh too much because the business web population has a manageable size due to its winner-take-all dynamics. Thus, it should be principally possible to analyse the whole business web sample.

Problems may arise in defining the entire sample. Here, the study has made an important contribution in defining constructs for the identification of business webs. The present sample of cases might serve as a starting point for a more general applicable theory of business web growth.

Subsequent research should focus on operating theoretical constructs, making them testable for larger data sets. A second research stream might also give a more holistic picture of the growth of business webs. The present study mainly focused the research on firms that successfully established a business web. The majority of firms presumably fail to introduce a product system. Therefore it seems promising to research the struggles for supremacy between competing shapers early in the infancy of a network industry and the differences in competitive strategies and resources.

On the theoretical side, the close observation of the influence of management and management skills on growth outcome seems promising. In fact, many of the shaper firm's growth histories are associated with ex-

---

[2] Eisenhardt (1989), p. 547.

[3] As Eisenhardt (1989), p. 545 writes: "The final product of building theory from case studies may be concepts (…), a conceptual framework (…), or propositions or possibly mid-range theory (…). On the downside, the final product may be disappointing. The research may simply replicate prior theory, or there may be no clear patterns within the data."

traordinary senior management individuals (such as Bill Gates at Microsoft, Steve Case at AOL, Pierre Omdyar at eBay, to name but a few). Further, the developed internal capability to compete in network markets is worth further research. As the mini-cases indicated, several firms have obviously created organisational routines to shape business webs around new product systems and in adjacent markets. This seems to be an important observation for survival of shaper firms and further growth. The relevance is also indicated in the empirical observation that several shaper firms play a important role in different business webs. Microsoft, Sun Microsystems, IBM, Apple are among the obvious examples.

References

Anonymous (2001). *Morning Report: eBay remains a Winner* [HTML]. Internetstockreport.com 2001 [cited 15.03.2003].

Achrol, R. S. (1997): Changes in the Theory of Interorganizational Relations in Marketing: Toward a Network Paradigm. *Journal of the Academy of Marketing Science* 25:56-71.

Adobe Inc. (1999): Annual Report.

────── (2002): Annual Report.

Afuah, A. (2000): How Much Do Your Co-Opetitors' Capabilities Matter In The Face Of Technological Change? *Strategic Management Journal* 21 (3):387-404.

────── (2001): Dynamic Boundaries of the Firm: Are Firms Better Off Being Vertically Integrated in the Face of a Technological change? *Academy of Management Journal* 44 (6):1211-1228.

────── (2003): Redefining Firm Boundaries in the Face of the Internet: Are Firms Really Shrinking. *Academy of Management Review* 28 (1):34-53.

Afuah, A. and Tucci, C. L. (2003): *Internet Business Models and Strategies: Text and Cases*. 2nd. ed. New York: McGraw-Hill.

Aldrich, H. E. and Fiol, C. M. (1994): Fools rush in?: The Institutional Context of Industry Creation. *Academy of Management Review* 19 (4):645-670.

Allee, V. (2000): Reconfiguring the Value Network. *Journal of Business Strategy* 21 (4):36-39.

Alvarez, S. and Busenitz, L. W. (2001): The Entrepreneurship of Resource-based Theory. *Journal of Management* 27:755-775.

Amaha, E. (1999): A la i-mode. *Far Eastern Economic Review* (August 12):44.

Anderson, J. and Wood, R. (2002): Seven Management Lessons from Microsoft. *Business Strategy Review* 13 (3):28-33.

Andersson, C. and Svensson, P. (1999): Mobile Internet: An Industry-Wide paradigm shift? *Ericsson Review* (4):206-213.

Antonelli, C. (1994): Localized Technological Change and the Evolution of Standards as Economic Institutions. *Information Economics and Policy* 6 (3-4):195-216.

────── (1998): Localized Technological Change and the Evolution of Standards as Economic Institutions. In *The Dynamic Firm*, edited by A. D. Chandler / P. Hagström and Ö. Sölvell. Oxford: Oxford University Press.

Aoki, M./ Gustafsson, B. and Williamson, O. E., eds. (1990): *The Firm as a Nexus of Treaties*. London: Sage.

Arango, T. and Eavis, P. (2001). *Listing Numbers Cast Doubt on eBay's Growth Plans* [HTML]. TheStreet.com 2001 [cited 15.03.2003].

Arrow, K. J. (2000): Increasing Returns: Historiographic Issues and Path Dependence. *European Journal of the History of Economic Thought* 7 (2):171-180.

Arthur, B. W. (1989): Competing Technologies, Increasing Returns, and Lock-In by Historical Events. *The Economic Journal* 99:116-131.

———— (1994): Positive Feedbacks in the Economy. *The McKinsey Quarterly* (1):81-95.

Auerbach, J. G. (1999): Online: Internet Giants Pool their Bids For Auction Site to Rival EBay. *The Wall Street Journal*, B1.

Augier, M. and Simon, H. A. (2003): Commentary: The Architecture of Complexity. In *Managing in the Modular Age: Architectures, Networks, and Organizations*, edited by R. Garud / A. Kumaraswamy and R. N. Langlois. Malden, MA: Blackwell.

Autio, E. (1997): 'Atomistic' and 'Systemic' Approaches to Research on New, Technology-Based Firms: A Literature Study. *Small Business Economics* 9 (3):195-209.

———— (2000): Growth of Technology-Based New Firms. In *Handbook of Entrepreneurship*, edited by D. Sexton and H. Landström. Oxford: Blackwell Publishers.

Autio, E. and Garnsey, E. (1997): Early Growth and External Relations in New Technology-Based Firms. Otakaari.

Autio, E./ Garnsey, E. and Yli-Renko, H. (1997): Resources, Complementary Assets, and Growth in New, Technology-based Firms. Paper presented at 42nd ICSB World Conference, June, at San Francisco.

Autio, E./ Yli-Renko, H. and Sapienza, H. (1997): Leveraging Resources under Threat of Opportunism: Predicting Networking in International Growth. Cambridge.

Bahrami, H. (1992): The Emerging Flexible Organization: Perspectives from Silicon Valley. *California Management Review* 34 (4):33-52.

Bain, J. S. (1956): *Barriers to New Competition*. Cambridge, MA: Harvard University Press.

Baldi, S. and Pyu-Pyu Thaung, H. (2002): The Entertaining Way to M-Commerce: Japan's Approach to the Mobile Internet: A Model for Europe. *Electronic Markets* 12 (1):6-13.

Baldwin, C. and Clark, K. B. (1997): Managing in the Age of Modularity. *Harvard Business Review* 75:84-93.

———— (2000): *Design Rules: The Power of Modularity*. Cambridge, MA: MIT Press.

Bank, D. (1995). *The Java Saga* [HTML]. Wired 1995 [cited July 2, 2003].

Barnett, W. P./ Mischke, G. A. and Ocasio, W. (2000): The Evolution of Collective Strategies Among Organizations. *Organization Studies* 21 (2):325-354.

Barney, J./ Wright, M. and Ketchen, J., David J. (2001): The Resource-based View of the Firm: Ten Years After 1991. *Journal of Management* 27 (6):625-641.

Barney, J. B. (1991): Firm Resources and Sustained Competitive Advantage. *Journal of Management* 17 (1):99-120.

———— (1999): How a Firm's Capabilities Affect Boundary Decisions. *MIT Sloan Management Review* 40 (3):137-145.

Baron, D. P. (2001): Private Ordering on the Internet: The eBay Community of Traders. In *Research Paper Series, Graduate School of Business, Stanford University*. Stanford.

Batista, E. (2001). *Biz Wiz: She Knows What You Want* [HTML]. Wired News 2001 [cited 21.01.2003]. Available from http://www.wired.com/news/women/0,1540,43342-2,00.html.

Bayus, B. L./ Jain, S. and Rao, A. G. (2000): Truth or Consequences: An Analysis of Vaporware and New Product Announcements. *Journal of Marketing Research* 37 (4).

Berlind, D. (2002a). *IBM Pressures Sun to Free Java* [HTML]. ZDNet 2002a [cited July 2, 2002]. Available from http://www.zdnet.com/filters/printerfriendly/o,6061,2878892-92,00.html.

———— (2002b). *Sun Bets its Future on Java* [HTML]. ZDNet 2002b [cited July 2, 2002]. Available from http://zdnet.com/filters/printerfriendly/0,0661,2878378-92,00.html.

Besen, S., M. and Farrell, J. (1994): Choosing how to Compete: Strategies and Tactics in Standardization. *The Journal of Economic Perspectives* 8 (2):117-131.

Bettis, R. A. and Hitt, M. A. (1995): The New Competitive Landscape. *Strategic Management Journal* 16:7-19.

Betwee, J./ Meuel, D./ Bergquist, W. H. and Memel, D. (1995): *Building Strategic Relationships : How to Extend Your Organization's Reach Through Partnerships, Alliances, and Joint Ventures*: Jossey Bass.

Birkinshaw, J. (2000): Network Relationship Inside and Outside the Firm, and the Development of Capabilities. In *The Flexible Firm: Capability Management in Network Organizations*, edited by J. Birkinshaw and P. Hagström.

Birkinshaw, J. M. and Morrison, A. J. (1995): Configurations of Strategy and Structure in Subsidiaries of Multinational Corporations. *Journal of International Business Studies* 26 (4):729-753.

Bisenius, J. C. and Siegert, W. (2002): *Multi Media Mobile*. Berlin: Vistas.

Blau, J. (2003). *Vodafone: Services, not Technology, will fuel Growth* [HTML]. IDG News Services 2003 [cited June 16, 2003]. Available from http://www.infoworld.com/article/03/07/01/HNvodaserve_1.html.

Borrus, M. and Zysman, J. (1997): Globalization with Borders: The Rise of Wintelism as the Future of Global Competition. *Industry and Innovation* 4 (2):141-166.

Bovet, D. and Martha, J. (2000): *Value Nets: Breaking the Supply Chain to Unlock Hidden Profits*. New York: Wiley.

Bradely, S. P. and Porter, K. A. (2000): EBAY, INC. *Journal of Interactive Marketing* 14 (4):79-97.

Brandenburger, A. M. and Nalebuff, B. J. (1996): *Co-Opetition: A Revolutionary Mindset that Combines Competition and Cooperation in the Marketplace*. London: Harper Collins Publishers.

Bresser, R. K./ Hitt, M. A./ Nixon, R. D. and Heuskel, D., eds. (2000): *Winning Strategies in a Deconstructing World*. Chichester: Wiley.

Brewerton, P. and Millward, L. (2001): *Organizational Research Methods : A Guide for Students and Researchers*. London: SAGE.

Brock, G. W. (2002): Historical Overview. In *Handbook of Telecommunications Economics: Structure, Regulation and Competition*, edited by M. Cave and S. Majumdar. Amsterdam: Elsevier.

Brown, J. S./ Durchslag, S. and Hagel III, J. (2002): Loosening up: How process networks unlock the power of specialisation. *The McKinsey Quarterly*:50-69.

Bunell, D. and Luecke, R. A. (2000): *The eBay Phenomenon: Business Secrets Behind The World's Hottest Internet Company*. New York: Wiley.

Burgelman, R. A. and Rosenbloom, R., eds. (1997): *Research on Technological Innovation, Management and Policy*. Vol. 6. Greenwich, Conn. and London: JAI Press.

Byous, J. (1998). *Java Technology: An Early History* [HTML]. Sun Microsystems 1998 [cited July 2, 2003].

Campbell, A. (1996): Agility, Virtual Organisations and Enterprise Webs: Redefining the Scope of Business Organisations? *Computing and Information Systems* 3 (3):87-94.

Campell-Kelly, M. (2001): Not Only Microsoft: The Maturing of the Personal Computer Software Industry, 1982-1995. *Business History Review* 75:103-145.

Cartwright, P. A. (2002): Only Converge: Networks and Connectivity in the Information Economy. *Business Strategy Review* 13 (2):59-64.

Cartwright, S. D. and Oliver, R. W. (2000): Untangling the Value Web. *Journal of Business Strategy* 21 (1):22-27.

Cave, M. E./ Majumdar, S. K. and Vogelsang, I. (2002): Structure, Regulations and Competition in the Telecommunications Industry. In *Handbook of Telecommunications Economics: Structure, Regulation and Competition*, edited by M. Cave and S. Majumdar. Amsterdam: Elsevier.

Chakravorti, S. (2003): Theory of Credit Card Networks: A Survey of the Literature. *Review of Network Economics* 2 (2):50-68.

Chan, T. (2001): The End of Technology. *Telecom Asia* 12 (12):38.

Chandler, A. D. (1992): Organizational Capabilities and the Economic History of the Industrial Enterprise. *Journal of Economic Perspectives* 6:79-100.

——— (1997): The Computer Industry: The First Half Century. In *Competing in the Age of Digital Convergence*, edited by D. B. Yoffie. Boston: Harvard Business School Press.

Chandler, A. D./ Hikino, T. and Nordenflycht, A. V. (2001): *Inventing the Electronic Century: The Epic Story of the Consumer Electronics and Computer Science Industries*: The Free Press.

Chandler, A. D., Jr. (1962): *Strategy and Structure: Chapters in the History of the American Industrial Enterprise*. Cambridge, Mass.: MIT Press.

Choi, J. P. (1997): Herd Behavior, the "Penguin Effect", and the Suppression of Informational Diffusion: An Analysis of Informational Externalities and Payoff Interdependency. *RAND Journal of Economics* 28 (3):407-425.

Christensen, C. M. (2000): *The Innovator's Dilemma: When New Technologies Cause Great Firms to Fail*. New York: Harper Business.

——— (2001): The Past and Future of Competitive Advantage. *MIT Sloan Management Review* 42 (2):105-109.

Christensen, C. M./ Raynor, M. and Verlinden, M. (2001): Skate to Where the Money Will Be. *Harvard Business Review* 79:74-81.

Christensen, C. M. and Rosenblum, R. S. (1995): Explaining the Attacker's Advantage: Technological Paradigms, Organizational Dynamics, and the Value Network. *Research Policy* 24:233-257.

Church, J. and Gandal, N. (1992): Network Effects, Software Provision, and Standardization. *The Journal of Industrial Economics* XL (1):85-103.

Coase, R. H. (1937): The Nature of the Firm. *Economica N.S.* 4:386-405.

Cohen, A. (2002a). *Is This Any Place to Run a Business?* [HTML]. Fortune 2002a [cited 16 July, 2003]. Available from http://www.fortune.com/fortune/smallbusiness/managing/articles/0,15114,389897,00.html.

——— (2002b): *The Perfect Store: Inside eBay*. Boston: Little, Brown and Company.

Cohen, W. M. and Levinthal, D. A. (1990): Absorptive Capacity: A New Perspective on Learning and Innovation. *Administrative Science Quarterly* 35 (1):128-145

Collins, J. C. and Porras, J. I. (1994): *Building to Last: Successful Habits of Visionary Companies*. New York: HarperBusiness.

Combs, J. G. and Ketchen, D. J. J. (1999): Explaining Interfirm Cooperation and Performance: Toward a Reconciliation of Predictions from the Resource-based View and Organizational Economics. *Strategic Management Journal* 20 (9):867-888.

CommunicationWeek International (2002): Special Report: The CWI Carrier Survey. 23-25.

Computing Canada (1999): NTT DoCoMo Unveils Java Wireless Phones. *Computing Canada* 25 (28):32.

Conner, K. R. (1991): A Historical Comparison of Resource-Based Theory and Five Schools of Thought Within Industrial Organization Economics: Do We Have a New Theory of the Firm? *Journal of Management* 17 (1):121-154.

Conner, K. R. and Prahalad, C. K. (1996): A Resource-based Theory of the Firm: Knowledge Versus Opportunism. *Organization Science* 7 (5):477-499.

Conner, K. R. and Rumelt, R. (1991): Software Piracy: An Analysis of Protection Strategies. *Management Science* 37:125-139.

Coyne, K. P. and Dye, R. (1998): The Competitive Dynamics of Network-Based Businesses. *Harvard Business Review*:99-109.

Credit Suisse First Boston (2002): GPRS 2002: Show me the money!

Cusumano, M. A. and Gawer, A. (2002): The Elements of Platform Leadership. *MIT Sloan Management Review* 43 (3):51-58.

Das, T. K. and Teng, B.-S. (2000): A Resource-Based Theory of Strategic Alliances. *Journal of Management* 26 (1):31-61.

Datamonitor (2002): i-mode in Europe. London.

David, P. A. (1985): Clio and the Economics of QWERTY. *Economic History* 75 (2):332-337.

Demsetz, H. (1993): The Theory of the Firm Revisited. In *The Nature of the Firm*, edited by O. E. Williamson and S. G. Winter. Oxford: Oxford University Press.

Dietl, H. (1993): *Institutionen und Zeit*. Tübingen: Mohr.

——— (1995): Institutionelle Koordination spezialisierungsbedingter wirtschaftlicher Abhängigkeit. *Zeitschrift für Betriebswirtschaft* 65 (6):569-585.

DiMaggio, P. (1988): Interest and Agency in Institutional Theory. In *Institutional Patterns and Organizations: Culture and Environment*, edited by L. G. Zucker. Cambridge, MA: Ballinger.

Dosi, G. and Nelson, R. R. (1994): An Introduction to Evolutionary Theories in Economics. *Journal of Evolutionary Economics* 4:153-172.

Doz, Y. L. and Hamel, G. (1998): *Alliance Advantage : The Art of Creating Value Through Partnering*. Boston, MA: Harvard Business School Press.

Duysters, G. and Hagendoorn, J. (1995): Strategic Groups and Inter-Firm Networks in International High-Tech Industries. *Journal of Management Studies* 31 (2):359-381.

eBAY INC. (1998): FORM 10-K.

——— (1999): FORM 10-K.

——— (2000): Annual Report.

——— (2002): Annual Report.

——— (2003). *eBay Certified Developer: Preferred Solution Provider* [HTML]. eBay.com 2003 [cited June 24, 2003]. Available from http://pages.ebay.com/psp/index.html.

Economides, N. (1996): The Economics of Networks. *International Journal of Industrial Organization* 14 (6):673-699.

——— (2003): Commentary: The Economics of Networks. In *Managing in the Modular Age: Architectures, Networks, and Organizations*, edited by R. Garud / A. Kumaraswamy and R. N. Langlois. Malden, MA: Blackwell.

Eisenhardt, K. M. (1989): Building Theories from Case Study Research. *Academy of Management Review* 14 (4):532-550.

——— (1991): Better Stories and Better Constructs: The Case for Rigor and Comparative Logic. *Academy of Management Review* 16 (3):620-627.

Eisenhardt, K. M. and Brown, S. L. (1998): Time Pacing: Competing in Markets That Won't Stand Still. *Harvard Business Review* 76 (2):59-69.

Eisenhardt, K. M. and Martin, J. A. (2000): Dynamic Capabilities: What are They? *Strategic Management Journal* 21:1105-1121.

Eisenhardt, K. M. and Schoonhoven, C. B. (1990): Organizational Growth: Linking Founding Team, Strategy, Environment, and Growth Among US Semiconductor Ventures, 1978-1988. *Administrative Science Quarterly* 35:506-539.

Eisenhardt, K. M. and Sull, D. N. (2001): Strategy as Simple Rules. *Harvard Business Review*:107-116.

Evans, D. and Schmalensee, R. (1993): *The Economics of the Payment Card Industry*. Cambridge, MA: National Economic Research Associates.

———— (1999): *Paying with Plastic: The Digital Revolution in Buying and Borrowing*. Cambridge, MA: MIT Press.

Evans, P. and Wurster, T. S. (1999): *Blown to Bits*. Boston: Harvard Business School Press.

Fahy, J. (2000): The Resource-based View of the Firm: Some Stumbling Blocks on the Road to Understand Sustainable Competitive Advantage. *Journal of European Industrial Training* 11 (1):94-104.

Farrell, J. and Saloner, G. (1985): Standardization, Compatibility, and Innovation. *Rand Journal of Economics* 16 (1):70-83.

Ferguson, C. H. and Morris, C. R. (1994): *Computer Wars: The Fall of IBM and the Future of Global Technology*. New York, NY: Times Books.

Finkelstein, S. (1997): Interindustry Merger Patterns and Resource Dependence: A Replication and Extension of Pfeffer (1972). *Strategic Management Journal* 18:787-810.

Fligstein, N. (1999): Social Skill and the Theory of Fields. In *Department of Sociology, University Berkeley*. Berkeley, CA.

Foong, K. (2002): NTT DoCoMo: i-mode Wireless Internet Services: Gartner Research.

Foong, K. and Mitsuyama, N. (2001): Learning from the Success of NTT DoCoMo's i-mode: Gartner Research.

Frank, R. and Cook, P. (1995): *The Winner-Take-All Society: Why the Few at the Top Get So Much More Than the Rest of Us*. New York: The Free Press.

Fransmann, M. (2002): Mapping the Evolving Telecoms Industry: The Uses and Shortcomings of the Layer Model. *Telecommunications Policy* 26:473-483.

Franz, A. (2002): Das Management von Business Webs. In *Projektstudie im Rahmen des postgradualen Forschungsstudiums, Ludwig-Maximilians-Universität München*. München.

———— (2003): *Management von Business Webs: Das Beispiel Technologieplattformen für mobile Dienste*. Wiesbaden: DUV.

Frengle, N. (2002): *I-mode: A Primer*. New York: M&T Books.

Funk, J. L. (1999): Standards, Information, and Complementary Assets: How NTT DoCoMo and its Suppliers Dominate the Japanese Digital Mobile Phone Market. Kobe University, Graduate School of Business, Japan.

———— (2001a): *The Mobile Internet: How Japan Dialed Up and the West Disconnected*. Pembroke, Bermuda: ISI Publications.

———— (2001b): Network Effects, Openness, Gateway Technologies and the Expansion of a Standard's "Application Depth" and "Geographical Breadth": The Case of the Mobile Internet. Kobe University, Japan.

———— (2002): Technological Trajectories and the Origins of New Industries: The Case of Network Products. Kobe University, Japan.

Funk, J. L. and Methe, D. T. (2001): Market- and Committee-Based Mechanisms in the Creation and Diffusion of Global Industry Standards: The Case of Mobile Communication. *Research Policy* 30:589-610.

Gadiesh, O. and Gilbert, J. L. (1998): How to Map Your Industry's Profit Pool. *Harvard Business Review* 76 (3):149-162.

Galbraith, J. R. (2002): Organizing to Deliver Solutions. *Organizational Dynamics* 31 (2):194-207.

Galunic, C. D. and Eisenhardt, K. M. (2001): Architectural Innovation and Modular Corporate Forms. *Academy of Management Journal* 44 (6):1229-1250.

Garfinkel, M. R. (2001): Alliance Formation in Distributional Conflict. In *University of California-Irvine, Department of Economics*. Irvine.

Garud, R. and Jain, S. (1996): The Embeddedness of Technological Systems. In *Advances in Strategic Management*, edited by J. A. C. Baum and J. Dutton. Greenwich, CT: Jai Press.

Garud, R./ Jain, S. and Kumaraswamy, A. (2002): Institutional Entrepreneurship in the Sponsorship of Common Technological Standards: The Case of Sun Microsystems and Java. *Academy of Management Journal* 45 (1):196-214.

Garud, R. and Kumaraswamy, A. (1993): Changing Competitive Dynamics in Network Industries: An Exploration of Sun Microsystems' Open Systems Strategy. *Strategic Management Journal* 14:351-396.

———— (2003): Technological and Organizational Designs for Realizing Economies of Substitution. In *Managing in the Modular Age: Architectures, Networks, and Organizations*, edited by R. Garud / A. Kumaraswamy and R. N. Langlois. Malden, MA: Blackwell.

Garud, R./ Kumaraswamy, A. and Langlois, R. N. (2003a): Introduction: Managing in the Modular Age: Architectures, Networks, and Organizations. In *Managing in the Modular Age: Architectures, Networks, and Organizations*, edited by R. Garud / A. Kumaraswamy and R. N. Langlois. Malden, MA: Blackwell.

———— (2003b): *Managing in the Modular Age: Architectures, Networks, and Organizations*. Oxford: Blackwell.

Gawer, A. (2000): The Organization of Platform Leadership: An Empirical Investigation of Intel's Management Processes Aimed at Fostering Complementary Innovation by Third Party. In *unpublished Ph.D Thesis*. MIT Alfred P. Sloan School of Management.

Gawer, A. and Cusumano, M. A. (2002): *Platform Leadership: How Intel, Microsoft, And Cisco Drive Industry Innovation*. Boston, MA: Harvard Business School Press.

Ghiladi, V. (2003): The Importance of International Standards for Globally Operating Businesses. *International Journal of IT Standards & Standardization Research* 1 (1):54-56.

Ghosh, S. (1998): Making Business Sense of the Internet. *Harvard Business Review* 76:127-135.

Gibb Dyer Jr., W. and Wilkins, A. L. (1991): Better Stories, Not Better Constructs, To Generate Better Theory: A Rejoinder To Eisenhardt. *Academy of Management Review* 16 (3):613-619.

Glaser, B. and Strauss, A. (1967): *The Discovery of Grounded Theory: Strategies for Qualitative Research*. Chicago: Aldine Publishing Company

Gnyawali, D. R. and Madhavan, R. (2001): Cooperative Networks and Competitive Dynamics: A Structural Embeddedness Perspective. *Academy of Management Review* 26 (3):431-445.

Gomez-Casseres, B. (1994): Group Versus Group: How Alliance Networks Compete. *Harvard Business Review* 72:62-74.

———— (1995): *International Alliances in High Technology*. Boston: Harvard Business School Press.

———— (2001). *eBay: A Concise Analysis* [HTML]. Brandeis University 2001 [cited 07.03.2003].

Göpfert, J. (1998): *Modularisierung in der Produktentwicklung. Ein Ansatz zur gemeinsamen Gestaltung von Technik und Organisation*. Wiesbaden: Gabler.

Gosling, J. (2003). *A Brief History of the Green Project* [HTML]. Sun Microsystems 2003 [cited July 2, 2003].

Grindley, P. (1995): *Standards, Strategy, and Policy. Cases and Stories*. Oxford: Oxford University Press.

Größler, A./ Thun, J.-H. and Milling, P. M. (2001): The Diffusion of Goods Considering Network Externalities: A System Dynamics-Based Approach. Mannheim.

Grove, A. S. (1996): *Only The Paranoid Survive: How to Exploit the Crisis Points That Challenge Every Company And Career*. New York: Doubleday.

Gulati, R./ Nohria, N. and Zaheer, A. (2000): Strategic Networks. *Strategic Management Journal* 21:203-215.

Gulati, R. and Singh, H. (1998): The Architecture of Cooperation: Managing Coordination Costs and Appropriation Concerns in Strategic Alliances. *Administrative Science Quarterly* 43:781-814.

Gustafsson, B. (1990): Foreword. In *The Firm as a Nexus of Treaties*, edited by M. Aoki / B. Gustafsson and O. E. Williamson. London: Sage.

Häcki, R. and Lighton, J. (2001): The Future of the Networked Company. *The McKinsey Quarterly* (3):26-39.

Hagel III, J. (1996): Spider Versus Spider. *The McKinsey Quarterly* (1):4-19.

Hagel III, J. and Singer, M. (2000): Unbundling the Corporation. *The McKinsey Quarterly* (3):148-161.

Hamel, G./ Doz, Y. L. and Prahalad, C. K. (1989): Collaborate with Your Competitors - and Win. *Harvard Business Review* 67 (1):133-139.

Hamel, G. and Prahalad, C. K. (1991): Corporate Imagination and Expeditionary Marketing. *Harvard Business Review* 69 (4):81-92.

Hamel, J. (1993): *Case Study Method*. Beverly Hills, CA: Sage Publications.

Hart, J. A. and Kim, S. (2000): Power in the Information Age. In *Of Fears and Foes: Security and Insecurity in an Evolving Global Political Economy*, edited by J. V. Ciprut. Westport, CT: Praeger.

———— (2002): Explaining the Resurgence of U.S. Competitiveness: The Rise of Wintelism. *The Information Society* 18:1-12.

Hartman, M./ Ragnevad, J. and Linden, J. (2000): Lessons from i-mode. Colchester: Baskerville Communications.

Hass, B. H. (2002): *Geschäftsmodelle von Medienunternehmen: Ökonomische Grundlagen und Veränderungen durch neue Informations- und Kommunikationstechnik*. Wiesbaden: DUV.

Haucap, J. (2003): Endogenous Switching Costs and Exclusive System Applications. *Review of Network Economics* 2 (1):29-35.

Hedlund, G. (1993): Assumptions of Hierarchy and Heterarchy, with Applications to the Management of the Multinational Corporation. In *Organisation Theory and the Multi-*

national Corporation, edited by S. Ghoshal and E. D. Westney. New York: St. Martin's Press.

Heise News (2002). *HypoVereinsbank/Vodafone-Tochter memIQ stellt Insolvenzantrag.* Heise 2002 [cited 09.02.2003]. Available from http://www.heise.de/newsticker/data/ anw-26.08.02-003/.

────── (2003). *Paybox stellt Endkunden-Geschäft in Deutschland ein* 2003 [cited 09.02.2003]. Available from http://www.heise.de/newsticker/data/uma-23.01.03-000/.

Henderson, R. M. and Clark, K. B. (1990): Architectural Innovation: The Reconfiguration of Existing Product Technologies and the Failure of Established Firms. *Administrative Science Quarterly* 35:9-30.

Hess, T. (2000): Netzeffekte: Verändern neue Informations- und Kommunikationstechnolgien das klassische Marktmodell? *Wirtschaftswissenschaftliches Studium (WiSt)* (2):96-98.

────── (2002): *Netzwerkcontrolling: Instrumente und ihre Werkzeugunterstützung.* Wiesbaden: Gabler.

Hill, C. W. (1997): Establishing a Standard: Competitive Strategy and Technological Standards in Winner-Take-All Industries. *Academy of Management Executive* 11 (2):7-25.

Himelstein, L. (1999). *Q&A with eBay's Meg Whitman* [HTML]. BusinessWeek online 1999 [cited 11.03.2003]. Available from http://www.businessweek.com/1999/99_22 /b3631001.htm.

Hite, J. M. and Hesterly, W. S. (2001): The Evolution of Firm Networks: From Emergence to Early Growth of the Firm. *Strategic Management Journal* 22 (3):275-286.

Hitt, M. A./ Keats, B. W. and DeMarie, S. M. (1998): Navigating in the new Competitive Landscape: Building Strategic Flexibility and Competitive Advantage in the 21st Century. *Academy of Management Executive* 12:22-42.

Hodgson, G. M. (1998): Competence and Contract in the Theory of the Firm. *Journal of Economic Behavior & Organization* 35 (2):179-201.

Hof, R. D. and Himelstein, L. (1999). *eBay vs. Amazon.com* [HTML]. BusinessWeek online 1999 [cited 11.03.2003]. Available from http://www.businessweek.com/1999/ 99_22/b3631001.htm.

Hofacker, I. (2000): Unternehmensnetzwerke zur Durchsetzung eines Standards. *Zeitschrift für betriebswirtschaftliche Forschung* 52 (7):643-661.

Höfer, S. (1997): *Analyse des Bildungsprozesses strategischer Allianzen und planungsunterstützender Einsatzmöglichkeiten der Theorie der strategischen Spiele.* Köln: Eul.

Holmström, B. and Milgrom, P. (1994): The Firm as an Incentive System. *American Economic Review* 84 (4):972-991.

Holmström, B. and Roberts, J. (1998): The Boundaries of the Firm Revisited. *Journal of Economic Perspectives* 12 (4):73-94.

Holmström, B. R. and Tirole, J. (1989): The Theory of the Firm. In *Handbook of Industrial Organization*, edited by R. Schmalensee and R. D. Willig. Amsterdam: Elsevier.

Hoovers Inc. (2001a): Hoover's Company Profile eBay Inc. Austin, Texas.

────── (2001b): Hoover's Company Profile Intel Corporation. Austin, Texas.

────── (2001c): Hoover's Company Profile SunMicrosystem, Inc. Austin, Texas.

Hunt, R. M. (2003): An Introduction to the Economics of Payment Card Networks. *Review of Network Economics* 2 (2):80-96.

Ireland, R. D./ Hitt, M. A. and Vaidyanath, D. (2002): Alliance Management as a Source of Competitive Advantage. *Journal of Management* 28 (3):413-446.

Jarillo, J. C. (1988): On Strategic Networks. *Strategic Management Journal.*

———— (1995): *Strategic Networks: Creating the Borderless Organization*. Oxford: Butterworth Heinemann.

Johnson, G. (2001): Early Wireless Web Services: Gartner.

Jones, C./ Hesterly, W. S. and Borgatti, S. P. (1997): A General Theory of Network Governance: Exchange Conditions and Social Mechanism. *Academy of Management Review* 22:911-945.

Katz, M. L. and Shapiro, C. (1985): Network Externalities, Competition, and Compatibility. *American Economic Review* 75 (3):424-440.

———— (1986): Technology Adoption in the Presence of Network Externalities. *The Journal of Political Economy* 94 (4):822-841.

———— (1992): Product Introduction with Network Externalities. *Journal of Industrial Economics* 40:55-83.

———— (1994): Systems Competition and Network Effects. *The Journal of Economic Perspectives* 8 (2):93-115.

Keil, T. (2002): De-facto Standardization through Alliances: Lessons from Bluetooth. *Telecommunications Policy* 26 (3-4):205-213.

Keil, T. and Autio, E. (1997): Embeddedness, Power, Control and Innovation in the Telecommunications Sector. *Technology Analysis & Strategic Management* 9 (3):299-317.

Kelly, K. (1998): *New Rules for the New Economy: 10 Radical Strategies for a Connected World*. New York: Viking Pinguin.

Kim, S. and Hart, J. A. (2001): The Global Political Economy of Wintelism: A New Mode of Power and Governance in the Global Computer Industry. In *Information Technologies and Global Politics: The Changing Scope of Power and Governance*, edited by J. N. Rosenau and J. P. Singh. Albany, NY: Suny Press.

Kirzner, I. M. (1982): The Theory of Entrepreneurship in Economic Growth. In *Encyclopedia of Entrepreneurship*, edited by C. A. Kent / D. L. Sexton and K. H. Vesper. New Jersey: Prentice-Hall

———— (1985): *Discovery and the Capitalist Process*. Chicago: University of Chicago Press

Kleiner, A. (2002): Professor Chandler's Revolution. *strategy + business*:1-8.

Kraemer, K. L. and Dedrick, J. (2002): Strategic Use of the Internet and E-Commerce: Cisco Systems. *Journal of Strategic Information Systems* 11:5-29.

Krogh, G. v. and Cusumano, M. A. (2001): Three Strategies for Managing Fast Growth. *MIT Sloan Management Review* 42 (2):53-61.

Krugman, P. (1987): Strategic Sectors and International Competition. In *U.S. Trade Policies in a Changing World Economy*, edited by R. M. Stern. Cambridge, MA: MIT Press.

Kuchinskas, S. (2000). *Mad for i-mode: In Japan, at Least, Wireless Rules* [HTML]. Business 2.0 2000 [cited 28.01.2003]. Available from http://business2.com/articles/mag/print/0,1643,14005,00.html.

Langlois, R. N. (1986): Rationality, Institutions, and Explanations. In *Economics as a Process: Essays in New Institutional Economics*, edited by R. N. Langlois. New York: Cambridge University Press.

———— (1992a): External Economics and Economic Progress: The Case of the Microcomputer Industry. *Business History Review* 66:1-50.

———— (1992b): Transaction-Cost Economics in Real Time. *Industrial & Corporate Change* 1 (1):99-127.

——— (2001a): Knowledge, Consumption, and Endogenous Growth. *Journal of Evolutionary Economics* 11 (1):77-93.

——— (2001b): The Vanishing Hand: The Changing Dynamics of Industrial Capitalism. Paper presented at INSI 2001 Conference, at Berkeley.

——— (2002): Modularity in Technology and Organization. *Journal of Economic Behavior & Organization* 49:19-37.

Langlois, R. N. and Robertson, P. L. (1992a): Networks and Innovation in a Modular System: Lessons from the Microcomputer and Stereo Component Industries. *Research Policy* 21 (4):297-313.

——— (1992b): Networks and Innovation in a Modular System: Lessons from the Microcomputer and Stereo Component Industries. *Research Policy* 21 (4):297-313.

——— (2003): Commentary: Networks and Innovation in a Modular System: Lessons from the Microcomputer and Stereo Component Industry. In *Managing in the Modular Age: Architectures, Networks, and Organizations*, edited by R. Garud / A. Kumaraswamy and R. N. Langlois. Malden, MA: Blackwell.

Lawrence, T. B./ Hardy, C. and Phillips, N. (2002): Institutional Effects of Interorganizational Collaboration: The Emergence of Proto-Institutions. *Academy of Management Journal* 45 (1):281-290.

Lee, C./ Lee, K. and Pennings, J. M. (2001): Internal Capabilities, External Networks, and Performance: A Study On Technology-based Ventures. *Strategic Management Journal* 22:615-640.

Leonard-Barton, D. (1995): A Dual Methodology for Case Studies: Synergetic Use of a Longitudinal Single Site with Replicated Multiple Sites. In *Longitudinal Field Research Methods: Studying Process of Organizational Change*, edited by G. P. Huber and A. H. Van De Ven. Thousand Oaks: SAGE.

Li, F. and Whalley, J. (2002): Deconstruction of the Telecommunications Industry: From Value Chains to Value Networks. *Telecommunications Policy* 26:451-472.

Limerick, D. and Cunnington, B. (1993): *Managing the New Organization. A Blueprint for Networks and Strategic Alliances*. San Francisco: Jossey-Bass.

Lockett, A. and Thompson, S. (2001): The Resource-Based View and Economics. *Journal of Management* 27 (6):723-754.

Lopatka, J. E. and Page, W. H. (1995): Microsoft, Monopolization, and Network Externalities: Some Uses and Abuses of Economic Theory in Antitrust Decision Making. *Antitrust Bulletin* 40 (2):317-70.

Lovas, B. and Sumatra, G. (2000): Strategy as Guided Evolution. *Strategic Management Journal* 21:875-896.

Margherio, L./ Henry, D./ Cooke, S. and Montes, S. (1998): *The Emerging Digital Economy*. Washington, D.C.: U.S. Department of Commerce.

Marshak, D. S. (2003): eBay Creates Technology Architecture for the Future. Boston: Patricia Seybold Group.

Marx, K. (1867): *Das Kapital - Erster Band*. 4th ed. Frankfurt a. M.: Verlag Marxistische Blätter, 1972.

Mathews, J. A. (1994): The Governance of Inter-Organizational Networks. *Corporate Governance* 1:14-19.

——— (2001): Competitive Interfirm Dynamics within an Industrial Market System. *Industry and Innovation* 8 (1):79-107.

Miller, D. and Garnsey, E. (2000): Entrepreneurs and Technology Diffusion: How Diffusion Research Can Benefit From a Greater Understanding Of Entrepreneurship. *Technology in Society* 22:445-456.

Mintzberg, H. and Lampel, J. (1999): Reflecting on the Strategy Process. *Sloan Management Review*:21-30.

Mitsumori, Y. (2000). *Mobile Carriers Go Java.* J@pan Inc 2000 [cited 28.01.2003].

Molony, D. (2002): NTT Feels on Top of the World. *CommunicationsWeek International*, 7 October 2002, 1.

Moore, G. A. (1995): *Inside the Tornado: Marketing Strategies from Silicon Valley's Cutting Edge.* New York: HarperCollins.

Moore, G. A./ Johnston, P. and Kippola, T. (1999): *The Gorilla Game: Picking Winners in High Technology.* Rev. Ed. ed. New York: HarperCollins.

Moore, J. F. (1993): Predators and Prey: A New Ecology of Competition. *Harvard Business Review* 71 (3):75-86.

——— (1997): *The Death of Competition: Leadership and Strategy in the Age of Business Ecosystems*: HarperCollins Publishers.

Morris, C. R. and Ferguson, C. H. (1993): How Architecture Wins Technology Wars. *Harvard Business Review.*

Moss, F. (2000): Beyond B2B: Why Business Webs and Web Services Will Drive an E-Business Renaissance: Bowstreet.com.

Munir, K. A. (2003): Competitive Dynamics in Face of Technological Discontinuity: A Framework for Action. *The Journal of High Technology Management Research* 14 (1):93-109.

Murtha, T. P./ Lenway, S. A. and Hart, J. A. (2001): *Managing New Industry Creation: Global Knowledge Formation and Entrepreneurship in High Technology*: Stanford University Press.

Natsuno, T. (2003): *i-mode Strategy.* Chichester: Wiley.

Negroponte, N. (1995): *Being Digital.* New York: Knopf.

Nelson, R. R. (1991): Why Firms Differ, and How Does it Matter? *Strategic Management Journal* 12:61-74.

Nelson, R. R. and Winter, S. G. (1982): *An Evolutionary Theory of Economic Change.* Cambridge: Belknap.

Normann, R. and Ramírez, R. (1993): From the Value Chain to the Value Constellation: Designing Interactive Strategy. *Harvard Business Review* 71:65-77.

North, D. C. (1991): *Institutions, Institutional Change and Economic Performance.* Cambridge: Cambridge University Press.

NTT DoCoMo (2003a). *Application for New Information Providers.* NTT DoCoMo 2003a [cited 12.04.2003]. Available from http://www.nttdocomo.co.jp/english/p_s/i/tag/newip.html.

——— (2003b). *Corporate Data* [HTML]. NTT DoCoMo 2003b [cited 07.04.2003]. Available from http://www.nttdocomo.com/investor_relations/corporate_data.html?sendto=revenue.

Orton, J. D. and Weick, K. E. (1999): Loosely Coupled Systems: A Reconceptualization. *Academy of Management Review* 15:203-223.

Park, C. (1998): Value Appropriation in an Interconnected World. In *Managing Strategically in an Interconnected World*, edited by M. A. Hitt / J. E. Ricart i Costa and R. D. Nixon. Chichester: Wiley.

Park, S. H. (1996): Managing an Interorganizational Network: Framework of the Institutional Mechanism for Network Control. *Organization Studies* 17 (5):795-824.

Parolini, C. (1996): The Value Net: A Methodology for the Analysis of Value Creating Systems. Paper presented at Strategic Management Conference 1996.

────── (1999): *The Value Net: A Tool for Competitive Strategy.* Chichester: Wiley.

Patsuris, P. (1998). *Bidding Frenzy* [HTML]. Forbes.com 1998 [cited 10.03.2003]. Available from http://www.forbes.com/1998/09/23/flash.html.

PCTECH Guide (2003). *Origin, History, and Evolution of PDAs* [HTML]. PCTECH Guide 2003 [cited July 2, 2003]. Available from http://www.pctechguide.com/25mob3.htm.

Peak, M. H. (1996): Turning Entrepreneurial Ideas Inside Out. *Management Review* 85 (2):7-10.

Pearce, R. (1999): The Evolution of Technology in Multinational Enterprises: The Role of Creative Subsidiaries. *International Business Review* 8 (2):125-148.

Penrose, E. (1959): *The Theory of the Growth of the Firm.* 2nd ed. Oxford: Oxford University Press.

Pescatore, P. (2001): i-mode Phenomen: Lessons from Europe: IDC.

Pfeffer, J. and Salancik, G. R. (1978): *The External Control of Organizations: A Resource Dependence Perspective.* New York: Harper & Row.

Pfiffner, P. (2003): *Inside the Publishing Revolution: The Adobe Story.* Berkeley, CA: Peachpit Press.

Picot, A. (1982): Transaktionskostenansatz in der Organisationstheorie: Stand der Diskussion und Aussagewert. *Die Betriebswirtschaft* 42 (2):267-284.

────── (1991): Ein neuer Ansatz zur Gestaltung der Leistungstiefe. *Zeitschrift für betriebswirtschaftliche Forschung* 43 (4):336-357.

────── (1993): Contingencies for the Emergence of Efficient Symbiotic Arrangements. *Journal of Institutional and Theoretical Economics* 149 (4):731-740.

────── (1999): Management in Networked Environments: New Challenges. *Management International Review* 39 (3):19-26.

────── (2003): Telekommunikation und Kapitalmarkt: Eine Einführung. In *Telekommunikation und Kapitalmarkt*, edited by A. Picot and S. Doeblin. Wiesbaden: Gabler.

Picot, A./ Dietl, H. and Franck, E. (2002): *Organisation: Eine ökonomische Perspektive.* 3 ed. Stuttgart: Schäffer Poeschel.

Picot, A./ Laub, U. and Schneider, D. (1990): Comparing Successful and Less Successful New Innovative Businesses. *European Journal of Operational Research* 47:190-202.

Picot, A. and Reichwald, R. (1994): Auflösung der Unternehmung? Vom Einfluß der IuK-Technik auf Organisationsstrukturen. *Zeitschrift für Betriebswirtschaft* 64 (5):547-570.

Picot, A./ Ripperger, T. and Wolff, B. (1996): The Fading Boundaries of the Firm: The Role of Information and Communication Technology. *Journal of Institutional and Theoretical Economics* 152 (1):65-79.

Picot, A. and Scheuble, S. (2000): Hybride Wettbewerbsstrategien in der Informations- und Netzökonomie. In *Praxis des strategischen Managements*, edited by M. K. Welge / A. Al-Laham and P. Kajüter. Wiesbaden: Gabler.

Piller, F. T. (2000): *Mass Customization ein wettbewerbsstrategisches Konzept im Informationszeitalter.* Wiesbaden: Deutscher Universitäts-Verlag.

Pine, J. B. (1993): *Mass Customization the New Frontier in Business Competition.* Edited by S. M. Davis. Boston, MA: Harvard Business School.

Porter, M. E. (1985): *Competitive Advantage.* New York: Free Press.

────── (1998): *Competitive Strategy.* New York: Free Press.

Powell, W. W. (1987): Hybrid Organizational Arrangements: New Form or Transitional Development? *California Management Review* 30 (1):67-87.

────── (1990): Neither Market Nor Hierarchy: Networks Forms of Organization. In *Research in Organizational Behavior*, edited by B. v. Staw and L. Cummings. Greenwich: Jai Press.

Prahalad, C. K. and Hamel, G. (1990): The Core Competence of the Corporation. *Harvard Business Review* 68 (3):79-91.

Quélin, B. (1997): Approbiability and the Creation of New Capabilities Through Strategic Alliances. In *Strategic Learning and Knowledge Management*, edited by R. Sanchez and A. Heene. Chichester: John Wiley & Sons.

Ratliff, J. (2000): DoCoMo as National Champion: I-Mode, W-CDMA, and NTT'S Role as Japan's Pilot Organization in Global Telecommunications. Department of Sociology, Santa Clara University.

Ratliff, J. M. (2002): NTT DoCoMo and Its i-mode Success: Origins and Implications. *California Management Review* 44 (3):55-71.

Rayport, F. R. and Sviokla, J. J. (1996): Exploiting the Virtual Value Chain. *The McKinsey Quarterly* (1):21-36.

Reichheld, F. F. (1996): *The Loyality Effect: The Hidden Force Behind Growth, Profits, and Lasting Value*. Boston: Harvard Business School Press.

Robertson, P. L. and Langlois, R. N. (1995): Innovation, Networks, and Vertical Integration. *Research Policy* 24:543-562.

Rose, P. (2001). *Pocket Monster*. Wired 2001 [cited 20.02.2003]. Available from http://www.wired.com/wired/archive/9.09/docomo.html.

Rühli, E. (1995): Ressourcenmanagement. *Die Unternehmung* 49 (2):91-105.

Sanchez, R. and Mahoney, J. T. (1996): Modularity, Flexibility, and Knowledge Management in Product and Organizational Design. *Strategic Management Journal* 17 ((winter special issue)):63-76.

Scheuble, S. (1998): *Wissen und Wissenssurrogate: Eine Theorie der Unternehmung*. Wiesbaden: Gabler.

Schilling, M. (2000): Towards a General Modular Systems Theory and Its Application to Inter-Firm Product Modularity. *Academy of Management Review* 25:312-334.

────── (2002): Technology Success and Failure in Winner-Take-All Markets: The Impact of Learning Orientation, Timing, and Network Externalities. *Academy of Management Journal* 45 (2):387-398.

────── (2003): Commentary: Towards a General Modular Systems Theory and Its Application to Inter-Firm Product Modularity. In *Managing in the Modular Age: Architectures, Networks, and Organizations*, edited by R. Garud / A. Kumaraswamy and R. N. Langlois. Malden, MA: Blackwell.

Schilling, M. A. and Steensma, K. H. (2001): The Use of Modular Organizational Forms: An Industry-Level Analysis. *Academy of Management Journal* 44 (6):1149-1168.

Schneider, D. (2001): Der Unternehmer - eine Leerstelle in der Theorie der Unternehmung? *Zeitschrift für Betriebswirtschaft* (4).

Schumpeter, J. A. (1993a): *Kapitalismus, Sozialismus und Demokratie*. Tübingen: Francke.

────── (1993b): *Theorie der wirtschaftlichen Entwicklung: Eine Untersuchung über Unternehmergewinn, Kapital, Kredit, Zins und den Konjunkturzyklus*. 8. ed. Berlin: Duncker u. Humblot.

Schwartz, E. I. (1997): *Webonomics : Nine Essential Principles for Growing your Business on the World Wide Web*. 1st ed. New York: Broadway Books.

Selz, D. (1999): *Value Webs: Emerging Forms of Fluid and Flexible Organizations, MCM.* Bamberg: University of St. Gallen.

Sexton, D. and Landstrom, H., eds. (1999): *The Blackwell Handbook of Entrepreneurship, Blackwell Handbooks in Management.* Oxford: Blackwell.

Shan, W. (1990): An Empirical Analysis of Organizational Strategies by Entrepreneurial High-Technology Firms. *Strategic Management Journal* 11 (2):129-139.

Shankland, S. (1999). *Sun Tries New Sales Channel: eBay* [HTML]. CNET News.com 1999 [cited 16 July, 2003]. Available from http://news.com.com/2100-1017-234549.html?tag=rn.

———— (2002). *Sun Looks for Payoff to Java Addiction.* ZDNet 2002 [cited July 16, 2003]. Available from http://news.com.com/2009-1001-866365.html.

Shapiro, C. (2000): Setting Compatibility Standards: Cooperation or Collusion? In *Prepared for presentation at "Intellectual Products: Novel Claims to Protections and Their Boundaries," Conference of the Engelberg Center on Innovation Law and Policy, La Pietra, Italy, June 25-28, 1998.*

Shapiro, C. and Varian, H. R. (1999): *Information Rules: A Strategic Guide to the Network Economy.* Boston, MA: Harvard Business School Press.

Shy, O. (1996): Technology Revolutions in the Presence of Network Externalities. *International Journal of Industrial Organization* 14 (6):785-800.

Simon, H. (1955): A Behavorial Model of Choice. *Quarterly Journal of Economics* 69:99-118.

Simon, H. A. (1962): The Architecture of Complexity. *Proceedings of the American Philosophical Society* 106 (6):467-482.

Smith, A. (1776): *An Inquiry into the Nature and the Causes of the Wealth of Nations.* Modern Library ed. New York: Random House, 1937.

Snow, C. C./ Miles, R. E. and Coleman, H. J. J. (1992): Managing 21st Century Network Organizations. *Organizational Dynamics* Winter:5-20.

Song, S.-H. (2000): Changes in the Value Chain for the Third-Generation Era: Gartner Group.

Stabell, C. B. and Øystein, F. D. (1998): Configuring Value For Competitive Advantage: On Chains, Shops, And Networks. *Strategic Management Journal* 19:413-437.

Stanford Technology Ventures Program (STVP) (2001): The Handheld Computing Industry: Stanford University.

Steiner, F. (2002): M-Business: Chancenpotenziale eines Mobilfunkbetreibers. In *Mobile Kommunikation: Wertschöpfung, Technologien, neue Dienste,* edited by R. Reichwald. Wiesbaden: Gabler.

Suchman, M. C. (1995): Managing Legitimacy: Strategic and Institutional Approaches. *Academy of Management Review* 20 (3):571-610.

Sydow, J. (1991): On the Management of Strategic Networks: Freie Universität Berlin.

———— (1992): *Strategische Netzwerke: Evolution und Organisation.* Wiesbaden: Gabler.

Takezaki, N. (1999): Killer App for Mobile Comms? *Computing Japan* 6 (9):50-51.

Tapscott, D. (2001): Rethinking Strategy in a Networked World (or Why Michael Porter is Wrong about the Internet). *strategy + business* 24:34-40.

Tapscott, D./ Lowy, A. and Ticoll, D. (2000): *Digital Capital: Harnessing the Power of Business Webs.* Boston, Mass.: Harvard Business School Press.

Teece, D. J. (1982): Towards an Economic Theory of the Multiproduct Firm. *Journal of Economic Behavior and Organization* 3:39-62.

——— (1986): Profiting from Technological Innovation: Implications for Integration, Collaboration, Licensing and Public Policy. *Research Policy* 15:285-305.

——— (1992): Competition, Cooperation, and Innovation: Organizational Arrangements for Regimes of Rapid Technological Progress. *Journal of Economic Behavior & Organization* 18:1-25.

——— (1998): Design Issues for Innovative Firms: Bureaucracy, Incentives and Industrial Structure. In *The Dynamic Firm*, edited by A. D. Chandler / P. Hagström and Ö. Sölvell. Oxford: Oxford University Press.

Teece, D. J./ Pisano, G. and Shuen, A. (1997): Dynamic Capabilities And Strategic Management. *Strategic Management Journal* 18 (7):509-533.

Tewary, A. (2003). *It's Hard to Beat "Network Effects"* [HTML]. BusinessWeek online 2003 [cited 11.03.2003]. Available from http://www.businessweek.com:/print/investor/content/feb2003/pi20030228_4861_pi044.htm?tc.

Thomke, S. and Hippel, E. v. (2002): Customers as Innovators: A New Way to Create Value. *Harvard Business Review* 80:78-81.

Timmers, P. (1998): Business Models for Electronic Markets. *Electronic Markets* 8 (2):3-8.

Tripsas, M. (2000a): Adobe Systems Incorporated. Boston, MA: Harvard Business School.

——— (2000b): Commercializing Emerging Technologies through Complementary Assets. In *Wharton on Managing Emerging Technologies*, edited by G. S. Day / P. J. H. Schoemaker and R. E. Gunther. New York: Wiley.

——— (2002): Adobe Systems Incorporated. In *Internet Business Models: Text and Cases*, edited by T. R. Eisenmann / H. Roger and M. Tripsas. Boston: McGraw-Hill.

Tsang, E. W. K. (1998): Motives for Strategic Alliance: A Resource-based Perspective. *Scandinavian Journal of Management* 14 (3):207-221.

Turowski, K. and Pousttchi, K. (2002): Komponentbasierte betriebliche Aussagesysteme. *das wirtschaftsstudium* 31 (8-9):1110-1117.

Tushman, M. L. and Anderson, D. (1986): Technological Discontinuities. *Administrative Science Quarterly*:439-465.

Tushman, M. L. and Rosenkopf, L. (1992): Organizational Determinants of Technological Change: Toward a Sociology of Technological Evolution. In *Research in Organizational Behavior*, edited by B. Staw and L. Cummings. Greenwich, CT: JAI Press.

Updegrove, A. (1993): Forming, Funding and Operating Standard-Setting Consortia. *IEEE Micro* 13 (6):52-61.

Utterback, J. M. (1974): Innovation in Industry and the Diffusion of Technology. *Science* 183:620-626.

Uzzi, B. (1996): The Sources and Consequences of Embeddedness for the Economic Performance of organizations: The Network Effect. *American Sociological Review* 61:674-698.

van Aken, J. E./ Louweris, H. and Post, G. J. J. (1998): The Virtual Organization: A Special Mode of Strong Interorganizational Cooperation. In *Managing Strategically in an Interconnected World*, edited by M. A. Hitt / J. E. R. i. Costa and R. D. Nixon. Chichester: Wiley.

Vanhaverbeke, W. and Noorderhaven, N. G. (2001): Competition between Alliance Blocks: The Case of the RISC Microprocessor Technology. *Organization Studies* 22 (1).

Varian, H. R. (1996): *Intermediate Microeconomics*. 4. ed. New York: Norton.

von Hippel, E. (1989): New Product Ideas From "Lead Users". *Research Technology Management* 32 (3):24- 27.

————— (1996): "Do it yourself" Versus Specialization: Customization of Products and Services by Users of ASICs and CTI.

Waldrop, M. M. (2001): Claude Shannon: Reluctant Father of the Digital Age. *Technology Review* 104 (6):64-71.

Wall Street Journal (2003). *Annual Earnings for NTT DoCoMo Inc.* [HTML]. Wall Street Journal 2003 [cited 08.04.2003]. Available from http://online.wsj.com /tafkam/ auth/mds/mds.cgi?route=BOEH&template=company-research-print&profile-name= Portfolio1&profile-version=3.0&profile-type=Portfolio&profile-format-action=include &profile-read-action=skip-read&profile-write-action=skip-write&p-sym=dcm&p-type =usstock&p-name=&section=annual-earnings&bb-fov-start-period=5&bb-fov-end-period=1&profile-end=Portfolio.

Waltenspiel, A. (2000): Management von Business Webs: Eine dynamische Betrachtung anhand von Shapern in Technology Webs. In *unpublished Master Thesis at the Institute for Information, Organisation and Management, Munich School of Business, Ludwig-Maximilians-University.* Munich.

Weber, B. (2001): A Flexible Data Set for the Analysis of Joint Product, Acquisition, and Alliance Decisions: The Internet Software Market. In *Department of Economics, University of Pennsylvania.* Philadelphia.

Weiber, R. (1992): *Diffusion in der Telekommunikation.* Wiesbaden: Gabler.

Weick, K. E. (1976): Educational Organizations as Loosely Coupled Systems. *Administrative Science Quarterly* 21:1-19.

Wernerfelt, B. (1984): A Resource-based View of the Firm. *Strategic Management Journal* 5:171-180.

Wigand, R. T./ Picot, A. and Reichwald, R. (1997): *Information, Organization und Management: Expanding Markets and Corporate Boundaries.* Chichester: Wiley.

Williamson, O. E. (1975): *Markets and Hierarchies: Analysis and Antitrust Implications.* New York: The Free Press.

————— (1985): *The Economic Institutions of Capitalism.* New York: Free Press.

————— (1991): Comperative Economic Organization: The Analysis of Discrete Structural Alternatives. *Administrative Science Quarterly* 36:269-296.

————— (1996): *The Mechanisms of Governance.* New York: Oxford University Press.

————— (1999): Strategy Research: Governance and Competence Perspectives. *Strategic Management Journal* 20 (12):1087-1108.

Windsberger, J. (1991): Der Unternehmer als Koordinator. *Zeitschrift für Betriebswirtschaft* 91:1413-1429.

Winter, S. G. (1987): Knowledge and Competence as Strategic Asset. In *The Competitive Challenge: Strategies for Industrial Innovation and Renewal*, edited by D. J. Teece. Cambridge, MA: Ballinger.

————— (1991): On Coase, Competence, and the Corporation. In *The Nature of the Firm: Origins, Evolution, and Development*, edited by O. E. Williamson and S. G. Winter. New York: Oxford University Press.

Witt, U. (1997): "Lock-in" vs. "Critical Masses": Industrial Change under Network Externalities. *International Journal of Industrial Organization* 15:753-773.

Wolff, B. (1994): *Organisation durch Verträge.* Wiesbaden: Gabler.

Yin, R. K. (1984): *Case Study Research: Design and Methods, Applied Social Research Methods Series.* Beverly Hills, CA: Sage Publications.

Yli-Renko, H./ Sapienza, H. J. and Hay, M. (2001): The Role of Contractual Governance Flexibility in Realizing the Outcomes of Key Customer Relationships. *Journal of Business Venturing* 16 (6):529-555.

Yoffie, D. B. (1996): Competing in the Age of Digital Convergence. *California Management Review* 38 (4):31-54.

Yoffie, D. B. and Kwak, M. (2002): Judo Strategy: 10 Techniques For Beating A Stronger Opponent. *Business Strategy Review* 13 (1):20-31.

Zerdick, A./ Picot, A./ Schrape, K./ Artopé, A./ Goldhammer, K./ Lange, U. T./ Vierkant, E./ López-Escobar, E. and Silverstone, R. (2000): *E-conomics: Strategies for the Digital Marketplace*. Berlin; Heidelberg; New York: Springer.

Zimmerman, M. A. and Callaway, S. (2001): Institutional Entrepreneurship and the Industry Life Cycle: The Legitimation of New Industries. Paper presented at USASBE/SBIDA 2001.

Zook, C. and Allen, J. (2001): *Profit from the Core: Growth Strategy in an Era of Turbulence*: HBS Press.

Abbreviations

3GPP	3rd Generation Partnership Project
3GPP2	3rd Generation Partnership Project 2
AOL	America Online
API	Application Programming Interface
ARPU	Average Revenue per User
ASP	Average Sales Price
ATM	Automated Teller Machine
B2B	Business to Business
B2C	Business to Consumer
CA	Computer Associates
CD	Compact Disc
CDMA	Code Division Multiple Access
CDMA2000	Code-Division Multiple Access IMT-2000
CEO	Chief Executive Officer
CFO	Chief Financial Officer
CGI	Common Gateway Interface
cHTML	Compact Hypertext Markup Language
DAT	Digital Audio Tape
DB	Database
DCC	Digital Compact Cassette
DEC	Digital Equipment Corporation
DIN	Deutsches Institut für Normung
DVB-T	Digital Video Broadcast – Terrestrial
DVD	Digital Versatile Disk
EDIFACT	Electronic Data Interchange for Administration, Commerce and Transport
ESA	External Sales Agent
ETSI	European Telecommunications Standards Institute
FCC	Federal Communications Commission
GIF	Graphics Interchange Format
GPRS	General Packet Radio Service
GSM	Global System for Mobile Communications
GSM-A	GSM Association
HP	Hewlett-Packard Company
IBM	International Business Machines Corporation
ICT	Information and Communication Technology
IEEE	Institute of Electrical and Electronics Engineers

IMT2000	International Mobile Telecommunication 2000
ISBN	International Standard Book Number
ISO	International Organization for Standardization
ISP	Internet Service Provider
ITU	International Telecommunication Union
IPO	Initial Public Offering
J2EE	Java 2 Platform, Enterprise Edition
Kbps	Kilobits per second
LAN	Local Area Network
MBA	Master in Business Administration
MIDI	Music Instruments Digital Interface
MSN	Microsoft Services Network
NDA	Non-disclosure Agreement
NTT	Nippon Telephone and Telegraph
OTWA	Online Traders Web Alliance
OEM	Original Equipment Manufacturer
OMA	Open Mobile Alliance
PCI	Peripheral Component Interconnect
PDA	Personal Digital Assistant
PDC	Personal Digital Cellular
PDC-P	Personal Digital Cellular-Packet Data
PDF	Portable Document Format
PERL	Practical Extraction and Reporting Language
PSTN	Public Switched Telephone Network
RISC	Reduced Instruction Set Computer
TCP	Transmission Control Protocol
TDMA	Time Division Multiple Access
TLP	Transport Level Protocol
UMTS	Universal Mobile Telephony Standard
URL	Unified Resource Locator
USB	Universal Serial Bus
VCR	Video Cassette Recorder
VHS	Video Home System
W3C	World Wide Web Consortium
WAP	Wireless Application Protocol
WBMP	Wireless Bitmap
W-CDMA	Wideband Code Division Multiple Access
WML	Wireless Markup Language
WWW	World Wide Web

List of Figures

List of Tables

Index

Printing and Binding: Strauss GmbH, Mörlenbach